THE FIVE TOOL NEGOTIATOR

THE FIVE TOOL NEGOTIATOR

The Complete Guide to Bargaining Success

RUSSELL KOROBKIN

LIVERIGHT PUBLISHING CORPORATION
A DIVISION OF W. W. NORTON & COMPANY
INDEPENDENT PUBLISHERS SINCE 1923

Printed in the United States of America
First Edition

For information about permission to reproduce selections from this book, write to Permissions, Liveright Publishing Corporation, a division of W. W. Norton & Company, Inc., 500 Fifth Avenue, New York, NY 10110

For information about special discounts for bulk purchases, please contact W. W. Norton Special Sales at specialsales@wwnorton.com or 800-233-4830

Manufacturing by LSC Communications, Harrisonburg
Book design by Daniel Lagin
Production manager: Julia Druskin

Library of Congress Cataloging-in-Publication Data

Names: Korobkin, Russell, author.
Title: The five tool negotiator : the complete guide to bargaining success / by Russell Korobkin.
Description: New York, NY : Liveright Publishing Corporation, A Division of W. W. Norton & Company, [2021] | Includes bibliographical references and index.
Identifiers: LCCN 2020053610 | ISBN 9781631490200 (hardcover) | ISBN 9781631490217 (epub)
Subjects: LCSH: Negotiation. | Negotiation in business.
Classification: LCC BF637.N4 K675 2021 | DDC 158/.5—dc23
LC record available at https://lccn.loc.gov/2020053610

Liveright Publishing Corporation, 500 Fifth Avenue, New York, N.Y. 10110
www.wwnorton.com

W. W. Norton & Company Ltd., 15 Carlisle Street, London W1D 3BS

1 2 3 4 5 6 7 8 9 0

For Sarah and Jessica

CONTENTS

USING THE TOOLKIT

CODA

THE FIVE TOOL NEGOTIATOR

INTRODUCTION

Baseball scouts prowl the globe for what are known as "five-tool" players: athletes with superior ability to hit for average, hit for power, field, throw, and run the bases. Five-tool baseball players are outstanding in all facets of the game. Willie Mays, Roberto Clemente, Hank Aaron, Frank Robinson, and the young Mickey Mantle (before knee problems slowed him) are generally considered the best five-tool players of all time. Each of these legends led his team to World Series championships.

Negotiation, like baseball, is a game in which success is achieved by using five, and only five, tools. Fortunately for most of us, none of them requires the ability to hit a big-league curveball. These tools are the keys to winning at the bargaining table in any league; that is, they are the same whether your goal in negotiating is an eight-figure corporate merger with a CEO, a seven-figure lawsuit settlement with a lawyer, a six-figure sales agreement with a purchasing agent, a five-figure Lexus with an automobile dealer, a four-figure raise with your boss, or even a workable bedtime with your child. By understanding how these tools work, anyone who negotiates in a business, professional, consumer, or family capacity can develop the depth of knowledge and the tactical flexibility to outperform the competition.

Tool #1, **Bargaining Zone Analysis**, enables you to identify the range of agreements that will benefit both parties.

Tool #2, **Persuasion**, convinces your counterpart, more than she otherwise would have recognized, that reaching an agreement will benefit her.

Tool #3, **Deal Design**, structures the terms of the potential agreement in ways that make it more valuable.

Tool #4, **Power**, forces your counterpart to reach an agreement on terms relatively more desirable to you.

Tool #5, **Fairness Norms**, provides a framework for sealing a bargain on terms that both parties can feel good about.

A baseball player need not be an expert at wielding all five of the tools of his game to excel. Even among elite professional athletes, very few are considered legitimate five-tool players. Superior hitting ability can make up for some weaknesses in fielding, and a great fielder with a strong arm and speed might enjoy a long career, even if he doesn't hit home runs. But only the five-tool player is truly *complete*.

The same can be said for negotiators. You don't need to be a master of all five tools to step onto the negotiation playing field. With some natural instincts for one or two tools, you can get into the game. Most professionals navigate the commercial world in just this way. But five-tool negotiators, or 5TNs, as I call them, play on a different level entirely. They are rare, even among those who routinely achieve good results in their particular line of work. This book will put you on the road to mastering all five tools and becoming a part of the negotiating elite.

The 5TN approach is ***universal***. Negotiation is a communication process that we use to engage the assistance of others to accomplish our goals. This book breaks down this critical social process into the core elements that are present in every negotiation, describes how they fit together, and provides a road map for navigating them. The five tools encompass the entire variety of tactics and techniques that provide an advantage in bargaining. You can use them to negotiate with your clients, your boss, a used-car dealer, or your spouse and kids.

The 5TN approach is ***rigorous***. The lessons you will learn have been honed over my 25 years of studying, writing about, and teaching negotiation to law and business students on four continents as well as to professionals in business and law. My approach is built on the platform of decades of research in a range of fields, including economics, decision theory, game theory, behavioral economics, cognitive psychology, social psychology, business, and law, and is also molded by my practical experience as a management consultant and a lawyer. This is a book for negotiators, not for scholars, but it is based on science. Throughout these pages, you'll learn about dozens of fascinating social science studies that underlie the 5TN framework.

And finally, the 5TN approach is ***manageable***. I provide a simple structure that you can easily learn, remember, and immediately apply. When you go to negotiate, you will have only five points you need to remember and put to use. You can then evaluate your performance and continue to improve your skills by critically assessing how well you were able to use each of the tools in your bargaining interactions.

TOOL #1

BARGAINING ZONE ANALYSIS

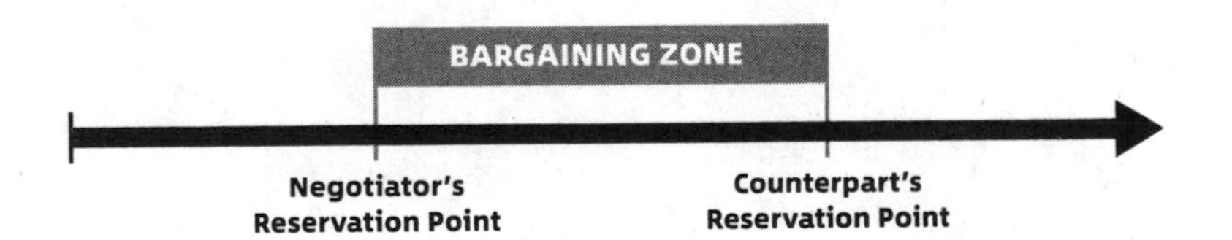

1

A TALE OF TWO PITCHERS

In August 2011, Jered Weaver, the pitching ace of the Los Angeles Angels baseball team, was offered $85 million by the team to extend the term of his contract for five seasons. This might seem like a lot of money, but most analysts thought it was a relative bargain for the Angels, even at the time. The prior season, Weaver had finished fifth in the voting for the American League's Cy Young Award, given annually to the best pitcher in the league, and he was performing even better in 2011. In April, he tied a Major League record for the speed with which he recorded his first six wins, and in July he was chosen to be the starting pitcher in Major League Baseball's All-Star game.

Weaver's agent, Scott Boras, urged him to decline the offer, wait a year until he was eligible for free agency, and then sign a long-term deal with another team, probably for much more money. Weaver rejected the advice and made the deal. Boras was so upset by his client's decision that he refused to attend the press conference at which it was announced.

Matt Harrington was another star pitcher from Southern California with a promising outlook, but his story had a very different ending. In 2000, Harrington was Gatorade's High School Baseball Player of the Year, and he was drafted by the Colorado Rockies with the seventh overall pick in the Major League Baseball draft. Harrington's agent, Tommy Tanzer, publicly demanded a $4.95 million signing bonus for his phenom, and after two months of hard bargaining he convinced the Rockies to increase their original offer of $2.2 million to $4.9 million, with some caveats. The team would go no further, and Harrington turned down the offer. A few years later, after several seasons playing amateur ball, Harrington found himself working in the tire department at Costco for $11.50 an hour.[1] He never made it to the major leagues.

Negotiation forces us to compare two possible futures: one in which we reach agreement with the other party, and one in which we reach impasse and do not make a deal. Unlike an exchange of goods or money ordered by a judge, the Internal Revenue Service, or a mugger, a *negotiated* agreement requires the consent of both (or several, as the case may be) negotiators. There is always a choice to be made between reaching agreement and walking away.

Bargaining Zone Analysis—the first of the five tools of negotiation—enables 5TNs to make the right choice between these alternative futures. It also enables them to predict how their counterparts will view the same choice, which in turn makes it possible to understand what can be achieved in the negotiation and what cannot. Negotiators who fail to use this tool, or do so incorrectly or half-heartedly, enter into agreements that they shouldn't, fail to seize opportunities that they should, and are often poorly equipped to obtain as much benefit from deals as is possible.

Jered Weaver was skilled at Bargaining Zone Analysis. Matt Harrington was not. Before I can explain, I need to define a few terms of art:

The *bargaining zone* is the range of agreements that both negotiators would be willing to accept, if they could do no better, rather than walking away from the table with no deal. (If there is no set of terms that both parties would prefer to an impasse, there is no bargaining zone.) If you and your boss would both prefer you to keep working for your company for a salary of $80,000, $90,000, or $100,000 rather than taking your services elsewhere, we can say all of those potential points of agreement fall within the bargaining zone.

The bargaining zone is bounded by the minimum set of terms that each party would be willing to accept, which I call the parties' *reservation points*. If a negotiation primarily concerns money, like a sales or salary negotiation, a reservation point can be described in dollars. In this situation, we can refer to it as a *reservation price*. If the minimum salary you are willing to accept (assuming that you cannot convince the company to give you any more) is $75,000, that is your reservation price. If the maximum the company is willing to pay you (if it cannot get you to work for any less) is $110,000, that is the company's reservation price. If you are negotiating for your toddler to go to sleep, your reservation point might be denominated in cookies, bedtime stories, or renditions of "Twinkle, Twinkle, Little Star." Whatever the currency of your negotiation, your reservation point should represent the amount of compensation you would have to give or receive such that you would enjoy the same amount of value, what economists call *utility*, from making the deal as from not making the deal.

Most negotiations concern multiple issues. For example, the negotiation with your boss might concern your job title and amount of vacation time, in addition to salary, and a bedtime negotiation with your child might concern treats, songs, and horsey rides. When this is the case, your reservation point can be described by several (or more) *reservation packages*: combinations of terms, each of which would provide you with an equivalent amount of utility, that would make you indifferent between agreement and impasse in the negotiation. If for paying off your difficult child you would be indifferent to choosing among (a) two cookies, (b) one cookie and five renditions of "Twinkle, Twinkle," or (c) one cookie and one pirate story, but you are not willing to give more than any of these combinations of bribes to secure a deal for a tantrum-free end to the evening, they are each reservation packages and can collectively be described as constituting your reservation point.

The wider the bargaining zone, the more total utility that the negotiators can create by reaching an agreement. If your boss wants your services so much that she has a high reservation point, and you love your job so much that you have a low reservation point, an agreement that allows you to stay in your position would be much more valuable to you and your boss jointly than if you were both lukewarm about the other and your reservation points were closer together. I'll refer to the total amount of value, or utility, that an agreement would create as the *cooperative surplus*.

Here's a simple example that puts together these three related concepts: Assume that Aphrodite has an opera ticket for tonight's performance, which she no longer wishes to attend. Beacher is interested in seeing the show, so the two decide to meet to negotiate. The most money that Beacher is willing to pay for the ticket—his reservation price—is $70. The least amount of money that Aphrodite is willing to accept—her reservation price—is $20. This means that the bargaining zone extends from $20 to $70. A sale for less than $20 or more than $70 is not possible, because one of the parties would refuse to agree to such a proposal. If Aphrodite agrees to sell the ticket to Beacher at any price within the bargaining zone, the agreement will create $50 of cooperative surplus, because the experience will now be enjoyed by the person (Beacher) who values it at $70 rather than the person (Aphrodite) who values it at only $20.

Notice that the price the parties agree upon affects the division of cooperative surplus but not the total amount of the cooperative surplus.

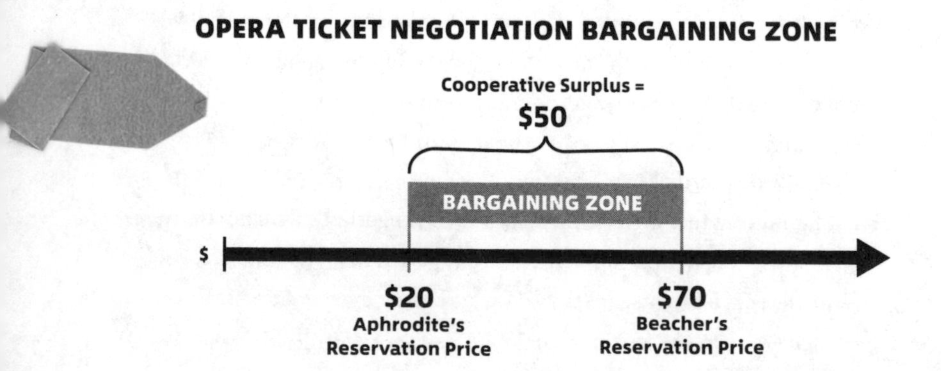

If they agree on a price of $60, for example, Aphrodite would enjoy $40 of the cooperative surplus (by trading an item worth $20 to her for $60), and Beacher would enjoy $10 of the surplus (by trading $60 for an item worth $70 to him). If they settle on a price of $45, each would receive $25 of the surplus.

No negotiator can avoid having a reservation point. Even if Beacher is desperate to attend the opera, some price would be so high that he would refuse to pay. And even if Aphrodite cannot attend the performance, some price would be too low for her to accept. Perhaps she would be willing to give away the ticket for free, but she probably wouldn't be willing to *pay* Beacher to take the ticket off her hands, so her reservation point is almost certainly not lower than $0.

Although negotiators cannot avoid having reservation points, they do have control over where they choose to set them. Aphrodite could set hers at $100, or $10, or $0; Beacher could set his at $5 or $500. The negotiator's reservation point should be set at precisely the point at which she would be indifferent between reaching a deal and accepting an impasse. When the reservation point is set correctly in this manner, negotiators know to refuse to enter any deal that is worse than their reservation point and, conversely, they know to accept the best deal they can negotiate that is better than their reservation point. (More later on the difficult problem of when to accept a deal that is better than one's reservation point and when to continue to press for an even better deal instead.)

The failure to establish the correct reservation point can lead directly to the two most serious errors a negotiator can make—what I call the two *cardinal sins* of negotiation:

- ***The first cardinal sin***

  Entering into an agreement when the negotiator would have been better off with no agreement at all. When this happens, the negotiator is left worse off than if he had never even entered into negotiations in the first place.

- ***The second cardinal sin***

  Reaching an impasse and walking away without an agreement when a deal was available on terms that would have been more desirable than not having a deal.

As a buyer, Beacher would place himself at risk of committing the first cardinal sin if he set his reservation price too high; he would place himself at risk of committing the second cardinal sin if he set his reservation price too low. As a seller, Aphrodite would risk committing the first cardinal sin by setting her reservation price too low and the second by setting her reservation price too high.

We know that Jered Weaver's reservation point was $85 million or less, because he accepted the offer for $85 million. Matt Harrington's reservation point appears to have been $4.95 million, or perhaps just a tad lower. We know this because his agent publicly stated that Harrington would sign a contract for that amount, and, although such proclamations are often bluffs (more on this in Part 4), history shows that he ended up accepting an impasse rather than accepting an offer of just $50,000 less than that amount.

Weaver understood that an impasse with the Angels in 2011 could have resulted in an even richer contract with another team the following year, but evidence suggests that setting a lower reservation point than his agent recommended, which led him to eventually sign for $85 million, was the correct decision for him. Having grown up in Southern California, as Weaver explained, he placed a high value on playing near home, where he could pitch in good weather and be sure his parents could attend every game. Locking down the five-year contract also enabled him to avoid the emotional ups and downs of the free-agency process and the risk that an injury or a bad season would reduce his market value. "Come on, it's $85 million," he told a newspaper reporter a year later, even after finishing second in the voting for the 2011 American League Cy Young Award. "It's more money than I ever thought I would make in my life."[2]

This sentiment doesn't mean Weaver shouldn't have instructed his agent to try to extract as many millions of dollars from Angels owner Arte Moreno as he possibly could—a reservation point is a minimum demand, not a goal. But when Boras determined that $85 million was the most that Moreno would offer, Weaver took the deal rather than waiting another year and testing the free-agent market.

In contrast, Harrington appears to have set a reservation point that was higher than it should have been. That mistake led him to commit the second cardinal sin—walking away from a deal that would have been better than no deal. Almost all courses of action that people pursue—those that follow from agreements and those that follow from not reaching agreement—entail some risk of a bad outcome, and risky choices are often justified by the potential reward. With better luck, Harrington's story could well have had a happier ending; he might have obtained a richer first contract the following year, as he had hoped, and then gone on to enjoy a long and successful pitching career. But Harrington's tremendous desire to play baseball for a living, his lack of financial independence, and the obviously large risk associated with declining the Rockies' offer all seem to suggest that a lower reservation point would have been appropriate.

2

DECISION ANALYSIS 101

Establishing a reservation point correctly is an exercise in decision analysis, a subfield of economics formalized in the mid-twentieth century.[1] This aspect of Bargaining Zone Analysis requires the negotiator to determine the minimum requirements of an agreement in what I will call the *focal negotiation*—that is, the negotiation at hand—such that she would maximize her utility by agreeing to the deal rather than accepting an impasse.

Conducting this analysis properly requires three essential steps:

- Identify your plan B.
- Compare the utility consequences of reaching agreement in the focal negotiation with pursuing that plan B.
- Calculate your reservation point.

This process is complicated, but it provides an absolutely essential foundation for understanding and using the other four tools of negotiation. Stay with me!

Step 1: Identify Plan B

I refer to the alternative course of action that the negotiator will take in the event of an impasse in the focal negotiation as his *plan B*.[2] Because the consequence of reaching an impasse in the focal negotiation is that the negotiator will have to pursue some other course of action, it doesn't make sense to try to determine your reservation point without first identifying your plan B—you'd just be making a wild guess. For example, Jered Weaver couldn't accurately determine the lowest salary that he should have been willing to accept from the Angels without first knowing that he had the option of becoming a free agent.

Step 2: Compare the Two Alternatives

The next step is comparing the benefits of reaching agreement to those you would enjoy if you pursued your plan B. In some situations, the two alternatives are similar—for instance, you might be negotiating the price of a new Buick with Joe's dealership and have a plan B of purchasing the same car from Sally's dealership. But in other situations, the focal negotiation and your plan B will be dissimilar options, which can make comparing them difficult.

To make matters worse, comparing these alternatives requires predicting how much utility you would obtain from each in the future, which is far from an exact science, for two different reasons. The first is that we humans are pretty good at anticipating whether an event will make us feel happy or unhappy (ice cream = delicious, castor oil = disgusting), but we are quite bad at predicting the *extent* of our future happiness or unhappiness.

The second complication stems from the fact that how much utility we will enjoy depends on how exactly the future unfolds, which is usually uncertain. If I am negotiating to purchase an ice-cream cone, I might be fairly confident about how I will feel if I eat the ice cream or, alternatively, if I pursued my plan B of eating a doughnut. But I can't be so confident concerning how I will feel about a new job after I start it. The job responsibilities might prove to be more or less interesting than I thought, or my boss might turn out to be unreasonable.

These difficulties with predicting the future mean that setting reservation points requires us to compare the *expected utility*, rather than the actual utility, of reaching agreement in the focal negotiation and of pursuing our plan B. This essentially means taking into account all the different futures that might result from either option, weighting these by the likelihood that each will come to pass, and then determining the average outcome. It also requires determining how we feel about risk, because one of these alternatives is often riskier than the other.

Step 3: Determine Your Reservation Point

In almost any two-party negotiation, you can think of one party as being a "buyer" and the other as being a "seller." (Classifying negotiators as buyers or sellers isn't necessary but doing so is helpful for diagramming the bargaining zone.) In salary negotiations, like Jered Weaver's, employees are sellers (they are negotiating to sell their labor) and employers are buyers (they are purchasing labor). In lawsuit settlement negotiations, plaintiffs are sellers (they are negotiating to sell their right to go to court) and defendants are buyers.

In negotiations that don't involve payments of money, it is often possible to think of either party as the buyer or the seller. For example, the United States has negotiated, on and off, with North Korea for nearly three decades to limit or eliminate the Hermit Kingdom's nuclear weapons program. You might think of these negotiations as the United States either seeking to "buy" nuclear nonproliferation with the currency of sanctions relief or peaceful nuclear technology, or, alternatively, seeking to "sell" economic liberalization and assistance in return for nuclear concessions. If friends are negotiating where to go for dinner and what movie to see, Friend A can be understood as seeking to "buy" a compromise of Friend B's movie preference with concessions on restaurant selection, or vice versa.

A buyer should set his reservation point at the maximum amount of compensation (financial or otherwise) that he could provide to the seller as part of an agreement in the focal negotiation and still enjoy at least as much expected utility as he would by pursuing his plan B. A seller should set her reservation point at the minimum amount of compensation that she could accept for an agreement in the focal negotiation and still enjoy at least as much expected utility from the agreement as she would if she were to pursue her plan B.

The correct reservation point might be different for different individuals (or firms) in exactly the same situation, because they are likely to have different subjective preferences for the benefits of reaching agreement in the focal negotiation compared to the features of their plan B. By any objective standard, Jered Weaver had a very good plan B when he was negotiating with the Angels: wait a year for free agency and sell his services to the highest bidder, possibly for an amount greater than $100 million. But the disadvantages of that plan B compared to re-signing with the Angels in the summer of 2011 loomed larger for Weaver than they might have for other players—those who cared more about their salary and less about playing in their hometown and avoiding a year of uncertainty and stress.

Let's consider how the analysis would work in our simple opera-ticket example. Recall that Beacher is interested in seeing the opera in town tonight, and Aphrodite has a ticket that she would like to sell. (For simplicity, let's assume the box office is sold out of tickets and Aphrodite is the only person Beacher knows who has one.) As Beacher prepares to negotiate for the ticket, what should his reservation price be?

Step 1: What will Beacher do tonight if he does not purchase the opera ticket? Let's suppose that he determines that he would attend a performance of the ballet instead, and that tickets for that event remain available at the box office for $50.

Step 2: Would Beacher prefer attending the opera or the ballet, and how much more would he prefer one to the other? Let's assume that, although he enjoys ballet, he would prefer to attend the opera tonight, and that the extra utility he would enjoy from the opera would be worth $20 to him.

Step 3: Since ballet tickets are available for $50 and attending the opera would be worth $20 more to him than attending the ballet, Beacher should set his reservation price for his negotiation with Aphrodite at $70. Of course, Beacher might hope to pay less than $70, and he can use tools #2–#5 of the 5TN to help him bargain for a lower price, but he should be willing to pay $70 if that is the best deal that he can negotiate. If he cannot obtain the ticket for $70, he should attend the ballet instead.

There are two factors that *should not* affect Beacher's reservation point. The face value of the opera ticket—whether it is $20 or $200—is irrelevant, because the price the opera company originally charged for tickets has nothing to do with how much more or less Beacher would prefer to attend the opera than the ballet. (Notice an important nuance, however: if a $200 ticket price were to suggest to him that the opera production will likely be outstanding—perhaps the ticket price is that high because of the quality of the tenor or the opulence of the costumes—that fact might increase his relative preference for the opera over the ballet, and that, in turn, would increase his reservation price.)

How much money Aphrodite is asking for the ticket is also irrelevant to Beacher's reservation point calculation. Remember that the reservation point draws a line of demarcation between agreements that would make the negotiator better off than impasse, and agreements that would make him worse off than impasse. If Beacher values the opera $20 more than the ballet, and Aphrodite will not part with the opera ticket for less than

$150, the correct conclusion for Beacher to draw is that he should go to the ballet, not that he should increase his reservation price above $70. In many negotiations, the best outcome is to not reach an agreement. Negotiators who are skilled at using the tool of Bargaining Zone Analysis always recognize when they find themselves in one of those situations and know to walk away.

This critical point can be difficult for many negotiators to fully understand because they intuitively sense that the amount of Beacher's offer should bear some relationship to the price Aphrodite is asking. The problem with this intuition is that it confuses the question "What should Beacher's reservation price be?" with the question "What should Beacher's bargaining strategy be to try to obtain the lowest price possible?" Whether Aphrodite asks for a high or low price might affect how Beacher uses the other four tools of negotiation to obtain the best deal that he can, but it should not affect his reservation price.

3

ADVANCED DECISION ANALYSIS I

INVESTIGATING PLAN B

Now that you understand how you should determine your reservation point, let's dig a level deeper into the process.

With a brief period of reflection, negotiators can usually identify their plan B at a general level of detail before beginning a negotiation. Beacher can determine that he will attend a different performance if he fails to reach agreement with Aphrodite. Jered Weaver knew that his plan B was to pursue free agency, and Matt Harrington knew his was to wait a year and reenter the Major League Baseball draft. Lawyers attempting to negotiate settlements know that their plan B is to take their case to court. Parents attempting to negotiate bedtime with their toddler know that their plan B is to physically deposit a screaming child in bed (or, depending on the parent, to allow the kid to watch cartoons until he passes out).

How much we know about our plan B will vary, however, and it is almost always the case that having more specific and detailed information would help to increase the accuracy of our reservation point. Beacher might not know what other performances are scheduled for tonight, or if he does, he might not know about their quality or the price of tickets. If he doesn't know that the only other performance that would interest him is sold out, for example, he might set his reservation price in his negotiation with Aphrodite too low. On the other hand, if it turns out that cheap tickets are available for a ballet that has received fabulous reviews, he will probably set his reservation price for the opera ticket too high.

This means that 5TNs must investigate the likely consequences of pursuing their plan B before negotiating. Jered Weaver couldn't adequately compare the consequences of free agency to reaching an agreement with the Angels if his agent did not first investigate which teams were likely to be interested in signing him and how much money free-agent pitchers at his level were likely to be offered the next year. Prior to attending a settlement negotiation, lawyers investigate the facts of their case and research the law so that they can estimate the likelihood that they will prevail if they must argue it before a court.

Obtaining this highly relevant information, however, is almost always costly in terms of time, effort, or money, or all three. This creates a very difficult problem: How much investment should negotiators make in investigating the nature, quality, and likely consequences of pursuing their plan B?

The amount of effort in exploring the intricacies of a plan B that is justified in any particular negotiation depends on two factors:

- The importance of the negotiation
- The degree to which the negotiator is likely to misestimate the quality of his plan B without more information

If Beacher does not research other performances that he could attend, he will be forced to implicitly estimate the quality of his plan B. If the estimate is inaccurate, he might set his reservation price for the opera ticket $20 or $30 higher or lower than his true point of indifference. Perhaps Beacher will set his reservation price at $70, but because, unbeknownst to him, his favorite ballet is playing and cheap tickets are still available, he should set his reservation point at only $45; that is, he will obtain the same amount of expected utility if he pays $45 for the opera ticket or if he attends the ballet. Alternatively, perhaps the only other performance that would even mildly interest Beacher is sold out, and this fact implies that he should set his reservation point at $80, because at that price he will obtain the same amount of expected utility from reaching agreement as from pursuing his plan B.

In either of these scenarios, the error that Beacher would make when setting his reservation price would be unfortunate but hardly a disaster. The stakes are low. Given the limited risk, the greater mistake would be for Beacher to spend hours learning everything there is to know about every other show in town. On the other hand, spending five minutes on the internet to see whether a ballet is being performed, find out the price of tickets, and perhaps read a review of the performance written by a favorite arts critic is probably worth the time involved in order to substantially minimize (but not completely eliminate) Beacher's risk of setting his reservation price inaccurately.

Jered Weaver's situation provides a stark contrast. Given the tens of millions of dollars at stake, doing anything less than analyzing every piece of available information about the free-agent market and how other teams were likely to evaluate Weaver would be negotiation malpractice. He would expect his agent to provide the best possible prediction of how many teams would be interested in his services, which ones, and how much money they would be likely to offer, almost without regard to the amount of time and effort needed to conduct this analysis.

Having conducted the appropriate amount of research into the qualities of your plan B, you are ready to compare its advantages and disadvantages to what you will get if you reach agreement in the focal negotiation, which will then enable you to decide what terms your counterpart must be willing to agree to for you to make a deal.

4

ADVANCED DECISION ANALYSIS II

COMPARING THE DIFFERENCES

Deciding what would make a deal in the focal negotiation preferable to pursuing your plan B requires focusing like a laser on the differences between the alternative paths. Specifically, there are five types of potential differences between the focal negotiation and your plan B to evaluate:

- The desirability of the features associated with each option
- The riskiness associated with each option
- The transaction costs associated with pursuing each option
- The timing of the costs and benefits associated with each option
- The indirect impacts on future opportunities or relationships associated with each option[1]

To make sure you don't overlook any of these, begin by estimating the expected cost or expected income that would come from pursuing your plan B. Then adjust up or down from this "baseline" to the extent that the differences between the options make agreement in the focal negotiation more or less desirable.

To demonstrate, let's consider how Jered Weaver might have determined his reservation price in his negotiations with the Angels:

Determine the "baseline" cost or value of plan B: Based on his agent's analysis of the market for free agents in general and for him in particular, Weaver might have concluded that the best estimate of what would happen if he were to pursue his plan B was that he would sign a $100 million contract at the end of the season with a team outside of California, most likely the New York Yankees or Boston Red Sox. He should then use $100 million as the baseline for his reservation price calculation.

If Weaver were perfectly indifferent between free agency and re-signing with the Angels, his reservation price would be $100 million. But the analysis is more complicated than this because, as is usually the case, there are important differences between the two options that affect their relative desirability to Weaver.

Adjust for differences in features: In some negotiating situations, the benefits or burdens at issue will be exactly the same whether the negotiator reaches agreement in the focal negotiation or reaches impasse and pursues his plan B. If you are negotiating to buy that Buick from Joe's dealership and your plan B is to buy exactly the same car from Sally's dealership, at the end of the day you will be driving home in either one of two automobiles that are identical in all relevant ways. But this type of situation is rare. Usually, an agreement in the focal negotiation promises to lead to a qualitatively different future than your plan B, making one path at least somewhat more desirable than the other, even when the two alternatives have a lot in common.

For Jered Weaver, pitching for the Los Angeles Angels would have been similar to pitching for another Major League team, but these two options were not exactly the same, and the difference was important to him. Re-signing with the Angels would better satisfy his personal preference of playing for his hometown team, whereas free agency would likely result in a move out of state. The subjective benefits of being an "Angels pitcher" rather than a "Yankees pitcher" or "Red Sox pitcher" dictated that Weaver should be willing to accept less than $100 million. He should have asked himself, "How much is this difference worth to me?" in whatever was the currency of the negotiation (in this case, money).

Let's assume that staying with the Angels rather than changing teams was worth $10 million to Weaver. This means that if location was the only difference between re-signing with the Angels and pursuing his plan B, his reservation point would be a salary of $90 million.

Adjust for differences in risk: Weaver's agent might estimate that free agency would yield a $100 million payday, but at the time of the negotiation, this was far from certain. With the benefit of hindsight, it seems clear that Weaver would have fielded higher offers after the 2012 season, during which he continued to be one of the league's top pitchers, had he become a free agent then. As it turned out, Weaver's Angels teammate Zack Greinke, another of the league's best pitchers but one who was not as successful as Weaver at that time, signed a free-agent contract at the end of that season with the Los Angeles Dodgers for $147 million over six seasons—the largest contract ever signed by a right-handed pitcher at that time. Had Weaver followed Boras's advice and opted for free agency, he probably would have earned more than $100 million.

The outcome that Greinke enjoyed, however, was hardly a certainty at the time Weaver had to make his decision. First, no one knew for sure that the Dodgers, or any other team, would pay any pitcher $147 million after the next season. Frugality might have hit the market. Second, any number of events could have reduced Weaver's individual market value. In fact, just one year after Weaver would have become a free agent, the speed of his fastball began to decline noticeably and, although he remained a quality pitcher, his performance faltered somewhat. Had this happened just one season earlier, he would have probably been far less marketable.

Some people have more aversion to risk than others, but given what economists call the declining marginal utility of money—that is, for any of us, our first $50 million is far more valuable than our second $50 million, which is much more valuable than our third $50 million—it seems safe to assume that Weaver would prefer a guaranteed amount of money from the Angels rather than a free-agent contract with the same expected value but potential variation on the upside or downside. Let's assume Weaver determined that the certainty of his compensation that would come from re-signing with the Angels would be worth $5 million.

Adjust for differences in transaction costs: Re-signing with the Angels would require much less of a time investment—lower "transaction costs," as an economist would call it—than testing the free-agent market. Although Weaver's agent would absorb much of these costs, the player himself would have to participate in generating free-agent offers, considering the pros and cons, meeting with teams bidding for his services, and so on. Devoting precious mental energy to the process of pursuing the best deal could distract Weaver from his more important goal of achieving excellence on the field. Let's assume that, to Weaver, the ability to avoid these costs by re-signing with the Angels would be worth $2 million.

Adjust for differences in timing: Re-signing with the Angels could be accomplished in 2011, whereas free agency would have to wait until the end of the following season. This meant that Weaver could begin enjoying the higher salary and the long-term job security earlier by reaching an agreement in the focal negotiation. Notice that there is a financial and a nonfinancial aspect of the timing difference in this particular situation. Because of what is known as the "time value of money" (the same amount of money is more valuable if it is received sooner rather than later), Weaver would certainly prefer $1 million in 2011 to $1 million in 2012; even if he had no plans to spend it right away, he could invest it and earn a positive return during the intervening time. But there was also a psychological benefit to him of having the next step in his career decided a year earlier rather than a year later. Let's assume the ability to sign earlier made reaching the agreement with the Angels $4 million more desirable to Weaver than his plan B, holding everything else equal.

As a side point, it bears noting that, although negotiators would usually prefer to enjoy the fruits of any agreement sooner rather than later, this is not always the case. Obtaining something desirable can have costs that make it undesirable in the short term (a great apartment in a new city is more valuable if the lease begins just as you move to town rather than three months earlier). In other situations, anticipation has its own benefits that can increase the longer a transaction is delayed (would you rather purchase a Caribbean cruise that departs in one week or in one month?).

Adjust for differences in effects on relationships and future opportunities between the alternatives: A small supplier might be willing to accept a lower price on its first order from a large manufacturer in hopes that doing a great job will earn it future business. Choosing to forgo free agency and re-sign with the local team would endear Weaver to the Anaheim fans, who would appreciate his loyalty and view him differently than many other star players who are perceived as mercenaries pursuing the highest paycheck. How much this benefit of the focal deal should affect Weaver's reservation point, of course, depends on Weaver's very subjective analysis of how much an uptick in fan appreciation is worth—let's assume $1 million.

Combine the difference adjustments to calculate the correct reservation point: In this example, all five of the differences between the focal deal and Weaver's plan B favor the focal deal, so, to determine the appropriate reservation price, Weaver would need to subtract from the baseline the monetary value he placed on each of those differences. Thus, Weaver's reservation price should be $78 million ($100M–$10M–$5M–$2M–$4M–$1M). He should accept the best deal he could negotiate that exceeds that amount, but he should choose impasse over any deal that would pay him less than that amount.

FROM PLAN B TO RESERVATION PRICE
(Jered Weaver Example)

BASELINE (Value of Plan B)	**$100 million**
DIFFERENCES (Compared to Focal Deal)	
1. **Features** (Relocation)	**- $10 million**
2. **Riskiness** (Injury, Market)	**- $5 million**
3. **Transaction Costs** (Free Agency)	**- $2 million**
4. **Timing** (Delay 1 Year)	**- $4 million**
5. **Relationships/Reputation** (Disappoint Local Fans)	**- $1 million**
RESERVATION PRICE	**$78 million**

Had free agency been more desirable than staying with the Angels on any of the five factors, the arithmetic would be slightly different. Assume, for example, that rather than preferring to remain in California, Weaver had dreamed since childhood of wearing Yankee pinstripes, and that the possibility of playing for New York next year would be worth $5 million to him compared to playing for the Angels. In this case, Weaver would have had to *add* $5 million to the $100 million baseline figure to indicate the extent to which free agency would be more appealing than signing with the Angels, based on the first of the five factors. He would then subtract the other sums to reflect the extent to which the other four differences favored striking a deal with the Angels. This would lead him to set a reservation price of $88 million. Under this hypothetical set of preferences, Weaver would have been better off turning down the $85 million offer and pursuing free agency.

The key to setting one's reservation point correctly is converting the benefits of the focal deal and those of pursuing plan B into the same currency in order to make an apples-to-apples comparison of the two alternatives possible. In the Weaver example, I used dollar values for the different features of the two alternatives in order to facilitate the comparison, but the features could have been denominated in units of utility or any other common currency.

This hypothetical analysis rather blithely assumes that Jered Weaver could place a dollar value on the nonmonetary differences between re-signing with the Angels and pursuing his plan B, such as on the ability of his parents to attend his games in Anaheim and the fan adulation he would receive by re-signing with the local team. But how could Weaver, or any of us, actually place dollar values on these sorts of intangible features with any degree of accuracy?

This analytical exercise is often very difficult, and no one can do it perfectly. 5TNs can only hope to set their reservation points so that they *approximate* the point at which they would truly be indifferent between reaching agreement in the focal negotiation and accepting impasse and pursuing their plan B.

So why bother? Is the game even worth the candle?

Unfortunately, the only alternative is plunging into a negotiation with only a vague idea of the terms that should be minimally acceptable and then deciding on whether to declare impasse on the basis of intuition or emotion in the heat of the moment. Weaver might struggle to put a dollar value on his parents' being able to attend his games, and it might seem crass to monetize his love for his family. But he was implicitly doing precisely these things when he decided to accept the $85 million deal rather than turn it down. When the only alternative is relying on gut instinct and hoping that you don't commit one of the two cardinal sins, setting a reservation point as carefully and accurately as possible seems like a pretty smart course of action.

This said, negotiators need to exercise judgment concerning the amount of time and effort they invest in Bargaining Zone Analysis in its entirety, in the same way that they need to balance the costs and benefits of investigating the likely consequences of pursuing their plan B. Here again, the importance of the specific negotiation matters. A multiyear Major League Baseball contract, valued in the millions of dollars, is a better candidate than an opera ticket for carefully and rigorously establishing the most precise reservation point possible, because the potential costs of making an error are orders of magnitude higher.

Although high stakes usually warrant a substantial investment in Bargaining Zone Analysis, there is one other factor to consider that is not necessarily related to the importance of the transaction: how likely it is that the counterpart's best offer will be close to the negotiator's reservation point. Here is why this matters:

If a deal is likely to be reached on terms that are far more desirable than the negotiator's reservation point, setting the reservation point imprecisely won't result in any harm, so the effort required to determine the precise desirability of plan B is likely to be wasted. For example, if Weaver was desperate to stay with the Angels and was willing to accept any serious offer from the team, he could safely agree to an $85 million extension without formally analyzing his reservation price. But if he could see merit in both staying with the Angels and seeking a new adventure elsewhere, a substantial investment in formally calculating his reservation point would be justified.

Matt Harrington's story suggests that more careful reservation point analysis might have paid a tremendous dividend. At the time that Harrington participated in the Major League Baseball draft, a player who did not sign a contract with the team that drafted him could reenter the draft the following year and hope to be drafted and signed by a different team. When Harrington and his agent assessed the offer made by the Colorado Rockies, they would have determined that reentering the draft the next year was Harrington's plan B. Although this plan B was not abysmal, it wasn't outstanding either.

Let's assume that Harrington and his agent estimated that the expected value of reentering the draft a year later would have been a contract from another team that included a $5 million signing bonus. (Even this seems aggressive, given that this amount had never been offered in the history of the Major League Baseball draft at that point.[2]) Pursuing his plan B meant spending at least one year doing something other than playing for a professional baseball franchise, taking on the significant risk that the passage of time would hurt his draft status the following year, and earning a reputation for being a difficult player to deal with, which could (and, in fact, did) cause teams to avoid him in future drafts.

This analysis suggests that Harrington's reservation price probably should have been set substantially below the $4.9 million that the Rockies offered him, and that his failure to accept that offer is an example of the second cardinal sin: failure to reach an achievable agreement that would have been more desirable than pursuing his plan B.

5

THE OTHER SIDE OF THE BARGAINING ZONE

The bargaining zone has two boundaries: the negotiator's reservation point, and her counterpart's reservation point. It follows that using the tool of Bargaining Zone Analysis requires the 5TN to estimate the location of both these points.

Unlike setting your own reservation point, knowing the point at which your counterpart would prefer impasse to agreement is not necessary to avoiding committing either of the two cardinal sins—you can completely avoid both merely by setting your own reservation point correctly. But this information is critical for deciding whether to accept an offer that is better than your own reservation point or to hold out for an even better deal. No matter how much Jered Weaver preferred the Angels' offer of \$85 million to his plan B of free agency, he might have rationally turned it down if he believed that Angels owner Arte Moreno's reservation point was substantially higher than \$85 million and that Moreno might thus increase his offer. Weaver said that \$85 million was more money than he could ever spend, but he still would have preferred \$90 million or \$100 million if he could have gotten it!

So, how do you estimate your counterpart's reservation point?

Reverse engineer his thought process; that is, put yourself in his shoes and evaluate his reservation point as you would if you were him.

In 2001, NBC was locked in negotiations with Paramount Television Studios over extending the run of the show *Frasier*, which Paramount produced and NBC had aired for eight years. The primary issue was the price NBC would pay per episode of the show for the right to continue to air it.[1] When approaching the negotiation, NBC executive Marc Graboff not only determined his own reservation point by estimating the revenue *Frasier* would generate compared to another show he might use to replace it (his plan B), he also estimated Paramount's reservation point.

Without the ability to read the mind of his negotiation counterpart on the Paramount side, Kerry McCluggage, Graboff couldn't hope to know Paramount's reservation point precisely, but he was able to estimate it with a substantial amount of confidence. Given that *Frasier* was the most successful television program at the time, having earned more than a billion dollars in its eight seasons, it was a safe bet that Paramount's plan B was to move the program to a competing network, such as ABC or CBS, rather than shutting down production. Not-so-subtle indications in the media of interest on the part of CBS, along with press reports of a meeting at CBS attended by the show's star, Kelsey Grammer, strongly suggested that selling the show to CBS was probably Paramount's precise plan B.

The more difficult question was how valuable it would be for Paramount to move the show to CBS, which in turn required an evaluation of how much CBS would be willing to pay Paramount for the rights. NBC analysts could have estimated this figure based on their general understanding of the economics of the television business combined with a series of reasonable assumptions about CBS's specific situation. But Graboff had a more reliable basis for conducting this part of the analysis: until moving to NBC just a year earlier, he had been the chief television-program buyer at CBS. Graboff later told professor and author Guhan Subramanian that he "knew better what CBS's economics were at that time than I knew what NBC's were." His estimate of the amount of money

CBS could pay Paramount per episode of *Frasier* and break even on the transaction was consistent with Paramount's analysis of its own reservation point.[2]

As is more typically the case, Jered Weaver lacked this kind of insider knowledge about how his negotiating counterpart, Angels owner Arte Moreno, was likely to analyze the team's plan B. But with information about the other top pitchers who would soon be available as free agents and with a fair amount of empathy, Weaver and agent Boras could reverse engineer an estimate of Moreno's reservation point nonetheless. Much of what successful agents like Boras earn their high fees for is their ability to use their experience in similar negotiations to estimate the reservation price of team owners.

While 5TNs consciously use the tools of decision analysis to determine a precise estimate of their counterpart's reservation point, most negotiations are characterized by a more intuitive, gut-level approximation of what the other negotiator is willing to accept in a given circumstance. Unfortunately, research suggests that most of us are quite bad at intuiting our negotiation counterparts' reservation points, so the time and energy required for careful calculation are well spent.

Negotiators tend to suffer from what psychologist Richard Larrick and economist George Wu labeled the *small-pie bias*.[3] We tend to underestimate how much the other negotiator is willing to give up in order to reach an agreement and thus tend to assume that the bargaining zone is smaller—and the available cooperative surplus less—than it actually is. This bias can cause negotiators to hand over to their counterpart a large portion of the cooperative surplus, mistakenly believing that pushing for a more advantageous deal would cause an impasse.

For an extreme example of the small-pie bias and its consequences, consider another negotiation involving baseball agent Scott Boras—one that ended far more to Boras's liking than the Jered Weaver negotiation did. In 2000, then–Seattle Mariners shortstop Alex Rodriguez (aka A-Rod), another Boras client, became a free agent. Boras assured the world

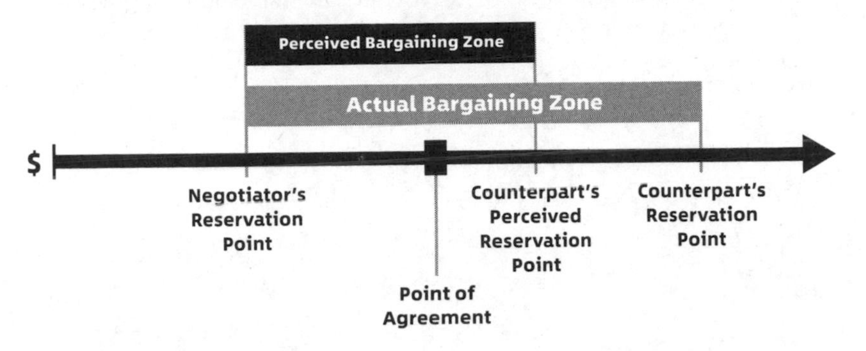

The small-pie bias can cause the negotiator to perceive the bargaining zone as being smaller than it actually is.

that astronomical offers were pouring in for A-Rod's services. After furious bargaining between Boras and Texas Rangers owner Tom Hicks, Rodriguez signed a 10-year contract with the Rangers for $252 million—by far the richest contract ever signed by a baseball player at that time.

No doubt, Hicks realized that he was paying dearly for the services of baseball's best player, but with all of A-Rod's potential and the considerable interest of every other team in the league, he believed that the Rangers would have to break the bank to have any hope of landing the star. In reality, however, A-Rod's plan B wasn't nearly as good as Hicks assumed. While many other teams would have been delighted to snag A-Rod at some price, at the end of the day he had only one other firm offer, and it was for only $102 million![4] Based on Hicks's assessment, the $252 million contract might have been better for the Rangers than an impasse, but the team probably could have signed the superstar for at least $100 million less than it paid.

6

THEN WHAT?

Once a negotiator has as accurate an estimate of the bargaining zone as possible, the next step is for her to decide how to put this analysis to work in the negotiation process. There are three different situations she could find herself in, each of which calls for a different strategy.

1. No Bargaining Zone

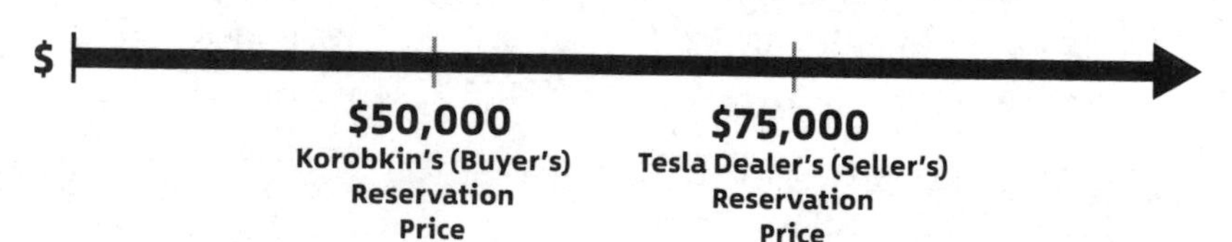

If using the tool of Bargaining Zone Analysis leads you to conclude that there is no bargaining zone—no possible agreements that both parties would prefer to an impasse—the obvious course of action is to *not* negotiate, thus saving the time, effort, and financial costs that would certainly be wasted.

In the part of Los Angeles in which I live, you can hardly throw a rock without hitting a Tesla Model S electric car. I love the combination of environmental friendliness and luxury that these cars represent, but I've never initiated negotiations with a Tesla dealer to try to purchase one. I know the retail price is over $80,000. Perhaps in a slow month a patient buyer might convince the dealer to knock $1,000, or maybe even $2,000, off that sticker price, but I'm pretty sure the dealer's reservation price is going to be above $75,000, even on the last day of a slow month. The dealer's plan B in any potential negotiation with me over a car he has in stock would be to wait for another customer who is willing to pay the sticker price or close to it. Because Teslas are popular and in short supply, I know that the dealer will expect this will happen in the near future, thus making his reservation price at, or at best just marginally below, the sticker price.

As for my reservation price, even if my perfectly good Volvo were to die tomorrow (and probably even if I were to win the lottery, to be honest), there is just no way that I would consider paying anywhere close to $75,000 or $80,000 for a car, no matter how much I like it, and no matter how good it is for the environment.

I know there would be no bargaining zone, so I never initiate a negotiation. Potential negotiations for which there would be no bargaining zone are far, far more common than potential negotiations for which there would be a bargaining zone. We all negotiate frequently, but we spend a lot more time *not* negotiating with others with whom we could conceivably negotiate.

2. Small Bargaining Zone

Another conclusion that could emerge from Bargaining Zone Analysis is that there is likely to be a very small bargaining zone: an agreement might be possible, but the parties' reservation points are probably located so close to each other that there are few—and perhaps only one—agreements that both would accept. This situation is not as uncommon as you might think. It is, in fact, typical of markets with many buyers and sellers of an identical or very similar product or service, instances of what economists call "perfect competition."

Imagine that, after having a nightmare in which Facebook CEO Mark Zuckerberg, wearing makeup like the Joker in "Batman," has taken over the entire world, you decide your mental health requires you to sell your 100 shares of Facebook stock. Coincidentally, on the same day, your colleague from the office is delighted by the fact that he received 75 "likes" for the photo of his lunch that he just posted on Facebook, and he tells you that he has decided to buy 100 shares of the company's stock.

Every day, somewhere around 20 million shares of Facebook stock are traded, and all of the shares are identical. Your shares are no better or worse than anyone else's, and, as a buyer, there is no reason for your friend to prefer your shares to the shares owned by anyone else. As a seller, you have no reason to prefer the money of any potential buyer over any other.

In this negotiation, your friend's plan B is to purchase shares on the

NASDAQ stock exchange at the current market price, and your plan B is to sell your shares on the NASDAQ, also at the current market price. Assuming that, in the case of impasse, each of you would have to pay a small brokerage fee to execute a trade online with a stranger, your friend's reservation price for buying your shares might be a few dollars higher than your reservation point for selling your shares, but the bargaining zone will be very small relative to the total size of the transaction.

There is really no point in either of you spending any time negotiating, because there is too little room to maneuver within the bargaining zone. Almost certainly, you will agree to sell the shares at the publicly available market price, so you should suggest that amount and close the deal.

3. Large Bargaining Zone

WEAVER NEGOTIATION: LARGE BARGAINING ZONE

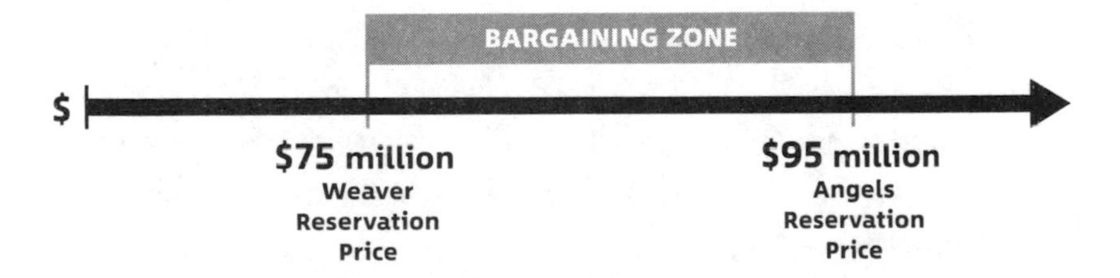

Finally, let's consider the most important situation from a negotiation perspective: you believe that a relatively large bargaining zone exists. Let's say, for example, that Jered Weaver determined that his reservation price was $75 million, and he and agent Scott Boras estimated that Angels owner Arte Moreno's reservation price was $95 million. Moreno tells Boras that $85 million is his "best and final" offer for Weaver's services; in other words, Moreno asserts that $85 million is his reservation price. Boras makes his living estimating how much owners are willing to pay for the services of athletes, and let's assume that he believes Moreno is bluffing and is actually willing to pay more. On the other hand, Boras lacks an unobstructed view into the recesses of Moreno's brain, so he has to recognize the possibility that Moreno's reservation price actually is only $85 million.

What should Weaver do? We know that he should choose to accept the offer rather than pursue his plan B of free agency, but there is obviously a third option: make a counteroffer for more money. Is this a better alternative than accepting the $85 million? Answering this question requires comparing the costs and benefits.

The potential benefit of demanding more money rather than accepting the $85 million is obvious: the Angels might increase their offer. If Weaver accepts the $85 million, there is no chance that the team will subsequently agree to pay him more than that. It is a truism of negotiation that you rarely get what you don't ask for.

But there are three significant risks to rejecting the offer and demanding more, which should be considered as well. First, this course of action could lead to an impasse, which, given our assumption that Weaver's reservation point was $75 million, would be catastrophic. It seems unlikely that Moreno would take back his $85 million offer, but it is not beyond the realm of possibility, especially if he had communicated firmly that $85 million was his best and final offer and that there would be no further concessions.

Second, rejecting the Angels' offer and continuing to negotiate means suffering transaction costs. Specifically, in this case, Weaver will not be able to enjoy the peace of mind that he would achieve by signing a new contract rather than waiting to become a free agent.

Third, continuing to hold out and demand more money might harm the pitcher's relationship with Moreno and the team management, especially if Moreno believes that $85 million is a fair salary (more on this issue when we get to tool #5).

If Weaver judges these risks to outweigh the benefit of potentially ending up with a richer contract, he should accept the offer. If not, he should reject it and make a counterproposal for a higher salary.

Earlier, I suggested that Matt Harrington probably set his reservation price too high in his negotiation with the Colorado Rockies, causing him to walk away from a deal that he should have accepted. But there is an alternative explanation of why his promising baseball career ended before it even began. Perhaps Harrington's reservation price was lower than the $4.9 million offered by the Rockies, but he and agent Tanzer estimated that the team's reservation price was higher than the $4.95 million Harrington demanded, and they believed the team would increase its offer if Harrington turned down the $4.9 million and demanded more. If so, he misestimated his counterpart's reservation price.

Harrington never played professional baseball because either (a) he erred in his analysis of his own reservation price, or (b) he erred in his analysis of his counterpart's reservation price. We will never know which.

7

WHO GOES FIRST?

"Should I make the first offer or encourage my counterpart to make the first offer?" This is the question that is asked most often, by students and professionals alike, in negotiation courses and training programs. For a 5TN, the answer depends on how confident you are in your Bargaining Zone Analysis—specifically, on how well you believe you are able to estimate your counterpart's reservation point.

In a panel discussion in which I participated, casino magnate Jack Binion told a great story that illustrates the perils of going first if you lack good information about your counterpart's reservation point. A casino company was interested in purchasing a piece of farmland in Mississippi that had been owned by a family for generations. The family considered asking $5 million for the property but was concerned that such a high demand might insult or scare away the buyer, so it decided to wait and let the casino company make the first offer. Much to the family's pleasant surprise, the company explained, somewhat apologetically, that the most it could pay was $20 million. By resisting the urge to celebrate and instead feigning hesitancy, the family was actually able to increase the sales price to $25 million.[1]

If you underestimate your buyer counterpart's reservation point, as Binion's landowners did, your initial offer is likely to be too modest, and you will sacrifice cooperative surplus. In Binion's story, the sellers accidentally avoided this outcome. If they had asked for $5 million, they certainly would not have received more than that, and they might have ended up settling for even less. At the other extreme, if you overestimate your buyer counterpart's reservation point, you might make an opening offer far outside the bargaining zone that leads to an impasse. Had the farm owners opened the negotiation by asking for $50 million, the buyer might have tipped his hat and walked away, concluding (incorrectly) that there was no bargaining zone.

Assuming that $25 million was less than the casino company's reservation price and that the deal was therefore still profitable for it, the company paid far more than it had to, essentially handing most of the available cooperative surplus to the sellers, because it failed at Bargaining Zone Analysis. Either it grossly misestimated the sellers' reservation price or, even worse, didn't even think about it! Without a carefully established estimate of that figure, it would have been better off waiting for the sellers to make an initial demand.

With an accurate estimate of the casino company's reservation point, the sellers could have availed themselves of three benefits that can come from making the initial offer: persuading the casino company to increase its reservation price (see Chapter 13), convincing the company that the sellers' reservation price was higher than it actually was (see Chapter 30), or framing subsequent concessions as leading to a fair compromise (see Chapter 39). But proper first-offer strategy begins with Bargaining Zone Analysis.

More generally, Bargaining Zone Analysis creates a framework for understanding what it is possible to achieve in a negotiation, setting the stage for a 5TN to use the other four tools to obtain the best deal possible.

SUMMARY OF KEY LESSONS FROM PART 1

- The bargaining zone is the range of possible agreements that both parties would prefer to an impasse and is thus bounded by the reservation points of each.
- Careful Bargaining Zone Analysis assures the 5TN that she will not commit either of the two cardinal sins of negotiation—reaching an agreement when she would have been better off with an impasse, or reaching an impasse when she had the opportunity to reach agreement on terms that would have made her better off—and provides a guide to what it is possible to achieve.
- To set your reservation point correctly, you must determine the term or terms of an agreement that would make you indifferent between making a deal and pursuing your plan B.
- In order to conduct this analysis, first determine how much time, effort, or money you should invest in researching your plan B, and then carefully compare all relevant differences between reaching agreement in the focal negotiation and pursuing that plan B.
- To estimate your counterpart's reservation point, place yourself in her position and conduct the same analysis.
- Use your estimate of your counterpart's reservation point to determine whether to agree to terms that your counterpart is willing to accept, or to continue negotiating for a more advantageous deal.
- If you lack confidence in your estimate of your counterpart's reservation point, allow him to make the initial offer in the negotiation.

TOOL #2

PERSUASION

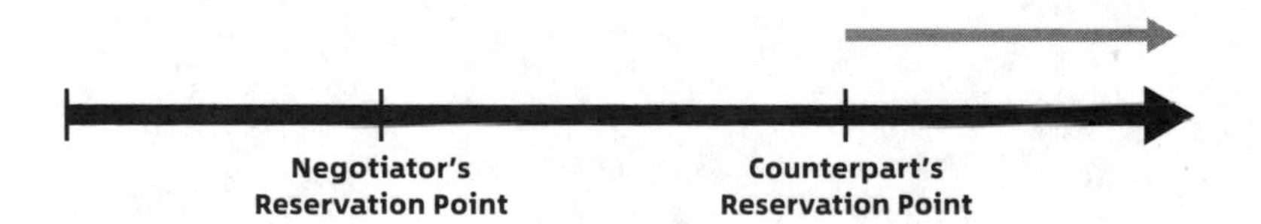

8

WE ARE ALL SALESPEOPLE

When he's not writing and performing music with U2, rock star Bono's passion is fighting poverty on the African continent. The Irish singer has championed this cause since 1985, when he first volunteered in an Ethiopian refugee camp, and he has raised millions of dollars from private sources—most notably by performing benefit concerts and by cofounding a product line (Red) that donates a portion of its profits to fighting disease. Believing that significant progress in the war on African poverty requires the full participation of the world's richest governments, Bono is a fixture in discussions on international development, from Washington, DC, to Davos, Switzerland, lobbying Western governments and international agencies to provide more aid.[1]

As the new millennium approached, Bono spearheaded an effort called Jubilee 2000 to convince Western governments to forgive large amounts of debt owed to them by the most impoverished African nations. In Washington, the Clinton administration originally favored forgiving two-thirds of the $6 billion owed to the United States, but Bono was not satisfied with what he viewed as a lukewarm commitment. Working through President Clinton's chief economic adviser, Gene Sperling, and

Treasury secretary, Lawrence Summers, Bono argued that only complete forgiveness of the African debt would be a suitably historic act by the American government. He was influential in ultimately convincing Clinton to revise his position and support 100 percent debt relief.[2]

Even more impressively, Bono was able to convince leading Republicans in Congress to support that position as well. His most unlikely and well-known success came in a meeting in September 2000 with Senator Jesse Helms of North Carolina, the arch-conservative legislator with little demonstrated interest in antipoverty programs and an outright hostility toward foreign aid (not to mention significant antipathy toward President Clinton). Bono, a devout Christian, emphasized to Helms the biblical imperative to help the poor and compared leprosy in scripture to AIDS in modern-day Africa. By the time he left the Capitol, Bono had won Helms's support for debt-forgiveness legislation. According to some reports, Helms was even moved to tears during the meeting. One month later, Congress voted to forgive the entire debt.[3]

The second of the five tools of negotiation, **Persuasion**, enables a 5TN to convince his counterpart that reaching an agreement in the focal negotiation would be more valuable to the counterpart than she initially recognized. By convincing her that she should be willing to sacrifice more than she thought to reach agreement in the focal negotiation, the 5TN effectively causes his counterpart to change her reservation point. In some situations, Persuasion can create a bargaining zone where none previously existed, thus making an agreement possible that at first appeared impossible. In other situations, Persuasion can make the bargaining zone larger, giving the persuasive negotiator an opportunity to obtain more desirable terms, and thus more cooperative surplus, than would have otherwise been possible.

Bono wasn't asking Clinton or Helms to write a personal check to African governments but to provide a currency far dearer to them: the use of their limited political capital to benefit people half a world away. In order to convince both Democrats and Republicans to part with *more* political capital than they planned on expending, Bono had to convince them that the debt-relief deal he was proposing was more valuable to members of both political parties than they recognized.

Persuasion is the sales aspect of negotiation. For people in the business of selling goods, services, or real estate, the centrality of sales to the negotiation process is so obvious that we call them "salespeople." What often goes unrecognized is that everyone who negotiates about anything is in the business of sales. To be a complete negotiator, you need to be able to sell your counterpart on the proposition that making a deal with you would be *really* good for her.

Many of us are busy selling without even realizing we're involved in a negotiation. For example, when an admitted UCLA Law School student discloses a particular interest in the subject of negotiation, our admissions office will often ask me to contact the student and discuss our course offerings in the field. I am playing a particular role in a larger negotiation, much of which is being handled by others, such as our dean of admissions. The dean knows that the student is comparing her plan B—which is probably attending another law school but could be forgoing law school altogether—to the option of attending UCLA. My job is to convince her to raise her reservation point for attending by increasing her perception of the value of the deal.

Every negotiation is different, of course, but Persuasion is the task that probably takes up the largest chunk of actual negotiating time. In researching his book *To Sell Is Human*, author Daniel Pink commissioned a study of thousands of full-time workers in the United States involved in all sorts of occupations. His survey respondents reported that, on average, they spent a whopping 41 percent of their work time "convincing or persuading people to give up something they value for something [the respondent has]." This was not 41 percent of the time the respondents were directly engaged in negotiating, or even 41 percent of the time they were directly interacting with other people—this was 41 percent of all their work time![4] Undoubtedly, had Pink asked what percentage of the time actually *engaged in negotiation* was devoted to convincing or persuading, the estimated proportion would have been much higher. Even novice negotiators intuitively understand that Persuasion is critical to obtaining the best deal possible.

The tool of Persuasion might at first seem inconsistent with the tool of Bargaining Zone Analysis. If Jered Weaver had determined his reservation price, wouldn't the Los Angeles Angels have found any efforts to persuade him to lower his reservation price to be a waste of time? Whatever pleas the team might make would, in theory, already be incorporated into Weaver's existing analysis. Similarly, how could Bono have been so successful in his efforts to persuade both President Clinton and Senator Helms to provide more African debt relief? Shouldn't these two sophisticated politicians have already known the maximum amount of debt relief they would be willing to provide, based on their analysis of the costs and benefits associated with enacting complete, partial, or no debt-relief legislation, before Bono lobbied them?

Persuasion is an important tool in any negotiation for the simple reason that determining one's reservation point is extremely difficult to do. Few negotiators attempt to use the careful, analytical process of Bargaining Zone Analysis that true 5TNs use. Most enter negotiations with only a general idea of how much they would value reaching an agreement. And even the most careful, analytical negotiators set their reservation points imperfectly. This is an unfortunate consequence of being a human being, but it creates a crucial role for Persuasion.

9

THINKING FAST

In recent decades, social scientists have come to believe that human beings have two decision-making modalities, sometimes labeled *System 1* and *System 2*. System 1 spontaneously makes intuitive judgments and decisions, often leaving us completely unable to explain their basis or struggling to gin up an after-the-fact explanation that seems logical. System 2 is deliberate and analytical, and can be used to review and, if necessary, override the snap judgments offered by System 1. The analytical approach to Bargaining Zone Analysis that I've described in Part 1 is a pure example of System 2 decision-making.

Here is an example of a question often used to illustrate the difference between these two modes of thinking:

> Assume that a bat and ball together cost $1.10, and that the bat costs $1 more than the ball. How much does the ball cost?[1]

If you are like most people, the answer "10 cents" immediately popped into your head. That's your System 1 mind responding. If you then stopped and thought, "Wait a minute—that's not right! If the ball cost 10 cents and the bat $1, the bat would cost only 90 cents more than the ball. I see now that the correct answer is 5 cents," that's System 2 asserting control.

System 2 is preferable if we want to maximize the accuracy of our judgments, but it is costly to operate in terms of both time and mental energy required. Evidence demonstrates, in fact, that the brain actually consumes more glucose when deep in thought! It would be literally impossible to make it through even a day if we called on System 2 every time a judgment, decision, or choice were required.[2] If you were to relentlessly insist on using System 2, you would have to pull out your laptop each morning and create a spreadsheet of costs and benefits in order to decide whether you should get up and start your day or stay in bed. And you would have to consult formulas in a physics textbook before deciding whether to cross the street if an oncoming car was in your field of vision, no matter how far away.

So, System 1 is our go-to method of thinking. This isn't a bad thing. The weight of expert opinion is behind the idea that System 1 intuition, while fast and automatic rather than slow and labored, is not as dissimilar to System 2 as it might seem. Our unconscious brains develop intuitions about the best choice among various options by recalling a variety of past choices and their resulting consequences and then using this information as the basis for predicting the future consequences, both costs and benefits, of current choices—a kind of immediate and automatic, if rough, expected utility analysis.[3] Our ability to listen and learn allows us to add to our subconscious database the knowledge and experiences of others as well, which is why recollections of our parents' long-ago warnings to us about crossing the street or a recent news report about a jaywalker being run over by an 18-wheeler can cause us to hesitate before stepping off a curb.

Remarkably, there is some evidence that System 1, as it has evolved, is even capable of accounting for uncertainty about future outcomes. In one experiment, scientists gave macaque monkeys a squirt of tasty fruit juice and measured the extent to which pleasure centers in their brains were activated in response. They then found that, by routinely turning on a light bulb 15 seconds before providing the juice sample, the same brain activation began to occur at the switch of the light, indicating that the macaques could anticipate the pleasure of the treat. Finally, the scientists found that they could control the extent of the activation by providing the juice at different probabilities after turning on the light. When experience suggested the macaques would receive the actual juice squirt only 50 percent of the time, the brain activation was about half the level it was when they received juice every time the light appeared; changing the probability to 25 percent or 75 percent caused decreased or increased activation levels, respectively.[4]

Often, our System 1 intuitions are experienced as feelings. Psychologist Paul Slovic coined the term *affect heuristic* to reflect his observation that people often choose between options based on which one feels better rather than on the logical framework of formal decision analysis.[5] Social scientists have recognized this relationship between emotion and cognition ever since.

As impressive as human intuition might be, however, there is little question that it sacrifices some accuracy in the pursuit of speed. Psychologist Daniel Kahneman won the 2002 Nobel Prize in Economic Sciences for his experimental work demonstrating the many ways that System 1 intuition, unsupervised by System 2's conscious deliberation, can cause us to make mistakes of judgment and to act against our interests.

The core lesson of Kahneman's best-selling book *Thinking, Fast and Slow* is that System 1 thinking relies on a variety of mental shortcuts, or *heuristics*. Kahneman explains that, when faced with difficult questions such as whether an $85 million contract with the Angels is better than testing the free-agent market in a year, System 1 substitutes a simpler question that it can answer much more easily, such as "Is $85 million a lot of money?" or "Would I prefer to live in Southern California than in New York or Boston?"[6] The answer that System 1 can quickly generate in response to one of the simpler questions ("Yes!") is then deployed, illogically, as the answer to the harder question. These unconscious mental shortcuts usually work well in enabling us to manage life in a fast-moving, complex environment, but they can lead to identifiable mistakes in judgment in particular situations, especially those that logically call for weighing a number of factors that are difficult to compare to one another.

Even 5TNs who overcome the siren's song of System 1 reasoning and harness the most explicit, labor-intensive System 2 approach possible—think of those few who crack open an Excel spreadsheet and attempt to identify and carefully assign a precise value to every difference between the focal deal and their plan B—cannot perform the necessary analysis perfectly. Conducting this analysis usually requires making apples-to-oranges comparisons. When political leaders considered Bono's proposal for African debt relief, they had to attempt to balance the benefits to Africa and their own historical legacies against what might otherwise be accomplished with the dollars and political capital that they would spend on that project.

These comparisons are exceedingly difficult for even the most analytical and well-prepared negotiators because our preferences, and particularly the strength of our preferences, are often completely unknown or only vaguely recognized. As human beings, negotiators can't help but struggle to determine exactly how much reaching an agreement is worth. For most negotiators, most of the time, the value of a potential deal, and thus their reservation points, are not fixed in the recesses of the brain just waiting to be accessed. Rather, we usually struggle to make value determinations in the course of bargaining, and we usually do so based, at least in part, on available contextual cues. Framing matters.

Jesse Helms probably didn't have a firm view as to whether African debt relief was a good or bad idea before Bono lobbied him. This lack of certainty opened the door for the tool of Persuasion. By framing information, the 5TN can influence the counterpart's determination of his reservation point.

10

TWO SIDES OF THE SAME COIN

In the 2014 movie *Draft Day*, Kevin Costner plays the character of Sonny Weaver, the general manager of the Cleveland Browns football team (and no relationship to the very real Jered Weaver!). Sonny's squad is coming off a losing season in which its quarterback was injured and missed the final 10 games. He faces intense pressure from the team's owner to do something that will make a splash and excite fans.

On the day of the NFL draft, the Seattle Seahawks general manager calls with an offer to trade Sonny the first pick in the draft, which would give him the opportunity to select star quarterback Bo Callahan. Sonny expresses interest but balks at the steep price Seattle is demanding: Cleveland's top pick for each of the next three years. The Seattle general manager tells Sonny that Callahan "is going to be a franchise player for someone." He continues: "I have the golden ticket, Sonny. If I give it to you, you get to save football in Cleveland." Alternatively, Sonny's Seattle counterpart warns, Cleveland can use its first-round pick for a "running back with a rap sheet" (referring to the legal problems of the player likely to be Cleveland's alternative in the draft) and take the field with a quarterback "who barely made it through half the season before getting injured last year."

Remember that the package of goods, services, or money that a negotiator is willing to give up in order to reach an agreement depends on the desirability of the focal deal *relative to* his plan B; the value of a ticket to a sold-out opera depends not only on how much you like Puccini but also on whether your alternative activity is a trip to Paris, France, or Paris, Texas. This means that the goal of Persuasion—convincing your counterpart that he should place a higher value on reaching agreement than he otherwise would have—can be accomplished by demonstrating *either* the desirability to him of the focal deal *or* the undesirability of his plan B. "Great focal deal" and "terrible plan B" are two sides of the same coin. The Seattle general manager in *Draft Day* uses both levers. First, he talks up Callahan's value, calling him a "franchise player" and indicating that the first draft pick is the "golden ticket"; then he deprecates Sonny's plan B of drafting a less desirable player and keeping his rickety incumbent quarterback. Sonny takes the deal.

Later in the movie, the draft is in progress. Because of last-minute rumors that Bo Callahan has personal problems, Cleveland and the next four teams to draft have surprisingly passed over the star quarterback. The Jacksonville Jaguars have the next choice, and the entire world expects them to select Callahan. Sonny badly wants this draft pick, however, so he approaches Jacksonville's young and inexperienced general manager and offers a trade.

TWO SIDES OF THE COIN

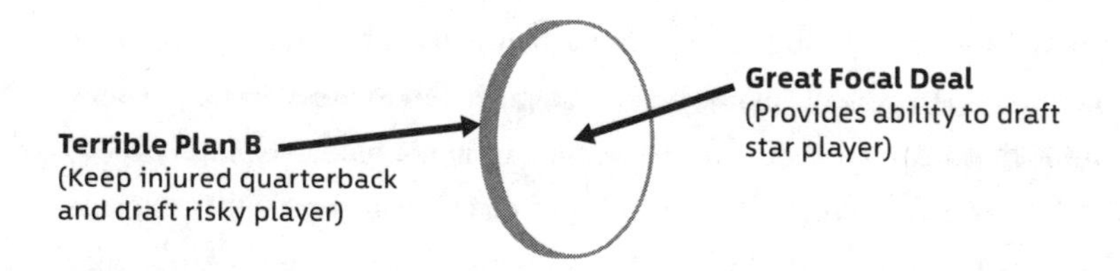

Sonny tells his Jacksonville counterpart that he thinks Callahan will be "a bust" in the pros and cryptically explains, "It's a character thing for me." He then says that if Jacksonville also isn't sold on Callahan, the Jaguars can trade the pick to Cleveland for future draft choices and the young general manager will "look like a seasoned pro." Every year, somebody emerges from draft day "looking like a donkey," Sonny warns, and "tomorrow I've got a feeling it could be you if you don't make this deal."[1]

Now it is Sonny who is working both sides of the coin: make the deal I'm proposing and you'll look like a savvy genius; pursue your plan B of drafting Callahan and you'll be remembered as a rube.

The *Draft Day* negotiations also demonstrate that negotiators can provide two different types of information: statements of fact (concerning elements of the deal or the counterpart's plan B) and assertions about the value of those facts to the counterpart. Sales training often refers to this as the difference between "features" and "benefits." Both types of information can be persuasive.

In the first negotiation, the Seattle general manager highlights undesirable facts (i.e., features) concerning Sonny's plan B: questions surrounding the player Sonny would draft and the quarterback he would bring back for another season. He leaves it to Sonny to draw the inference that these facts make his plan B a poor option. On the other side of the coin, the Seattle general manager stresses the high value to Sonny (i.e., the benefit) of making the deal and drafting Callahan by predicting that Sonny could become the "savior" of sports-mad Cleveland.

In the second negotiation, Sonny follows the same playbook. Having learned of an episode in Callahan's past indicative of dishonesty, he shares this factual information (Callahan has a "character" issue) with Jacksonville's general manager, from which that general manager may infer that his plan B of selecting Callahan is not valuable. Sonny seeks to increase the perceived desirability of reaching an agreement to trade the draft pick to Sonny for future selections by putting his positive spin on the benefits his counterpart would enjoy—appearing sophisticated to colleagues and fans.

Negotiators skilled at using the tool of Persuasion provide factual information about their counterparts' alternatives *and* their analysis of the implications of reaching or not reaching agreement: features *and* benefits.

11

ONE SIZE DOESN'T FIT ALL

What is most notable about Bono's success in convincing the U.S. government to forgive African debt is the understanding he demonstrated that Persuasion is not a one-size-fits-all proposition. Successful Persuasion requires framing a potential agreement in its best light relative to the counterpart's preferences, which vary from person to person and are often shaped by the context of the negotiation.

To the Democrats, African debt relief was immediately desirable, but it had to compete against other desirable policy initiatives that would cost the Treasury a lot of dollars and the president some political capital. Bono made it seem *even more* desirable—and thus worthy of spending greater political capital—by framing complete debt forgiveness as an act that would burnish President Clinton's historical legacy. With Jesse Helms and other congressional Republicans, Bono framed the benefits in terms of satisfying God's injunctions and the legislators' responsibilities as devout Christians.

Negotiators can learn a great deal about Persuasion from basic concepts routinely taught in sales training. The best salespeople start by investigating the customer's needs. Only after the salesperson understands the customer's problem does he describe how his product can help. Otherwise, he might be hawking attributes that have little or no perceived value. In *SPIN Selling*, sales guru Neil Rackham provides research that shows that the top performers in sales of big-ticket items are those who are most effective at the investigation stage of the process.[1]

The key to conducting this investigation is asking questions. This seems like a simple observation, but in my experience the single biggest tactical mistake that negotiators routinely make is beginning a negotiation by launching a stream of declarative statements designed to demonstrate the value of reaching agreement. Relatedly, when their counterpart is speaking, negotiators routinely begin to mentally formulate their next verbal volley rather than focusing on understanding what needs and desires the other person is trying to convey. Nearly every negotiator could improve his results by heeding the counsel often attributed to the Greek philosopher Epictetus that "we have two ears and one mouth so that we can listen twice as much as we speak."[2]

A great place to begin is with *open-ended questions* that might immediately help to uncover the counterpart's underlying interests: "What attributes of a business partner are most important to you?" "What features are you looking for in a new car?" "Why is receiving a larger weekly allowance important to you?" A skillful persuader can then demonstrate that an agreement would address these interests.

If there are multiple constituencies to serve, each might have different interests, which may or may not overlap or even be compatible. If the counterpart serves as an agent for others, his interests might not be the same as those he directly serves or indirectly represents. In *Draft Day*, Cleveland sports fans might have had a primary interest in putting together a team that wins football games in the future, but embattled general manager Sonny Weaver had an interest in making a splashy draft pick that would create an immediate public-relations buzz and save his job.

Successful Persuasion usually requires following up on responses to broad inquiries with more-pointed questions to home in on what is truly most important to the counterpart. Sales training sometimes describes these as *problem questions*—those that identify difficulties that the counterpart faces: "In what ways is your current supplier not meeting your company's needs?" This framing implicitly assumes that the counterpart's plan B is to maintain the status quo—that in the absence of a sale the potential buyer will do nothing. From the somewhat broader perspective of a negotiator, doing nothing at all might be the counterpart's plan B, but, of course, it might not be. The more general goal of asking problem questions is to unearth ways in which a counterpart's plan B will not fully satisfy his interests.

After identifying shortcomings with the counterpart's plan B, negotiators tend to become extremely excited and immediately launch into a spiel that describes all the ways in which an agreement in the focal negotiation would be superior. If the counterpart lacks information about how the features of an agreement will benefit her, this approach is sensible. But when the counterpart is already aware of the benefits of reaching an agreement, it is often more effective to resist the urge to overtly "sell" and instead continue to ask questions.

At this point, you want to pose questions that encourage the counterpart to identify the value that an agreement in the focal negotiation would have relative to her plan B. Remember that persuasive negotiators can provide factual information (features) or explain the value associated with that information (benefits). But we all want to be the hero of our own story, so a question that enables your counterpart to identify the value that would be created by reaching an agreement is more likely to persuade than if you assert that value proposition.[3] Bono *asking* Bill Clinton what it would mean for the president's legacy to offer full African debt relief would probably have been more persuasive than *telling* him.

Asking questions and allowing the counterpart to identify the value that he will obtain from an agreement in the focal negotiation ("How do you see my consulting services benefiting your company?") also has the advantage that it avoids the risk that the counterpart will reject or question the negotiator's assertion about the value of an agreement.

12

COMPARED TO WHAT?

Consider three social science experiments that demonstrate how people use System 1 mental shortcuts when determining the value of options:

First, imagine that, in an effort to better keep up with current events, you decided to purchase a subscription to *The Economist* magazine. When you investigated the options, you learned that for $125 you could purchase a one-year subscription that includes delivery of a printed copy of the weekly periodical plus internet access to every issue, or, for $59, a digital-only subscription. Which option would you prefer?

Behavioral economist Dan Ariely, the author of *Predictably Irrational*, asked research subjects this question, and approximately two-thirds chose digital only. He gave the same choice to a second group of subjects, but he added a third alternative to the other two: a print-only option, at a price of $125. As you might guess, no one chose the print-only option. After all, it cost the same amount as print-plus-digital. But what was fascinating is that 84 percent of this second group of subjects chose print-plus-digital rather than digital only, significantly more than those in the first group.[1]

Next, assume you are a college music major looking to purchase a music dictionary in a used bookstore for somewhere between $10 and $50. How much money would you be willing to pay (that is, what is your reservation price) for a dictionary with 10,000 entries that is in "like new" condition? Would your answer change if you were told there is also a dictionary that has 20,000 entries but a torn cover?

Psychologist Chris Hsee found that subjects asked to evaluate only the dictionary with 10,000 entries said they would pay $24, on average, but subjects told about both dictionaries were willing to pay an average of only $19 for that 10,000-entry dictionary (and $27 for the 20,000-word dictionary).[2]

Finally, imagine that, instead of a magazine subscription or a music dictionary, you are in the market to purchase a camera (or you were at a time when digital cameras were less advanced than they are today). One option is a Minolta SLR camera with several advertised features, including compact quartz-controlled aperture priority plus fully automatic/manual metering, 1/1000- to 4-second shutter speed, a self-timer, and a weight of three pounds. It costs $169. The second option is a different model of Minolta SLR camera with several specified advanced features, including a high-speed program mode, integrated dual-area metering, and an advanced automatic multiprogram selector, and it has a weight of one pound. This camera costs $239. Which camera would you prefer? Would it matter if you knew there was also a third alternative, at a price of $469, with a number of additional features?

It did to subjects in an experiment conducted by psychologists Amos Tversky and Itamar Simonson. Subjects given the choice between just the first two cameras were split, with half preferring each. But when the third, most expensive alternative was added to the choice set, not only did some subjects choose that alternative (no surprise there), only 22 percent of the subjects opted for camera number one (the cheapest alternative), and more chose camera number two than had when there were only two choices.[3]

All three of these experiments demonstrate that when faced with a difficult problem, our System 1 mind searches for an easier problem to solve. A magazine subscription that comes with the print version and internet access is clearly more valuable than a digital-only subscription, but is the value of the hard copy worth an additional $66 a year? For many people, that is a hard question. Whether the print-plus-digital version is worth more than the print-only version at the same price, however, is an easy question. Ariely's results in experiment number one suggest that at least some of the subjects in his second group answered the easier question, choosing print-plus-digital over the cheaper digital-only subscription because print-plus-digital is clearly preferable to the identically priced print-only selection.

In experiment number two, Hsee's subjects who were presented with only one dictionary had to determine the value of an item with two features, one of which (the condition) was clearly desirable, the other of which (the number of entries) was difficult to evaluate. Standing alone, this is a difficult problem, and in solving it the subjects appeared to put more weight on the feature that was easier to evaluate—the "like new" condition. But in a context that offered a comparison, the desirability of the other feature—number of entries—became seemingly easier to evaluate. Most people don't know whether 10,000 entries are many or few, but everyone understands that 10,000 is not as good as 20,000! Hence, in that context, the 10,000-entry dictionary doesn't seem so great.

Faced with three options of uncertain value, Tversky and Simonson's subjects in experiment number three favored the one that fell between the other two in terms of price and features, presumably because the intermediate choice appeared safer. When there were only two options, there was no intermediate choice.

Social scientists love to coin new terms, and the researchers who conducted these experiments named their findings "tradeoff contrast," "evaluability," and "extremeness aversion," respectively. But all three sets of results are closely related and illustrate a more general point: facing the need to assign a valuation to a particular potential deal, the System 1 mind, always in a hurry to take care of the day's business, looks for a readily available contextual clue for assistance. Unless the System 2 mind slams on the brakes and insists on thinking through the problem in a more careful but time-inefficient way, the value of a potential transaction is influenced by how attractive it appears in comparison to *reference points* that are readily accessible to the brain.

Savvy marketers can and do take advantage of the shortcomings of System 1 reasoning by providing consumers with reference points that make purchasing their products look desirable in comparison. Author William Poundstone tells the story of how Coach, the purveyor of expensive handbags, set out to persuade potential customers, uncertain of the value they placed on an elegant bag made out of ostrich leather, that they should have a reservation price for that item that exceeded its $2,000 price tag. In its store windows the company placed the $2,000 ostrich-skin bag next to a similar-looking alligator-skin bag with a $7,000 price tag.[4]

Determining whether your reservation price for the ostrich bag is higher or lower than $2,000 is difficult, at least for some members of Coach's customer demographic (that is, people who covet expensive handbags and have a lot of disposable income). The available alternatives to buying the handbag are virtually limitless, making it difficult to identify one's plan B. And whatever that plan B is, it will probably be some course of action that is very different from buying a handbag, thus requiring an apples-to-oranges comparison. On the other hand, it is easy to determine that the $2,000 ostrich bag is a better buy than the identical-looking $7,000 alligator alternative. This is the type of comparison that the ultrafast System 1 loves, and Coach undoubtedly sold many handbags by framing the purchasing decision in this way.

Negotiators can persuade their counterparts to place a higher value on reaching agreement by carefully framing the benefits of the focal deal in reference to a less attractive alternative, even if that alternative is not the counterpart's plan B. One of my favorite experiments provides a perfect example. Psychologist Robert Cialdini and his colleagues approached college students on a university campus and asked if they would be willing to volunteer to serve as counselors for juvenile delinquents for two hours a week for a two-year period of time. Perhaps not surprisingly, not a single busy college student agreed to the extremely burdensome request. Immediately, the researchers then asked the students if they would be willing to volunteer to chaperone the same delinquents on a single trip to the zoo. The contrast with the onerousness of the original request made the zoo trip seem much more desirable (or less undesirable) than it otherwise would. We know this because approximately half of the students who were first asked to serve as counselors for two years (and declined) agreed to be zoo chaperones, whereas only 17 percent of students who were not first asked to be counselors were willing to go to the zoo.[5]

5TNs understand that juxtaposing what they are offering with a less attractive alternative can make reaching an agreement *appear* more desirable.

13

DROPPING ANCHOR

You probably have no idea how often corporate managers commit fraud when reporting their financial results, but experienced professional auditors have a basis for estimating the incidence of such wrongdoing. In one study, one group of auditors estimated, on average, that the rate was about 16 incidents of fraud out of 1,000 companies, and another group of auditors estimated, on average, that the number was more than 43 out of every 1,000 companies. In other words, auditors in the second group thought that accounting fraud was more than twice as prevalent as auditors in the first group believed.

Members of both groups had been randomly selected from the same pool of professional auditors, so it was very unlikely that the members of the second group simply had more fraudster clients in the past, on average. But there was one difference between the two groups: before being asked for their estimate, auditors assigned to the first group were asked whether they thought the rate of fraud was more or less than *10* out of 1,000 companies, while subjects assigned to the second group were first asked whether they thought the rate was more or less than *200* out of 1,000 companies.[1]

The effect of exposure to the number 10 compared to the number 200 on the auditor's fraud estimates is known to social scientists as *anchoring*.[2] The usual explanation for the phenomenon is that numerical values can serve as easily available reference points for our predictions about the world, especially when we lack complete information, and that the System 1 mind fails to sufficiently adjust from those reference points. So, when an auditor in the first subgroup of the study is asked to estimate the rate of accounting fraud—a topic about which he possesses some but not complete knowledge—the number 10, prominent in his mind, is likely to affect his estimate.[3]

Numerical anchors can act as reference points not only for probability estimates but also for determinations of value. This makes them a valuable tool of Persuasion, especially in negotiations over price, in which numbers, in the form of offers and counteroffers, are almost certain to be part of the conversation. When we are trying to determine exactly what a deal would be worth to us—that is, our reservation price—we can be subconsciously pulled in the direction of an anchor value to which we have been exposed. A seller attempting to persuade his counterpart that what he is selling is particularly valuable can be helped by setting a high anchor, in the form of a negotiation demand, while a buyer attempting to persuade her counterpart that the subject matter of the negotiation has a low value can be aided by setting a low anchor, in the form of an offer.

A vivid example of this effect was demonstrated in an experiment involving real estate agents. Psychologists Max Bazerman and Margaret Neale asked agents to recommend to buyers and sellers what their reservation price should be in negotiations over the sale of a particular house.[4] To inform their advice, they provided the agents with a great deal of information about the house itself along with market data concerning other houses in the same neighborhood that had been sold recently. The experimenters varied a single piece of data: the purported listing price of the house (i.e., the seller's initial negotiating demand). On average, agents who were provided higher listing prices recommended that both buyers and sellers set higher reservation prices than agents who were provided with lower listing prices, even though the objective information about the house and the market conditions were exactly the same for all agents.

My colleague Chris Guthrie and I demonstrated this effect in an experiment concerning the settlement of a lawsuit over a new car that the buyer believed was defective.[5] The experimental subjects, all of whom were asked to play the role of the disgruntled purchaser, were advised that their lawyer believed the case was very close and a court judgment could go either way. All of the subjects were then told that the defendant in the case, the car dealership, had made a final offer, to pay them $12,000 to settle the case out of court, and they had to either accept that offer or take their chances in court before a judge. Half of the subjects were told that the dealership had previously offered a $2,000 settlement, before increasing its offer to $12,000. The other half were told that the dealership had previously offered $10,000.

Even though all the subjects were choosing between the same $12,000 settlement agreement in the focal negotiation and the same plan B (a risky trip to court), the initial offer, now superseded, clearly anchored the value they placed on settling the case. Those who were told they had originally received the lower ($2,000) offer were twice as likely as those in the higher-offer ($10,000) group to indicate that they would definitely or probably accept the $12,000 final offer. The results suggest that, in a context in which it is difficult to determine exactly how much money would make the recipient indifferent between reaching a negotiated settlement and pursuing her plan B, anchors can subconsciously affect valuation decisions.

This effect is one of the reasons why I suggested in Part 1 that a negotiator who is confident in Bargaining Zone Analysis can benefit by making the initial proposal rather than encouraging or even allowing his counterpart to do so. By making an offer below a seller's reservation point or a demand above a buyer's, you are likely to persuade a counterpart that reaching agreement with you would be at least a bit more desirable than

THE EFFECT OF AN ANCHOR

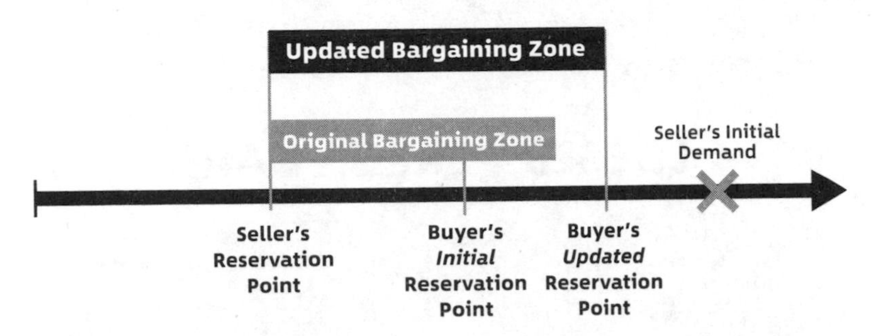

A seller's high initial demand can cause a buyer to determine his reservation point should be higher than previously thought, increasing the bargaining zone to include agreements that would be desirable for the seller.

he otherwise would think. She might reject that first offer, but with her estimate of the value of reaching agreement subtly shifted, a subsequent, more generous offer from you might now seem better than pursuing her plan B when she otherwise would not have thought so. Indeed, there is ample research that supports this theory directly. At least in the context of relatively simple negotiations over price, negotiators who make aggressive first offers tend to capture more cooperative surplus than those who do not, holding all else equal.[6]

14

LOSSES VERSUS GAINS

Imagine that a stranger walked up to you and a friend, gave one of you a coffee mug and the other a large chocolate bar, and then asked whether you would like to trade the item you received for the other one. If you are a chocoholic like me, you would probably trade the mug for the chocolate bar and not trade the chocolate for the mug. If you are a caffeine addict who prefers savory foods to sweets, you would probably have the reverse set of preferences. What is surprising is that research shows that a large number of people would not wish to trade, regardless of whether they were given the mug or the candy initially.

Similarly, research shows that if some people are given mugs (or chocolate bars, or lottery tickets, or anything else) while others are given cash, the people given a mug would demand a larger payment to sell it, on average, than the people given cash are willing to pay to buy it. In these experiments, the mugs clearly have no special sentimental value to the group of "mug owners," because the researchers hand them out only a couple of minutes before the subjects are given the opportunity to sell them, and there is no reason to think that subjects in one group enjoy mugs more than those in the other.

The explanation for these curious findings is that people tend to be more hesitant about losing something than they are enthusiastic about the possibility of gaining something of equal value. This phenomenon, that losses loom larger than gains, is known to social scientists as *loss aversion*.[1]

A negotiated agreement, of course, usually involves both parties obtaining something and giving up something else. This means that if both parties implicitly use the preagreement state of the world as their reference point for judging what constitutes a "loss" and what constitutes a "gain," fewer deals will be made than would be the case in a world without loss aversion. Potential mug purchasers, for example, would have lower reservation prices than we would otherwise expect. People who desperately love mugs will still buy them, but people with more neutral feelings about mugs will be less likely to, because the money (or chocolate bar or whatever else they would be trading) that they would *lose* would likely seem relatively more significant and the mug that they would *gain* relatively less significant. Social scientists call this effect of loss aversion the *status quo bias*.[2]

That's the bad news. But like the other quirky ways in which our System 1 mind relies on reference points to assess value, loss aversion also provides an opportunity for negotiators to benefit from the skillful use of Persuasion. The reference point that people use for comparison when deciding whether to mentally process a change as either a "gain" or a "loss" is rarely set in stone. The current state of the world is the most obvious reference point in many situations, but it is not the only one—an expectation or even a hope about the future can create a reference point.

The challenge for the negotiator is to convince your counterpart to implicitly adopt a reference point that would make *not* entering into an agreement feel like suffering a loss—which he will then take pains to avoid. A particularly useful tactic is describing a world in which a deal has already been consummated or, better yet, creating an opportunity for your counterpart to experience what that would be like. Car dealers do this by letting you take the vehicle for a test drive; Amazon's Kindle store does this by allowing you to download the beginning of a book without purchasing it. These sales tactics won't cause anyone to buy a car or book that they hate, but they will often increase customers' reservation points to some extent by making an impasse seem more like accepting a loss (which is painful) than like merely failing to capture a gain (less painful).

One particularly pernicious implication of loss aversion is that, to avoid having to accept a loss, people will often take risks that they would never willingly accept for the chance of obtaining an equivalent gain. If both parties view making a deal as accepting a loss, this increased tolerance for alternative risky courses of action can lead to calamitous impasses.

On October 7, 2001, the San Francisco Giants slugger Barry Bonds hit a record-setting 73rd home run of the season into the right-field seats of the team's stadium. Alex Popov appeared to snag the ball in the webbing of the baseball glove he had brought along in the hope that exactly this opportunity would arise, but a violent scrum ensued and the ball came loose. Another fan, Patrick Hayashi, somehow emerged from the melee with ball in hand and was escorted to safety by stadium security. Popov claimed the ball was his and sued Hayashi.

Experts at the time believed that the ball would bring $1 million at auction. Legal observers thought the outcome of a court case was highly uncertain—it really could have gone either way. If we assume that each man had a 50 percent chance of prevailing, Popov's reservation price in the settlement negotiation should have been less than $500,000 (given the expected value of the litigation along with its riskiness and the legal fees involved), and Hayashi's reservation price should have been more than $500,000.

Barry Bonds, along with many other observers, recommended that the two men sell the ball and split the proceeds. The two men, along with their lawyers, met and tried to negotiate an out-of-court settlement agreement, but to no avail. Even four sessions with a respected mediator could not help. There should have been a bargaining zone, but there simply wasn't, so Popov and Hayashi pursued their shared plan B of litigating the matter in court.

The fundamental barrier to agreement was that each man believed the ball was rightfully his. Viewed from the reference point of having complete dominion over the ball, the prospect of reaching a negotiated agreement to split its value felt to both of them like *losing a half-million dollars*. Like many people, both Popov and Hayashi were willing to pursue a risky plan B in an effort to avoid suffering such a large loss.

This perspective ended up being quite expensive for both of them. Fourteen months after the scuffle in the bleachers, a Solomonic San Francisco judge named Kevin McCarthy ruled that the two men shared legal ownership of the ball. He ordered it sold and the profits divided.[3] For a variety of reasons, which might or might not have been predictable, the value of the ball had declined precipitously during the time period of the litigation. It was ultimately sold at auction in the summer of 2003 for a disappointing $450,000. By this time, Hayashi owed one-third of his share of the net proceeds to his lawyer, who had taken the case on a contingent-fee basis, and Popov was billed $473,530 by his attorney, more than twice his share of the proceeds (which, in turn, led to another lawsuit, this one against the lawyer).[4]

If Popov and Hayashi could have persuaded each other to evaluate a potential negotiated agreement with reference to what they had before Barry Bonds hit the fateful home run (nothing), rather than with reference to what each felt he was entitled to (complete ownership), they almost certainly would have chosen agreement rather than rolling the dice on a risky plan B, and both men would be substantially wealthier today.

15

ROSE-COLORED GLASSES

Loss aversion helps elucidate why Alex Popov and Patrick Hayashi couldn't settle their dispute over the Barry Bonds home-run ball, but it doesn't provide a complete explanation. If either (or both) had believed he was certain to lose the court battle—meaning that he realized his plan B was terrible—that man would have probably been willing to accept some modest amount of money to settle the case out of court. Even accounting for loss aversion, few people will accept an enormous risk in an effort to avoid having to accept a small loss. Popov and Hayashi no doubt spent hundreds of thousands of dollars on lawyers to fight for a small leather-clad sphere made up of cork, rubber, and yarn because each of them believed that he would ultimately win the lawsuit.

It is well documented that, on average, people tend to think they are more likely to win a legal case than they actually are. Decision theorist George Loewenstein and colleagues gave pairs of both undergraduate and law-school students identical information about a lawsuit involving a collision between a motorcycle and a car. They designated one student the injured plaintiff (the motorcyclist) and one the defendant, and gave the defendant cash in proportion to the amount at stake in the lawsuit:

$1 for every $10,000 of damages suffered by the plaintiff. The subjects were told to try to negotiate a settlement, with the defendant paying the plaintiff some amount of money. If they failed to agree, the case would be decided by a local judge, and the cash redistributed (or not) according to the judge's decision.

Before the negotiations began, all subjects were asked to write down their prediction of how much money, if any, the judge would award to the plaintiff in the event they reached impasse in their negotiation. Subjects in the plaintiff role predicted significantly higher awards than did subjects in the defendant role, even though all subjects had the same set of information. Not surprisingly, subjects with wider disparities in their predictions were far less likely to reach a negotiated agreement than subjects whose predictions were closer together.[1] If both parties think they are highly likely to prevail, the expected value of litigating can exceed the value of settling for any possible amount for at least one of the parties, even if they properly take into account transaction costs (legal fees), risk aversion (the possibility of ending up with nothing at all), and reputational and relational costs of litigating.

I can personally vouch for the reliability of this finding. I provide law students in my negotiation class a file full of information about a much more complicated dispute over a construction contract and assign each of them the role of the plaintiff's or the defendant's lawyer. The students then review the relevant law of construction disputes and prepare a brief that argues their position to a court. Each pair of students then attempts to negotiate a settlement, understanding that if no agreement is reached, a judge (in this case, a professor) will consider the opposing students' individual briefs and render an all-or-nothing ruling in the case. I grade the students based on how their settlement agreement or court verdict (if they don't settle) compares to that of the other students assigned the same role.

Before the students negotiate, I have them write down their estimate of how likely the judge would be to rule for the plaintiff. While they negotiate, I calculate the average of the predictions made by the students in each role, and I present the averages when the negotiation period ends. This is the academic equivalent of performing a trapeze act without a net; it would be quite embarrassing if the demonstration failed. The difference between the average responses of the two groups varies somewhat from year to year, but, no matter the size of the class, I have never failed to demonstrate that the average student "plaintiff" is more likely than the average student "defendant" to believe that the plaintiff will prevail in court.

This effect has been reinforced by other studies conducted in the wilds of the real world, outside the setting of carefully controlled experiments. Psychologist Elizabeth Loftus and colleagues interviewed practicing lawyers before and after their cases were resolved. They found that, on average, the lawyers predicted more desirable settlement or court outcomes than they actually achieved.[2]

Social scientists call this tendency, which is in no way unique to lawyers or lawsuits, the *optimism bias*,[3] one specific illustration of a long list of egocentric dispositions that cause us to think better of ourselves and our prospects than is justified by the objective facts. One way that researchers often study the optimism bias is to ask subjects whether they are more or less likely to experience a desirable future outcome than the average member of some comparison group. If individuals are not biased—and if they don't live in Garrison Keillor's Lake Wobegon, where, famously, "all the women are strong, all the men are good looking, and all the children are above average"[4]—around half of the subjects should predict that they are more likely than average to experience a good outcome. But the vast majority of college students think they are more likely than average to earn a grade above the class average, most MBA graduates expect to receive a job offer with a higher-than-average starting salary relative to their peers, most taxi drivers think they are better drivers than the average of their compatriots, and a whopping 94 percent of college professors think they are better at their job than the average professor.[5]

A healthy amount of confidence in the future is certainly useful. Without sufficient optimism, no one would take any chances; few people would ever try to stretch their abilities, start a new business, try out a new hobby, or go on a date. And some amount of undue optimism seems to be necessary for mental health. Researchers have found that the clinically depressed are most likely to view their future prospects in an unbiased way.[6] The optimism bias can also produce social benefits. Studies show that people attribute higher amounts of skill and stature to those who display a high degree of confidence in their knowledge and ability.[7]

The bias seems to result from a combination of two psychological tendencies, both of which relate to the information on which we subconsciously focus our attention. First, we are more likely to notice facts that are consistent with the way we wish to see the world than with the way we do not wish to see the world. In a famous study from the 1950s, psychologists Albert Hastorf and Hadley Cantril showed students from Dartmouth and Princeton the tape of a particularly aggressive football game between the two Ivy League schools. Both groups of students identified relatively more penalties committed by players from the other school.[8]

Second, we tend to overestimate our own relative ability to affect outcomes, because we pay more attention to ourselves than we pay to others.[9] If I think a lot about the attributes that make me a good professor but don't spend much time focusing on the positive attributes of my colleagues, I'm likely to conclude that I'm above average at my job, even if I'm not. This point explains occasional findings of the exact opposite effect, a pessimism bias, in which most people believe they are worse than average.[10] This bias is observed in situations in which people recognize they lack relevant skills but don't fully account for the fact that others in the comparison group lack them as well. If asked, most college professors would probably believe they would be worse than the average college professor at performing brain surgery, because they would tend to focus more on the fact that they have had no training than on the fact that their colleagues are also ill equipped for the task.

Depending on the circumstances, the optimism bias can either increase or decrease a negotiator's interest in reaching an agreement and thus make his reservation point higher or lower than it would be in the absence of bias. To predict the effect, we need to know whether the potential consequences of reaching a deal or the potential consequences of pursuing one's plan B are more uncertain.

In legal-settlement negotiations, like the one engaged in by Popov and Hayashi, the consequences of settling the case are fairly certain: one party pays the other a specified amount of money and keeps the ball, or they sell the ball and divide the profits. The consequences of not settling and pursuing their plan B, in contrast, are uncertain: either party might win or lose the lawsuit, or there might be some intermediate outcome (which is, of course, what happened when the judge divided ownership of the ball). When the consequences of pursuing plan B are uncertain, the optimism bias will tend to make that plan B look more desirable than it otherwise would. This has the effect of reducing the perceived desirability of reaching agreement and narrowing the bargaining zone (i.e., why settle when I believe the outlook for court is so rosy?).

When a counterpart's plan B has uncertain consequences, Persuasion requires the negotiator to attempt to reduce the extent of the bias by emphasizing the negative outcomes that might result from pursuing that path. This is why, for example, lawyers emphatically argue their case to their counterparts during out-of-court settlement negotiations. There is exactly zero possibility that the adversary will concede defeat; the goal is to reduce, if only slightly, the other side's confidence in prevailing if the case were to go to court.

In other negotiation contexts, it is the future consequences of reaching agreement that are uncertain. When Bono was trying to convince Bill Clinton to entirely forgive African debts, Clinton's agreement could have led to a legacy of grandeur or one of weak-kneed naïveté. The less bold alternative of only partially forgiving the debts would appear to have more predictable, intermediate consequences. In this situation, we can predict that the optimism bias would have caused President Clinton to view the deal proposed by the rock star to be more desirable than an unbiased analysis would have likely concluded, thus increasing the likelihood of agreement.

In these situations, a negotiator can use the optimism bias as a tool of Persuasion by focusing his counterpart's attention, and thus her rose-colored glasses, on the more positive consequences that could stem from reaching agreement.

A little more optimism can make the difference between having a bargaining zone and not having one. In *Draft Day*, Cleveland general manager Sonny Weaver knew that trading several years' worth of his team's future draft picks for the opportunity to draft star quarterback Bo Callahan was a deal with a big potential payoff but also a lot of risk. The Seattle general manager's reminder that the trade could potentially save the city of Cleveland might have been the little extra push that was needed to cement the deal. Sonny, like most of us, probably believed he had a better-than-average chance of making magic happen.

16

PROMINENCE AND PROBABILITY

In 1978, three teenage girls driving a Ford Pinto to a volleyball game were rear-ended by a van. The Pinto's gas tank exploded and the car became an inferno. Two of the girls died immediately, and the third died hours later.

As author Malcolm Gladwell explained in the *New Yorker*, the cause of the deaths can be understood from a variety of perspectives, each of which suggests a different target for the blame. One problem was that the van, weighing in at 4,000 pounds, was twice as heavy as the Pinto, a compact car. Another was that the van's driver apparently looked down for his package of cigarettes shortly before the crash and didn't see the Pinto until just before impact. A third problem was that the Pinto was stopped in the road because a curb prevented the driver from pulling over to retrieve the gas cap that had just fallen off. A case could be made that primary responsibility should rest with the light steel used for the Pinto, the heavy construction of the van, the inattention of the van driver, or the poor design of the roadway.[1]

Public indignation was not directed at any of these causes of the tragedy, however, but at the engineers who chose to locate the Pinto's gas tank near its rear bumper. For this decision, prosecutors charged the Ford Motor Company with criminal homicide, and the Pinto brand soon disappeared from the market. But the Pinto was not actually poorly engineered. Statistically, it was no more dangerous than other cars in its class built by General Motors or the American Motors Corporation. Because of engineering choices, the Pinto was somewhat more prone to fire fatalities resulting from rear-end collisions than similar cars, but it was safer in other ways than its rivals, a fact that enabled Ford to ultimately prevail in court.[2] So why was nearly all of the public attention focused on the gas tank?

The answer lies in what is known as the *availability heuristic*,[3] another mental shortcut that System 1 relies on to make sense of a complicated world. For a variety of reasons, some events are more mentally prominent than others—that is, they stick in our minds—and we often use judgments about prominence (which are easy) to answer queries about frequency (which are hard), thus concluding that mentally available events are more likely to occur than they actually are. Like most other heuristics, this one is usually sensible but not always accurate. Events often stand out precisely because they occur frequently, but sometimes they are prominent for other reasons entirely.

Try asking yourself whether there are more words in the English language that begin with the letter *K* or that have *K* as their third letter. Psychologists who study the availability heuristic know that the latter choice is correct but that most people choose the former. It is easier to call to mind words that begin with the letter *K*—kitchen, king, and so on—than words that have that letter buried somewhere in the middle. But again, in this example, mental availability does not equate with frequency. Most Americans also believe that homicides occur more frequently than suicides, although the reverse is actually true. Here, the cause of the misunderstanding is probably that homicides often receive extensive media coverage, whereas suicides rarely do unless the victim happens to be a celebrity.

Every negotiation presents a choice between two possible futures, one in which the parties reach agreement, and the other in which both negotiators pursue their individual plan Bs. The consequences of this choice, as I've noted, are usually not completely certain. For Bill Clinton, agreeing to Bono's request for complete debt forgiveness might have made him an international human rights hero, and it might have provoked an angry backlash against the Democratic party by voters who thought the president should be more generous to American citizens in need and less so to foreign countries. For Alex Popov, litigation might have resulted in sole ownership of the prized home-run ball, shared ownership, or nothing at all. Bono and Patrick Hayashi could increase the odds of obtaining the agreement they wanted by making available in the minds of Clinton and Popov positive visions of the future that could occur if an agreement were reached and negative visions of a future that could occur in the case of impasse.

Imagine being a salesperson in 1979 trying to sell a Chevrolet Vega, a primary competitor of the Ford Pinto, to a customer. The Vega was not actually safer overall than the Pinto—both cars had some unsafe features[4]—but the image of a car igniting into a fireball was extremely vivid and mentally available. Mentioning that the gas tanks of Pintos were known to explode would almost certainly cause the customer to increase his reservation price for a Vega! It is hardly a surprise that Ford discontinued production of the Pinto in 1980. Chevy salespeople no doubt suggested to potential customers that an agreement to purchase a Vega would lead to a future of rainbows and unicorns and an impasse could lead to an exploding fuel tank.

17

FOLLOWING THE CROWD

Consider two famous experiments, conducted in the mid-twentieth century by founding fathers of modern social psychology, that illustrate how important the actions of others are to our behaviors:

In 1951, Solomon Asch showed subjects two pictures. One had a single vertical line. The other had three vertical lines of different lengths, one of which was clearly equal in length to the single line in the first picture. Asch asked the subjects an exceedingly simple question: Which of the three lines in the second picture is equal in length to the line in the first picture? Almost every subject in the control group answered the question correctly. Subjects assigned to the experimental condition had been placed in a room with a group of people who were supposedly other subjects but were actually working for Asch. Asch posed his question to his assistants first, and several of them confidently gave the wrong answer. When the real subjects were then asked the question, more than one-third provided the obviously incorrect answer that the assistants had given.[1]

A decade later, Stanley Milgram, who became famous for demonstrating the willingness of ordinary people to provide seemingly painful electric shocks to others when ordered to do so by an authority figure,

SOLOMON ASCH'S VERTICAL LINE EXPERIMENT

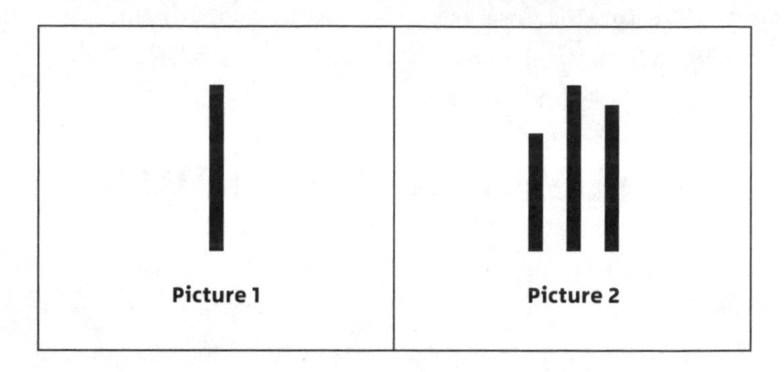

One-third of subjects said that the line in Picture 1 matched the wrong line in Picture 2 after observing someone else provide the wrong answer.

placed an assistant on a street corner looking upward. Occasionally a pedestrian walking past would stop and look upward too, but few people broke stride. When Milgram placed a group of assistants on the same corner gazing upward, however, many people stopped and joined the group. The more of Milgram's assistants in the group, the more likely that passersby would stop and gaze skyward.[2]

These experiments demonstrate two different ways in which people use social cues as heuristics. The Milgram experiment shows how, when constructing our preferences, we often rely on the behavior of others as cues. When you are walking down the street and come to a corner, if you see many people standing still and looking skyward, you are likely to figure that there is something to be seen that might interest you and, therefore, that your time would be better spent stopping, at least briefly, than by going about your business.

You have probably seen signs in hotel bathrooms giving you the choice between having your towel replaced every day and reusing it in order to conserve resources and help the environment. These signs are quite successful at persuading guests to reuse their towels. But for many a bleary-eyed hotel guest just starting the day, the best choice isn't obvious. Sure, reusing the towel saves water, which is clearly a good thing. But having a fresh towel each day is a nice luxury. And how much harm is really caused by washing one more towel?

When faced with the towel decision, would you care what total strangers do? Psychologist Robert Cialdini and his colleagues discovered that the answer, for many people, is a decided "yes." By placing on those ubiquitous signs the information that a majority of hotel guests reuse their towels, rates of reuse increased by 26 percent compared with signs that stated only that guests could help save the environment and show respect for nature by reusing their towels.[3]

The Asch experiment demonstrates how we often rely on others to interpret factual information in the world around us, which will indirectly affect our analysis of a negotiation situation. Imagine that you noticed a sidewalk vendor hawking wool scarves for $19.95. This might seem like a good deal if the scarves are made from cashmere but a bad deal if they are made from a lower-quality wool. If you are not a textile expert, determining whether your reservation price for a scarf in this situation is more or less than $20 would be difficult. If there is a long line of shoppers waiting to purchase scarves, you would be more likely to buy than if the vendor were standing by himself.

Will following the social consensus actually lead to better decisions—that is, to more utility? Sometimes, but not always. As author James Surowiecki explains in *The Wisdom of Crowds*, group decisions about factual information are usually better than individual ones if the members of the group are diverse and they reach their determinations individually.[4] If you want to know how many jelly beans are in a jar, you are better off asking 20 people to guess and then taking the average of their responses than relying on your own pair of eyes. But if the members of the group are too similar to one another, sharing the same biases and worldviews, or—even worse—if they make their determinations sequentially and are affected by the determinations of those who went before, the crowd might prove to be foolish rather than wise. If the last 19 guessers base their jelly-bean estimates on that of the first, and if the first guesser has poor eyesight or is inattentive, the group average might be wildly inaccurate. And, of course, when it comes to matters of subjective utility—how much a jar full of jelly beans is worth, for example—the group consensus is useful only to the extent that its members have preferences similar to yours.

As a general matter, however, in a complex world characterized by too much information, too little cognitive power to analyze it all perfectly, and too little time to use the brainpower that we do have, relying on social signals can be a very useful heuristic device. This, in turn, gives negotiators the opportunity to use information about social consensus as a tool of Persuasion. Holding all other things equal, we all would prefer to buy a scarf from a popular vendor than from one with no customers, to work for a company that ranked highest in a survey of "best employers" than for one that isn't ranked at all, and to take a course from the professor who received the best student ratings, even though we know that none of these indicators absolutely guarantees high quality. It follows that a 5TN should always point out to her counterpart that other people value what she has to offer.

Which social group's behavior or testimony will prove most persuasive depends, as one might expect, on context. When we are trying to determine the value of some goods or services, not everyone's observations or preferences are equally relevant, and people seem to intuitively recognize this. Research on advertising has shown that the most effective endorser of a product depends on what exactly the seller is trying to promote.

When functionality is the key to value but difficult to assess, the opinions of experts in the field carry the most weight: think of the old Trident sugarless gum commercials that for years reported, "Four out of five dentists recommend sugarless gum for their patients who chew gum."[5] (What kind of gum, by the way, do the other 20 percent of dentists recommend?) When an item reflects social status, celebrities can make better endorsers, perhaps explaining why basketball coaching legend Phil Jackson drove an Audi automobile (at least in the commercials) and actor Matthew McConaughey drove a Lincoln (and claimed that he did even before he was paid to do so). When value is determined by subjective personal enjoyment, testimonials provided by regular people, who we will probably assume have proclivities similar to ours, are usually most effective, which might explain why McConaughey doesn't shill for chocolate chip cookies or toilet paper.[6]

Negotiators can deploy the tool of Persuasion by demonstrating that the appropriate reference group would place a high value on reaching agreement in the focal negotiation or a low value on pursuing the counterpart's plan B.

18

WANTING WHAT WE CAN'T HAVE

Colleen Szot is a legendary writer of scripts for direct-response infomercials—the television programs that typically air late at night or on specialized cable channels and invite viewers to immediately purchase the products being advertised, usually online or by telephone. In 2012, she wrote the scripts for 7 of the year's top 50 infomercials,[1] and her scripts have sold more than $1 billion in products. But her best-known line of dialogue had nothing directly to do with the product she was trying to sell.

At the end of an advertisement for NordicTrack exercise equipment, Szot decided to replace the usual notice that "operators are standing by" with a reworded call to action: "If operators are busy, please call again." According to an article in the *Harvard Business Review*, this slight change "turned the exercise machine into one of the best-selling products in infomercial history."[2] NordicTrack is a famously successful infomercial brand, but the claim that its entire success can be attributed to this single script change should perhaps be taken with a grain of salt. Still, the simple change in language apparently did cause a notable increase in sales. Why?

The traditional "operators are standing by" language implicitly suggests low demand. Would the operators be "standing by," just waiting to take your call, if many viewers wanted to purchase a NordicTrack machine at the advertised price? Probably not. If the machine were popular, the operators would be occupied taking orders, and you would receive a busy signal when you tried to call. In the face of such popularity, it would be important for NordicTrack to remind you to call again rather than give up.

What made the revised NordicTrack infomercial persuasive can be traced back to the psychological principle known as *reactance*, first articulated by psychologist Jack Brehm in 1956.[3] We tend to want something more if we fear that we might be unable to obtain it. Sure, that NordicTrack machine looks like fun, and who wouldn't want to have six-pack abs like the model we are watching working out with it while we are splayed out on the couch eating Cheetos? But would we use it, would we look like that model even if we did, and is it worth its hefty price tag? The machine's desirability might depend, at least in part, on whether we might be unable to get one. If other people are so desperate to buy that all the operators might be busy, we had better hurry up and get in on the deal while we can.

The same concept was illustrated more recently on an episode of the ABC television sitcom *Modern Family*. Bumbling real estate agent Phil Dunphy, played by actor Ty Burrell, has just shown a house—for the seventh time—to a couple who say they love it but just can't decide if they are "in love" with it. While the lookie-loos poke around, Phil takes a call from his wife, Claire, who is concerned that the garbagemen might not haul away the crumbling old easy chair Phil has left on their front curb. Phil assures Claire that "if they won't take it, someone else will." When Claire questions this prediction, Phil confidently explains that "it's warm and cozy and someone is going to snap it up." Eavesdropping on only one side of the conversation, the indecisive couple suddenly fear that the house is about to be purchased. In an absolute panic, their indecision vanishes, and they agree to buy.[4]

Maybe Hollywood scriptwriters study reactance, or maybe this particular principle is particularly good for laughs, because it seems to pop up in a lot of sitcoms. HBO's *Silicon Valley* chronicles the travails of tech genius Richard Hendricks, played by Thomas Middleditch, and his crew of super-nerd programmers and business advisers as they try to launch a new startup. When Hendricks and the gang are trying to attract investment money from venture capitalists for their suddenly hot idea, one firm goes so far as to rent the San Francisco Giants baseball stadium (where Barry Bonds hit the ill-fated home-run ball) in order to throw a party on the field for the crew and plaster Hendricks's image on the jumbotron scoreboard in the outfield. When Hendricks then visits the firm's office to discuss financing, though, the venture-capital guys are suddenly unenthusiastic, pointing out problems with Hendricks's business plan and telling him to come back and see them after he has worked out some of the issues. Sensing his road to riches might be less smooth than it first appeared, Hendricks gets nervous, but his blowhard consigliere, Erlich Bachman (T. J. Miller), senses a negotiation tactic.

Rather than using the term *reactance*, Bachman explains to Hendricks that the firm is "neg-ing" them, a tactic he describes as one usually used as a form of sexual manipulation by men trying to spark the interest of women by pretending that they are not interested. Furious about being manipulated, Hendricks storms back into the boardroom and screams that he will never return and never let that firm invest in his company. Now the venture capitalists panic, sensing that their opportunity to get in on the ground floor of the next big thing is slipping away.[5]

Just as scarcity can increase the perceived value of reaching an agreement to a negotiator, availability can decrease the perceived value. If Phil Dunphy suggests that the house you are considering is about to be sold out from under you, its value in your eyes might increase. Relatedly, if he tells you it is yours for the asking, its value in your eyes is likely to decline. Real estate agents (the real kind) are known, in fact, to remove listings of houses that have not sold from the multiple listing service and then repost them in order to reset the "number of days on the market" statistic back to zero.[6] As this practice suggests, buyers tend to be skeptical of the quality of a house that has been sitting on the market for too long.

Sometimes, as in the case of a stale real estate listing, the availability of a potential deal indicates that other people have already turned it down. Logically, we can interpret this fact as a signal that, if we knew all the information, we would be likely to determine that the deal is undesirable to us too. This won't always be the case, of course. Other people might be mistaken about the facts, or they might have preferences that are different from ours. But the heuristic seems to be a reasonable one, especially if we don't have the time to investigate every house on the market. What problems lurk deep inside a house that no one else will buy?

Research on the phenomenon, named *reactive devaluation* by psychologist Lee Ross and colleagues,[7] suggests a slightly different effect at work as well: knowing that our potential negotiation counterpart is willing to make a particular deal can reduce its value in our eyes, even if no one else has had the opportunity to take the deal and declined. One study, for example, found that a specific proposal to settle the Israeli-Palestinian conflict received support from students in both groups when they were told it was advanced by their political leaders. But the students opposed the proposal when told that the leaders of the other side had initiated it.[8]

Part of the explanation for this result, undoubtedly, is that resolving centuries-old ethnic and political disputes is complicated, and students are smart enough to realize that they don't have all the relevant information. If a long-standing adversary proposes a negotiated agreement, you should be concerned that its utility for you might be less than it appears for reasons you simply don't understand. If the fear is that our counterpart has information that we lack, any initial hesitancy to accept an offer solely because the other side is willing to agree to the terms should fade when we have the time and opportunity to carefully investigate the fine print. But people also tend to reactively devalue available deals when there is less risk of hidden information, suggesting that availability can affect our actual preferences.

In a study that illustrates this point, students were told that they had worked as a research assistant for a professor and that the work they performed on one of the professor's articles was far more significant than the usual student-assistant contribution, thus justifying either a cash payment or credit as the coauthor of the article when published. Half of the students were told that the professor had offered them the cash payment, while the other half were told that the professor had offered them the coauthor credit. The subjects were then asked which form of compensation they preferred. Those offered the cash preferred coauthorship, on average, whereas those offered coauthorship preferred the money.[9] Unlike proposals designed to resolve centuries of complicated ethnic hatred, college students can presumably determine how much utility they would get from a coauthorship credit and how much from a cash payment. There isn't any potentially hidden information here, which suggests that the availability of a type of compensation negatively affected the students' determination of how much utility it would provide.

Scarcity can enhance Persuasion, and too much availability can undermine it. This means that, for a 5TN, success often requires subtlety. On the one hand, you need to suggest that an agreement *is* possible. Otherwise, why would the counterpart even bother to investigate the opportunity? On the other hand, you should imply that a deal *might not* be possible, in order to maximize its perceived value to the counterpart.

19

PREFERENCES ABOUT PREFERENCES

Persuasion can also be accomplished by appealing to the ways in which striking a deal can reinforce the counterpart's broader self-conception or self-image, rather than his more narrow, immediate interests.

As Senate majority leader prior to his election as vice president and then president, Lyndon Johnson was known as one of the most successful dealmakers ever to operate in the U.S. Senate. No negotiation was tougher than his attempt to push the landmark Civil Rights Act of 1964 through a divided Congress—especially as a new president following the assassination of John F. Kennedy. Johnson's Democratic Party was split between northern liberals, who supported the bill, and segregationist southerners, who steadfastly opposed it. Worse, the southerners in his own party were filibustering the bill, preventing it from even coming up for a vote in the Senate. Obtaining the votes of the 60 senators needed to break the filibuster would require the support of Republicans, so Johnson called Senate minority leader Everett Dirksen to the Oval Office to court his support.

Conservative by disposition and generally wary of expansions of federal power, Dirksen was initially disinclined to support the new president's revolutionary bill, and he paraded out a list of practical and ideological reasons for his hesitancy. Johnson won Dirksen's backing only after he challenged the Republican leader to "decide if you want to be remembered as someone who changed the course of history, or someone who just liked to hear himself talk." Rather than trying to satisfy Dirksen's immediate goals and desires, the president appealed to the senator's preferences about his preferences—or, put another way, about the type of person that he would like to be—expanding Dirksen's view of what interests of his might be served by agreeing to the president's proposal.

Dirksen rallied Republican votes to break the filibuster, which led to the bill's passage. Johnson signed the historic legislation into law with 75 separate pens. He gave the very first one to Dirksen.[1]

The principle is also demonstrated by an academic study of the much more mundane but critically important activity of hand washing. It has long been known that the number of hospital-acquired infections can be substantially reduced by health-care providers washing their hands more often, but hospitals have had a difficult time fostering behavioral change. Psychologists Adam Grant and David Hofmann placed signs in a hospital that stressed that hand washing protects either providers or patients from catching diseases, and they found that the latter message significantly increased the behavior but the former did not.[2] Health-care professionals find constantly stopping to wash their hands annoying, but most are willing to perform this task more often, it turns out, if doing so is necessary to maintaining their self-image as people who care about their patients above all else.

Appeals to preferences about preferences can be spotted in common commercial transactions nearly every day once you know to look for them. Recently, the water heater in my home stopped working and needed to be replaced. One salesman who came to my house was peddling a technologically advanced, top-of-the-line model from South Korea that cost twice the price of the other options. After rattling off a list of technological specifications that I couldn't understand, he became very serious and said, "You seem like a man who wants the very best for his family."

I didn't buy his product, but perhaps that is because I fancy myself a prudent consumer interested in overall value for money rather than the type of person who wants the best that money can buy. I love my family very much, but I really don't care about them having the very best water heater—one that will reliably provide hot water is quite sufficient! I suspect, however, that this appeal to preferences about preferences does enable that salesman to persuade other customers to reevaluate their reservation price for his water heater, just as Michelin's long-running advertising campaign featuring cute babies and the tag line "Because so much is riding on your tires" helps it to sell tires to people who know nothing at all about the relative performance of Michelins compared to other brands.[3]

20

THE LIKABILITY BONUS

In an episode of the HBO political satire *Veep*, the vice president of the United States, Selina Meyer, played by Julia Louis-Dreyfus, is in the process of creating a task force to study "clean jobs," and she is looking forward to rewarding political contributors from the energy industry with seats on the commission. Then, at the request of a liberal senator, she promises to do exactly the opposite: to exclude energy-industry representatives. When her flummoxed staff asks her how she could have made such a commitment, Meyer blames her flip-flop on having been "niced." "He had a sparkle in his eyes, and he was nice to me," she explains apologetically.[1]

The reaction is not unique to bumblers like Vice President Meyer. As members of a fundamentally social species, we all have an instinct to be more generous to people we like than to people we don't. Just as we are more likely to do favors for or bestow gifts on such people outside of the quid pro quo context of negotiation, we are more likely to make concessions to them in the negotiation context. Part of the reason is that we are more inclined to trust people with whom we feel an affinity, a point we will explore in Part 6. But a different and equally important reason is that we obtain utility from doing things that benefit the people we like. It feels good.

If your child promises to immediately head to bed without delay in return for an extra scoop of ice cream, you experience pleasure both from *the relief you feel* about not having to fight the bedtime wars tonight and *the joy he experiences* from more chocolate. The opposite can also be true. If we dislike our counterpart, we sometimes do not want the agreement to make her happy. At some point, you have probably decided not to make a purchase from a merchant who you believe mistreated you in the past, even though this meant doing without a product or service you desired or paying more for it elsewhere, because you didn't want that business to benefit from the transaction.

Being a likable person can, in itself, increase the desirability of reaching an agreement for your counterpart, effectively shifting his reservation point. You can think of the utility that your counterpart will gain from reaching an agreement as arising from two sources: the material benefits that he will obtain, and the good feelings he will enjoy by doing something that you want and that will benefit you. The more he likes you, the more of this second type of utility is at stake.

When negotiators think about Persuasion, they usually focus on convincing their counterpart that reaching agreement will provide them with the first type of utility. But a complete negotiator benefits by ensuring that her counterpart can enjoy the second type of utility as well. Best of all, providing it doesn't cost you anything.

SUMMARY OF KEY LESSONS FROM PART 2

- Persuasion convinces the other negotiator that an agreement would be more valuable to her than she previously believed or realized. This pushes her reservation point further from yours, increasing the size of the bargaining zone and making it possible for you to obtain a more favorable agreement.
- Persuasion can be accomplished by conveying features and benefits of reaching agreement or shortcomings of the counterpart's plan B.
- To tailor Persuasion tactics, start with questions to understand the counterpart's unique needs and concerns rather than assuming that one size fits all.
- Persuasion can be employed by framing the possibility of a deal in the best possible light based on the many ways the System 1 mind relies on heuristics when assessing the value of options. These include reliance on reference points and anchors, loss aversion, the optimism bias, the availability heuristic, and reactance.
- Persuasion can also be enhanced by signaling that relevant third parties would find the focal deal desirable.
- Efforts at Persuasion need not be limited to emphasizing the material benefits of the deal. Negotiators also obtain utility from providing a benefit to someone they like and from acting in ways that are consistent with their self-image.

TOOL #3

DEAL DESIGN

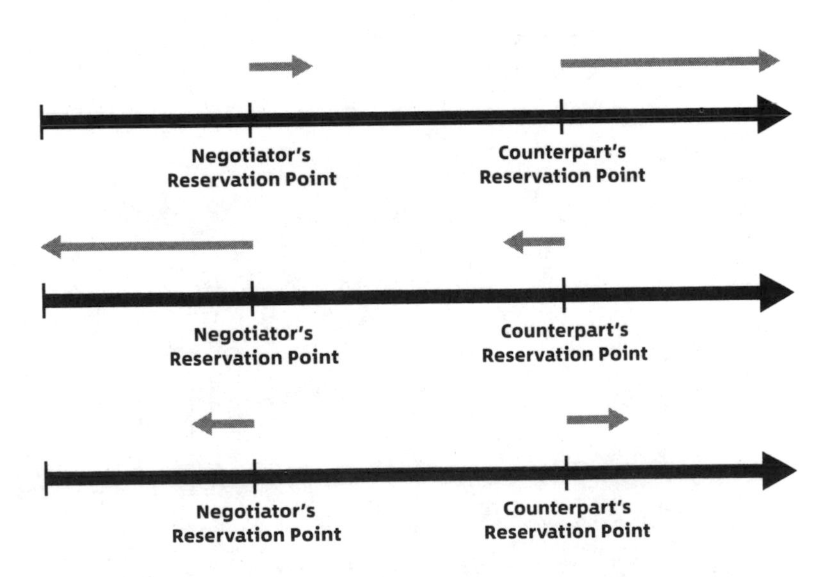

21

CREATIVITY IN NEGOTIATION

In the Roaring Twenties, entrepreneur Ivar Kreuger won fame on both sides of the Atlantic as a financier to European nations, an adviser to American presidents, and the architect of the Swedish Match company, an international industrial juggernaut that at one point manufactured two-thirds of all the phosphorus matches consumed in the world. For his innovations in the development of financial instruments, he has been called the forerunner of much of modern Wall Street. For his financial misdeeds, which came to light in the wake of the 1929 stock market crash, he earned infamous comparisons to fraudster Charles Ponzi and even gangster Al Capone.[1] But two decades earlier, Kreuger earned his first fortune in part due to his ability to creatively redesign a common transaction.

In 1908, the young Kreuger established a London construction firm called Kreuger & Toll. At that time, standard construction contracts came without guarantees of timely completion, which meant that the clients effectively bore all the risk of delays. Although some construction delays result from events beyond the contractor's control, builders have more ability than their clients to minimize that risk by selecting reliable subcontractors, managing them efficiently, procuring supplies with sufficient lead time, and so on. Builders are also often in a better position than their clients to insure against delays that they can't control and to diversify the risk that they cannot insure over a portfolio of projects. Kreuger learned that in return for his guaranteeing timely completion of his projects, many clients were willing to pay a premium price. He began including such guarantees in his contracts, and by the outbreak of World War I, Kreuger & Toll was one of the leading construction firms in Europe.[2]

Relying on habit and custom, and on the reams of fine print that accompany most consumer and business contracts, many negotiators assume that most types of deals will be structured in a particular way with a static set of features, and that the variables that are subject to negotiation are both limited and fixed. Using the third tool, **Deal Design**, 5TNs structure agreements in noncustomary ways to increase the total amount of cooperative surplus that they generate. These structural changes alter both parties' reservation points and, when used correctly, increase the size of the bargaining zone.

Kreuger understood how careful attention to Deal Design can increase a transaction's potential value. Bearing the risk of delays would undoubtedly increase Kreuger's expected costs of doing business, which would increase his reservation price for selling construction services. But the timeliness guarantee increased the reservation prices of many potential customers even more, compared to the typical contract, thus expanding the size of the bargaining zone and increasing the amount of cooperative surplus created by each contract. This allowed Kreuger to charge prices that more than compensated for his increased costs, while simultaneously offering his customers deals that were better for them than what the competition offered.

22

WINE, WOOL, AND THE WEALTH OF NATIONS

Before Kreuger's innovation, most builders and their customers assumed that the negotiable elements of a construction contract were limited. The extent of the project was subject to negotiation, of course, as was the price for the job. But financial responsibility for delays was simply ignored as an issue that could potentially be assigned to either party. Just because no one raised the issue during contract negotiations did not mean that it did not exist; in the event of a delay in completion, someone was going to bear a cost, either by losing money or by not being able to use the property advantageously. Failure to explicitly consider the issue meant that the risk would be implicitly allocated to one party. In this case, by custom, the loss would fall on the customer, who would not be able to use or rent out the new building during the time that it was under construction.

In some cases, this might create an annoyance but not a serious problem. But let's assume, for example, that a new home is due for completion on June 20, the customer plans to host her daughter's wedding at the house on July 1, and the cost of arranging for a suitable substitute site at the last minute would be $20,000. To avoid this risk and enjoy greater peace of mind, the customer might be willing to pay a $10,000 premium for the house in return for the builder agreeing to design the deal with an on-time guarantee, perhaps by assuming responsibility for any costs the customer suffers in the event of a delay.

It isn't enough that the customer would prefer that the builder guarantee the completion date, or even that the customer would be willing to pay some amount of money in return. For a guarantee to be an appropriate use of the tool of Deal Design, the expected cost to the builder of providing the guarantee must be less than its expected benefit to the customer. This could be the case for several reasons. Perhaps the contractor can avoid all risk of delay by working with more reliable suppliers of materials than he usually would, and this will cost him only $3,000. Alternatively, perhaps there is no way for the contractor to completely control the risk of delay—some unforeseen issues usually arise during complicated projects, and the behavior of his subcontractors is not completely within his control—but he can estimate that the likelihood of a delay is low and thus estimate that the average, expected cost of assuming liability is only $3,000.

In either case, if the customer's reservation price for the project alone was $500,000, her reservation price for the project with the guarantee should be $510,000, and if the builder's reservation price for doing the work without the guarantee was $470,000, his reservation price for a con-

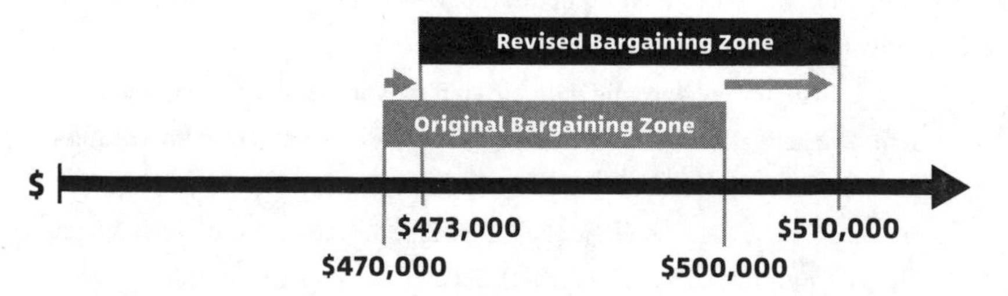

tract including the guarantee should be $473,000. Adding the guarantee to the parties' agreement creates an additional $7,000 in value compared to the typical structure of the deal, increasing the cooperative surplus enjoyed by the two parties from $30,000 to $37,000.

The basic insight that underlies how negotiators can design deals that are as profitable as possible is often called *integrative bargaining* in the academic literature on negotiation.[1] The concept can be traced back to core economic principles developed in the eighteenth and nineteenth centuries. Focusing on international trade, Adam Smith wrote in *The Wealth of Nations* that two nations could both be made better off if each specialized in producing products in which it had an absolute advantage and then traded with each other. In Smith's famous example, Portugal could produce excellent wine more cheaply than could England, while England was more efficient at producing wool, so rather than each nation growing grapes and raising sheep, Portugal should do the former and England the latter, and they should then trade their products with each other.[2]

Shortly thereafter, the political economist David Ricardo added the important observation that such specialization could make two countries better off even if one could produce both of the goods under consideration more cheaply than could the other. In that case, each country should specialize in the product in which it held a comparative advantage.[3] If Portugal could produce good wool slightly cheaper than could England, but Portugal could produce good wine much cheaper, for example, it would be better off producing only wine and trading it to England for wool. The reason is that the opportunity cost of producing wool—in this case, forgoing some very efficient wine production—would be greater than the cost of having to purchase wool from England.

The logic explains why individuals find it advantageous to trade with one another rather than investing their energy in self-sufficiency: growing all of their own food, building their own house, doing their own dry cleaning, providing their own medical care, and so on. The principle is also easily expanded to demonstrate that two parties can be made better off if they structure a deal in a way that recognizes comparative advantage in various elements of production.

Imagine, for example, that Portugal enjoys a comparative advantage in growing wine grapes due to better soil, while England has a comparative advantage in producing wine from the grapes due to better technology or cheaper labor. Rather than allowing Portugal to specialize in all elements of wine manufacture because it enjoys an overall comparative advantage in that trade, the two countries can be better off if Portugal grows the grapes and England turns them into a table beverage.

Comparative advantage analysis demonstrates how the total cooperative surplus enjoyed by two negotiators can be increased by thoughtful Deal Design, but this alone is not enough to guarantee that they will agree to the more profitable arrangement. If a contractor can prevent or minimize construction delay for $3,000, whereas the guarantee of early completion would be worth $10,000 to the owner, designing the deal so that liability for delay falls on the contractor would increase total cooperative surplus.[4] But the contractor, quite reasonably, might be unimpressed with the suggestion that he agree to accept a $3,000 cost in order to provide his customer with $10,000 of extra benefit. Even if the contractor cares deeply about his client, he is not likely to want to be legally liable under the contract for any shortcoming.

This explains why professional economists almost uniformly love free trade but many workers have become decidedly less enamored in recent years. Because of the principle of comparative advantage, the total benefits of trade outweigh its total costs. But the benefits and costs often fall on different groups of people, so not everyone will be happy. Unless the local shepherds whose jobs move abroad are compensated with some of the increased profits enjoyed by the local winemakers who profit from their expanded markets, the outcome will not meet with unanimous acclaim.

In the political arena, the winemakers who stand to benefit might be able to outvote the shepherds who would be made worse off and enact a free-trade agreement. But in a negotiation, both parties have veto power over any potential deal. This means that unless one negotiator makes a mistake and enters into an agreement that is worse for him than pursuing his plan B, which does happen (remember the pitcher Matt Harrington, who never played in the major leagues), the gains from trade that arise from the principle of comparative advantage must be shared in a way that makes both parties better off than they would otherwise be.

For two negotiators to favor a change in Deal Design, then, the change must not only increase the total amount of cooperative surplus, it must make both of them better off.[5] If, to use our example of assigning responsibility for delays to the contractor, the owner pays the contractor *at least* $3,000 more, but *not more than* $10,000 more than she otherwise would have been willing to pay, the change in Deal Design satisfies this standard. Both parties win.

23

ROULEZ LES BON TEMPS

As the American population expanded westward after the Revolutionary War, access to the Mississippi River and the port of New Orleans became extremely important for settlers looking to sell their agricultural products. Spain, which had gained control of New Orleans and the Louisiana Territory from France in 1762 as a result of the French and Indian War, signed a treaty in 1795 that provided Americans the rights to both navigate the Mississippi and deposit goods in New Orleans for shipment through the Gulf of Mexico.

In 1802, however, a revitalized and expansionist France, under Napoleon Bonaparte, pressured Spain to return the Louisiana Territory and ordered the local authorities to end American access to the storage facilities at the port of New Orleans. With the primary trade route for the western American territories threatened, President Thomas Jefferson sent James Monroe to Paris to negotiate the purchase of New Orleans and navigation rights on the river, along with the territory of Florida, if possible. Jefferson set Monroe's reservation price in this negotiation at $10 million.

Before Monroe could get to France, however, Napoleon's dreams of reestablishing a French empire in the Americas soured. The French army had failed to suppress a rebellion of slaves and free blacks in what is now Haiti, and the French emperor's aides had convinced him that Louisiana would be easily captured by the British in the event of war between the European powers, which loomed on the horizon.

When Monroe arrived in Paris, the French foreign minister proposed the sale of the entire Louisiana Territory. Just weeks later, Monroe finalized the Louisiana purchase—828,000 square miles stretching from the Mississippi River to the Rocky Mountains and containing all or part of what would later become 13 American states—for approximately $15 million, or just $5 million more than the U.S. government had been willing to pay merely to guarantee access to the Gulf of Mexico.[1]

The Louisiana Purchase exemplifies the most common method of using the tool of Deal Design: *adding an issue* to what is initially assumed to be the negotiation's scope. Social norms understood by a group of people, or communication between two parties prior to bargaining, usually result in the parties approaching a negotiation with common assumptions about the structure of the potential deal. Expanding the scope of the negotiation requires the parties to determine that adding some good, service, or legal right to the mix would create more value to the party that would stand to obtain that new item than it would cost the party that would stand to lose it.

If your reservation price for buying my house is $1 million and my reservation price for selling it is $900,000, we have the basis for a mutually profitable transaction. The bargaining zone extends from $900,000 to $1 million and we stand to create $100,000 in cooperative surplus. But that doesn't mean that we should expand the agreement's scope to include my furniture (or my clothes, or my dog!) for a higher price. Most of the time, the seller of a house values its furnishings more than the buyer does. So, furniture is usually not included in home sales. But if there is a custom-built buffet that fits the dining room precisely and would be difficult to fit in a different house, the buyer might place a higher value on that particular item than the seller. If the negotiators are skilled at using the tool of Deal Design, they will add the buffet to the transaction's scope.

To the United States in 1803, the Louisiana Purchase presented an opportunity for future expansion for a growing and restless population. Napoleon had decided that, for France, it was largely useless land—far from home, difficult to access, and impossible to defend from the British. Adding this territory to a deal that was originally assumed to be only for New Orleans greatly increased the cooperative surplus available from the transaction. With hindsight, at about three cents an acre, it seems like the Americans probably captured most of the extra cooperative surplus. But this was also a beneficial deal at the time for France, which received millions of dollars for a parcel of land it judged to be more trouble than it was worth.

In the Louisiana Territory negotiation, the value of the agreement was increased by the seller adding to the transaction a tangible piece of property that had greater value to the buyer. Benefits of greater value to the buyer than to the seller, though, can take all kinds of forms. Ivar Kreuger is one example: as a seller, he added responsibility for the risk of delay to what he was selling, a feature that most buyers valued more than his cost of providing it.

Another real estate company's product demonstrates how time, rather than land or risk, can be yet another source of value in negotiation. When homeowners decide to sell their houses, their time constraints can vary greatly. A person interested in selling his house in the city and retiring to a quieter life in the country might be in no great hurry to find an interested buyer. But someone who has just had his job transferred across the country and needs to get his children enrolled in a new school right away might place a high value on a fast sale. The residential real estate market in most locations is not nearly as liquid as the market for, say, shares of stock, which can be sold in literally a fraction of a second over the internet. A typical home sale could take weeks or months.

Once a home seller finds a buyer, the two parties can design their deal to include an unusually speedy closing date if the value of this to the seller exceeds the cost to the buyer (or if it is valuable to both the seller and the buyer), but this type of additional term obviously can't be added to a deal's design before the buyer is identified. Enter Opendoor, a company that will buy your house almost immediately. The company harnesses the power of big data to estimate, often in just a couple of hours, the price that a seller's house will eventually sell for when the right buyer comes along. Opendoor makes the seller a cash offer for the house, usually within 24 hours of being contacted, based on what it thinks a buyer who wants to live in the house will eventually pay. The company then patiently waits for that buyer to find the house and resells.

Opendoor's offer price is a bit lower than it thinks the house can eventually be sold for, of course, to compensate it for the transaction costs of reselling and the time value of the capital tied up in the property while it waits. But if these costs are lower to Opendoor than the value of a fast sale is to the seller, which is sometimes the case, we can understand the company's approach as adding "speed" to a normally slow transaction in a way that increases the total amount of cooperative surplus shared by the parties.[2]

Usually, adding an issue will increase costs to one party, even if the benefit to the other party is greater. Parting with the Louisiana Territory outside of New Orleans was a "cost" rather than a benefit to Napoleon (he wouldn't have given the land away or paid the United States to take it off his hands), and the ability to price a house in just hours requires a substantial investment by Opendoor. In some situations, however, negotiators can identify additions that work to the benefit of both parties simultaneously, even holding price and other terms of the transaction constant. Consider, as an example, the perhaps apocryphal story of

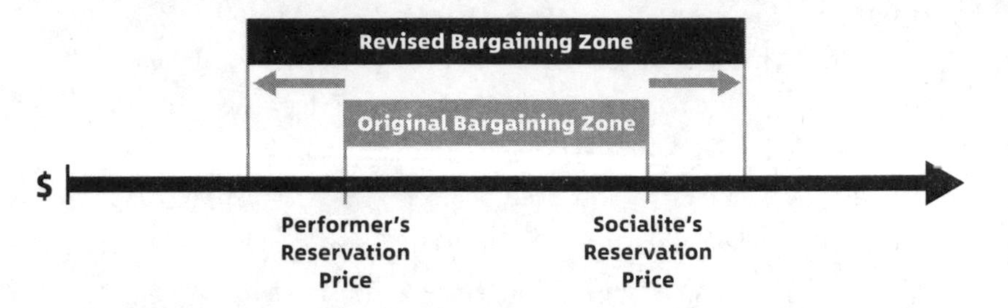

In unusual circumstances, a change in a deal's design can make it more desirable to both parties simultaneously, rather than increasing the desirability to one and reducing the desirability to the other.

a snobbish socialite and an antisocial virtuoso performance artist: The socialite inquired as to how much the artist would charge to perform at a private party. The artist responded with a price quote of $5,000. The socialite said that a condition of the engagement would be that the artist could not mingle with the guests at the event, to which the artist dryly responded that the price would then be $2,000.[3]

24

DIVIDE AND SUBTRACT

Cars are almost always sold with tires. You have probably purchased a car, or many cars, without paying the slightest bit of attention to this customary feature of automobile sales agreements. Virtually every car buyer intends to drive her vehicle, not use it as an enormous paper weight or display it as a sculpture, so she is going to need four tires. It saves transaction costs for sellers of automobiles to include tires with the body as opposed to buyers having to investigate and purchase their tires separately. Notice, though, that the bundling of automobile chassis and tires is a choice, not an immutable law of nature.

Most negotiated agreements bundle together items that could theoretically be separated—such as cars and tires—because doing so maximizes the total amount of cooperative surplus that can be produced most of the time. Many negotiators limit their negotiation to what is included in the established bundle rather than carefully considering the implicit choices that it embodies. But because negotiators' preferences and circumstances vary, the customary bundle does not create the most cooperative surplus for every pair of negotiators. 5TNs search for opportunities to design their deal in nonstandard ways that increase the amount of cooperative surplus that they can create.

As the prior chapter illustrated, this can often be done by adding issues to the bundle. The typical house sale in the United States does not include furnishings because sellers will usually value their furniture more than buyers will. But sometimes this won't be the case. Maybe the seller plans to travel the world in a mobile home and has no need for any furniture, while the buyer is moving from a small apartment and owns little, such that the buyer would value all (or nearly all) of the seller's furniture more than the seller would. This situation calls for the parties to deviate from custom and add the seller's furniture to the scope of the transaction.

The same logic suggests that cooperative surplus can also be increased in many situations by *subtracting issues* from the standard bundle. Although furniture is not usually included with the sale of a home, fixtures attached to the walls or ceiling are customarily included. Unlike ordinary furniture (but perhaps like custom-built furniture), fixtures will probably not be useful in the seller's new accommodations, and thus will usually be more valuable to the buyer than to the seller. But, just as furniture is sometimes more valuable to the buyer and should be added to the deal, fixtures are occasionally more valuable to the seller and should be subtracted from the deal. If the crystal dining room chandelier is a family heirloom beloved by the seller, whereas its ornate styling clashes with the buyer's modern architectural sensibilities, negotiators skilled at Deal Design will increase the cooperative surplus available from the sale by subtracting the chandelier from the transaction, thus allowing the seller to keep it.

The principle of subtracting is easy to understand when the subject matter of a negotiation is a collection of tangible items like automobile chassis and tires or houses and chandeliers. But the principle is also embedded within a surprising range of situations that are more difficult to recognize. Once you understand the concept, examples abound almost everywhere you look.

On April 1, 2001, a U.S. Navy airplane flying a surveillance mission over the South China Sea collided with a Chinese fighter jet. The Chinese plane crashed, and its pilot was killed. The pilot of the American plane successfully made an emergency landing on the Chinese island of Hainan without the permission of the Beijing government. All 24 crew members survived, but a diplomatic incident ensued.

Accusing the United States of spying, Chinese president Jiang Zemin claimed that the American plane was responsible for the collision and demanded an apology from the American government. Washington took the position that the Chinese jet was responsible, and U.S. Secretary of State Colin Powell responded that the United States had "nothing to apologize for." The American government did express "regret" over the death of the Chinese airman, but Beijing rejected this language as insufficient. China refused to release the plane and crew, and tempers flared. Illinois congressman Henry Hyde referred to the crew as "hostages," and a poll showed most Americans agreed with that characterization.

Meanwhile, behind-the-scenes negotiations between the two governments continued. But which side would yield? The Chinese president had made it abundantly clear that the return of the plane and crew would require an American apology, and the highest officials in the Bush administration, including the president himself, were on record as refusing to apologize. There didn't seem to be a bargaining zone: the price that China demanded (an apology) for an agreement was higher than what the United States was willing to pay.

On the 11th day of the standoff, the Bush administration delivered a letter to China stating that the United States was "very sorry" both for the loss of the Chinese pilot and for the American plane entering Chinese airspace and landing without permission. No mention was made of responsibility for the mid-air collision itself. The next day, China released the American crew.[1]

The settlement of the Hainan Island incident can be understood as the result of taking what appeared to be a unitary negotiation issue (whether the United States would apologize), dividing that issue into parts, and then subtracting one part in order to expand the bargaining zone—or, in this case, perhaps creating a bargaining zone where none originally existed. The price China demanded for the navy crew was an apology for the accident, but the resulting stalemate suggested that the reputational cost of providing one was above the reservation point of the United States. And while the Americans were willing to pay the lesser price of announcing "regret," the Chinese claimed this was insufficiently meager payment.

It took nearly two weeks of feverish diplomacy, but the negotiators were finally able to divide the demanded "apology" into two parts: (1) an expression of being "very sorry" for the incident, and (2) acceptance of responsibility for the collision. By subtracting that acceptance from the subject matter of the settlement, the cost to the United States of apologizing declined substantially, and the benefit of gaining the crew's freedom outweighed that cost. Although the Chinese government would have obtained more value from an expansive apology, the more limited apology proved more desirable than an impasse; that is, its value exceeded China's reservation point.

In this way, the settlement of the Hainan incident was similar in design to a more famous international agreement that has been a staple of books about negotiation since it appeared as an example in Roger Fisher and William Ury's seminal book, *Getting to Yes*, in 1981. On June 5, 1967, the Six-Day War between Israel and its Arab enemies broke out. After destroying most of the Egyptian and Syrian air forces on the ground, the Israel Defense Forces (IDF) quickly captured the Gaza Strip and Sinai Peninsula from Egypt and the Golan Heights from Syria. When the Jordanian army shelled Israeli positions, the IDF drove it out of East Jerusalem and the West Bank of the Jordan River.[2] A decade later, Israel and Egypt found themselves in stalemated peace negotiations over the status of the Sinai. Egypt refused to sign a peace agreement without the return of the Sinai, and Israel was just as firm in its refusal to relinquish the territory.

The logjam was broken when Israel agreed to return control of the peninsula and Egypt agreed to keep that desert province demilitarized, leading to the Camp David Accords.[3]

The usual negotiation lesson drawn from the Camp David Accords, per *Getting to Yes*, is that the two parties made peace by focusing on their underlying interests rather than maintaining conflicting positions.[4] Had both sides stood firm on the incompatible desires to possess the Sinai, impasse would have resulted. But Israel's primary "interest" was security, which would be undermined by Egypt again stationing tanks and soldiers on the small and besieged nation's southwestern border, while Egypt's core interest was in regaining sovereignty over territory that it had ruled for over 5,000 years. Demilitarizing an Egyptian Sinai could serve the interests of both, and recognizing this paved the way for a peace treaty that served the primary interests of both sides and has survived the test of time.

This analysis is certainly correct, but the case study can be understood, more specifically, as an example of Deal Design using the tactic of subtraction. On the surface, the parties appeared to be contesting a unitary item—a chunk of desert that could be controlled by either Israel or Egypt but not both. But if "the Sinai" is understood as a combination of two sources of value, one could then potentially be subtracted from the package of concessions that Israel might exchange for a peace agreement.

The Sinai was valuable both as (1) an area of land over which a nation could fly its flag and demonstrate sovereignty, and as (2) a forward staging ground useful for locating military equipment. By subtracting the latter item from the subject matter of the peace agreement, the cost to Israel of returning the Sinai to Egypt declined dramatically because the deal would not undermine Israel's self-defense capabilities, while the reduction in the benefits of the deal to Egypt was far smaller. With the subject matter of the negotiation thus redefined, both parties decided that a trade of normalized diplomatic relations in return for sovereignty of the (demilitarized) Sinai territory was more desirable than pursuing their common plan B of maintaining a state of hostility.

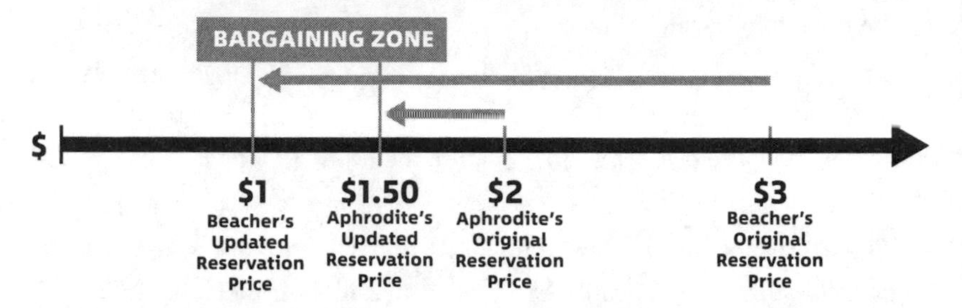

By removing the peel from the sale and allowing the seller to keep it, the seller's reservation price is reduced more than the buyer's, creating a bargaining zone.

The value of subtraction is also readily demonstrable in more prosaic commercial transactions. Imagine that Aphrodite craves citrus, so she is willing to pay up to $2 for Beacher's orange. Beacher does not particularly like eating oranges, but he is planning on cooking a meal that requires the zest from an orange, so he is reluctant to sell. His reservation price is $3. If the orange is reimagined as an amalgamation of flesh and peel, the peel can be subtracted from the negotiation's subject matter. Aphrodite had little use for the peel, so her reservation price would decrease only slightly, to $1.50. Since Beacher could keep the portion of the orange that he values, his reservation price for what is left would drop substantially, to $1. Subtraction can now turn a negotiation that was destined to end in impasse into an opportunity for an agreement that will generate 50 cents worth of cooperative surplus.

25

LOGROLLING

On the early American frontier, neighbors recognized the value in helping each other move their timber to a river for transporting or to a homestead for burning or cabin construction. The end result was the same as if each person had labored alone, but the sum total of all the effort needed was less. Put another way, this particular form of social organization maximized the cooperative surplus generated by the community's total efforts and everyone was made better off, sharing in that surplus.

Davy Crockett, the frontiersman turned U.S. congressman, is credited with being the first person to borrow the term *logrolling* from the frontier and use it to describe the process of legislators helping each other by trading votes.[1] By pledging a vote on an issue of lesser concern in return for a colleague's vote on an issue of greater concern, two legislators can obtain more total utility than if each were to vote his preference on both matters. The practice continues to be common in politics, whether lawmakers are trading votes across different pieces of legislation or across features within a single piece of legislation.

In this way, President Ronald Reagan, who wanted to cut Social

Security benefits, and Democratic Speaker of the House Tip O'Neill, who wanted to expand that program's scope, famously reached agreement on legislation to improve the financial stability of the Social Security Trust Fund in 1983. Reagan secured O'Neill's support for reducing annual cost-of-living increases in return for Reagan's agreeing to require government employees to join the system and to tax a portion of the benefits paid to high earners. Reagan signed the resulting bill into law after it passed both the Democratic House and the Republican Senate.[2]

Three years later, the same two adversaries reached agreement on the Tax Reform Act of 1986. O'Neill agreed to Reagan's demand that the highest marginal tax rate be reduced to 28 percent in return for the president's acceptance of equalizing the tax rate on capital gains and earned income so that the investor class would not pay a lower rate than the working class.[3]

You don't have to look to Capitol Hill to see logrolling in action; it is a fundamental principle of Deal Design in a wide range of negotiating situations. The opportunity for logrolling nearly always arises whenever a negotiation includes multiple issues, which all complex negotiations do. The parties usually have different preferences, different available resources or talents, or different tastes for risk, all of which suggest the opportunity to increase the cooperative surplus of an agreement by trading concessions across issues.

In 1977, movie director and producer George Lucas was looking to cast what he was then calling his "space opera," which eventually became known as *Star Wars*. His available budget didn't match his grand ambitions, which forced him to cast many lesser-known actors in key roles—some of whom, of course, went on to become quite famous. For the role of Obi-Wan Kenobi, however, Lucas wouldn't compromise: he wanted Academy Award–winning actor Sir Alec Guinness for the part. Of course, Guinness preferred a substantial up-front fee, but his comfortable financial position made him open to taking a risk on the success of a new movie concept and an unknown filmmaker. So, Guinness agreed to take a lower-than-usual salary in return for 2 percent of the gross royalties earned by Lucas, creating a bargaining zone and making a deal possible (and, as it turned out, making Guinness tens of millions of dollars in the long run).[4]

As obvious as logrolling is as a potentially valuable negotiation tactic, and as common as it is in virtually all types of negotiations, several psychological barriers can impede its successful use, leaving negotiators with agreements that are less beneficial to both parties. Logrolling requires one party to propose a concession that is less important to her than to her counterpart. *Reactive devaluation* (Chapter 18), the psychological tendency to want something less if it is available, threatens to cause negotiators to be less enamored of concessions once these are offered than if the concessions were analyzed in the abstract. And because negotiators are likely to use the customary deal structure as the reference point against which they evaluate Deal Design proposals, *loss aversion* (Chapter 14) can cause the potential sacrifice that is a necessary aspect of logrolling to loom larger than the offsetting benefit.

Another impediment, labeled the *fixed-pie bias* by psychologists Max Bazerman and Margaret Neale,[5] causes people to assume, without exploration, that their counterpart will value issues in the same way and to the same extent that they do. In a negotiation simulation that I conduct in classes and workshops, one negotiator plays the role of a movie-studio executive and another a star actor's agent in a movie-contract negotiation. One of many issues they need to resolve is whether the studio or the actor will have control over the choice of director for the film. The negotiators can resolve this issue by allocating control to either party or agreeing to "joint control" (in which case both sides have veto power and must agree on a director). The way the simulation is written, the actor is very particular about his directors, and he would greatly prefer to have sole control. The studio would also prefer to have director control, but its preference is weak—that is, it has only a slight preference for sole control compared to either joint control or actor control—because it has confidence in the star's judgment.

Quite often, the actor's agent assumes, incorrectly as it turns out, that since his client has a strong preference for selecting the director, the studio must also have a strong preference. When this happens, the parties often agree to the apparent compromise solution of joint control. But the deal can create more cooperative surplus, and both parties can individually enjoy more utility, if they allocate director control to the actor, who cares more about the issue, and logroll that issue in return for a concession on another issue or issues in which the studio has a stronger preference for a particular outcome.

In some cases, the fixed-pie bias can obscure Deal Design opportunities that would actually benefit both parties (as opposed to opportunities that would benefit one party more than it would cost the other). Consider, again, the example of the seller who adores the old-fashioned crystal chandelier hanging in the dining room. Because the seller loves the antique, she might assume that the buyer would as well, and thus she might never suggest subtracting it from the agreement to sell the house, only to have the buyer, who favors more modern décor, pay to deposit it in the local landfill after the sale closes. In this example, subtracting the chandelier would have reduced the seller's reservation price for the house (since she could have used the fixture in her new residence) and increased the buyer's reservation price (because he would not have had to pay for disposal), increasing the amount of total cooperative surplus and making both parties individually better off, even without adjusting the sales price. Failing to take advantage of this type of opportunity has been called, appropriately enough, "lose-lose" negotiation.[6]

The antidote to the fixed-pie bias is fighting the urge to assume that your counterpart values elements of a deal the way that you do. Logrolling opportunities abound. 5TNs raise for discussion all potential trades across issues that have *even a slight possibility* of increasing the total cooperative surplus.

26

SOLVING THE "LEMONS" PROBLEM

George Akerlof won the Nobel Prize in Economic Sciences primarily for his 1970 article "The Market for Lemons," which has gone on to become one of the most cited economics articles in history. Although not about the bargaining process specifically, the article provides substantial insight into an important use of Deal Design.

Using the sale of used cars as his primary example, Akerlof theorized about the marketplace consequences of differences in information possessed by buyers and sellers. There are aspects of a used car's quality that buyers can easily observe—make and model, for instance, and whether the car's body is free of scratches and dents. But other aspects of a car's quality are known to sellers but unobservable to buyers: whether the seller rode the brakes constantly, whether the car has trouble starting on cold mornings, whether a prior accident caused nonvisible damage, and so on. Due to these unobservable features, you can think of every used car with a particular set of observable qualities as sitting somewhere on a spectrum ranging from very high quality (Akerlof called these excellent cars "peaches") to very low quality ("lemons").

Since buyers can't tell whether a used car is a peach or a lemon, you might think they would set their reservation price at the value they would place on a car of average quality. Not so, according to Akerlof, based on the following logic: Sellers who own peaches would not be willing to sell for less than a price suitable for a peach. So, if buyers were willing to pay only average-quality prices, only sellers with cars that are either average quality or below-average quality would offer to sell. Realizing that any car they purchased would be at best average and at worst a lemon, buyers would be willing to pay only a price appropriate for a lower-than-average-quality car. Knowing this, only sellers with much-lower-than-average-quality cars would enter the marketplace, and so on.

The ultimate consequence of sellers knowing more about their wares than buyers do, Akerlof argued, would be a "lemons" market—only sellers with lemons would sell, and, anticipating this, buyers would be willing to pay only the low price appropriate for lemons. In extreme cases, in which unobservable characteristics could potentially make products close to worthless, there would be no market at all.[1]

At least one respected economics journal rejected Akerlof's "Lemons" article on the grounds that it was obviously wrong. Markets abound, the editors observed, and certainly everything sold isn't of shabby quality![2] But the fact that markets exist doesn't undermine Akerlof's reasoning; it suggests, rather, the need for negotiators to implement measures that reduce the extent of the problem.

The lemons problem, also referred to as *adverse selection*, is routinely discussed in the context of insurance markets, in which it is buyers, rather than sellers, who have private information unknown to the other party. If buyers of life insurance, for example, know whether they are likely or unlikely to die young but insurance companies do not know the relative risk of different buyers, people with shorter-than-average life expectancy will be more likely to buy a policy sold at a price that is actuarially appropriate for the average person, causing insurance companies to lose money. Companies can substantially minimize, if not completely solve, this problem by investigating the health of the buyer before agreeing to sell a life-insurance policy, usually by requiring potential buyers to share their medical records and submit to a medical examination. The seller can then charge a low price to the "peaches" (i.e., those who are least likely to die) and a high price to the "lemons" (i.e., those more likely to die).

Similarly, buyers of used cars can counteract the adverse-selection problem they face by hiring an independent mechanic to inspect the vehicle prior to purchase. After the inspection reveals the car's quality, the buyer can determine whether his reservation price should be high or low. Even though Opendoor, the home-purchasing company, is selling its ability to purchase houses incredibly fast, it won't actually buy your house without first inspecting it. If it bought sight unseen, it would almost certainly attract customers who disproportionately have leaky roofs, broken furnaces, and foundations with subsidence problems.

Most Americans think that people with medical problems should not have to pay more for health insurance than healthier people, which is why the Affordable Care Act—also known as Obamacare—prohibits insurance companies from charging higher rates to people with "preexisting conditions." The problem with charging lemons and peaches the same amount is that many peaches, who in this case are the people less likely to need medical care this year, are likely to decline to purchase insurance rather than pay a price that reflects the average cost of medical care for everyone. The Affordable Care Act addressed the adverse-selection problem by requiring everyone—healthy or unhealthy—to purchase the product (or else pay a fine). If the lemons and the peaches all purchase insurance, so goes the theory, insurance companies can sell policies to everyone for an average price.

This feature of the Affordable Care Act, known as the "individual mandate," was the single most controversial feature of the law.[3] It barely survived a constitutional challenge in the U.S. Supreme Court on a 5–4 vote,[4] and when Republicans took control of both houses of Congress in 2016 they essentially abolished it, reducing the penalty for not buying insurance to zero. The controversy surrounding the individual mandate was attributable to a libertarian streak in the American polity that rebels against government requiring citizens to act in a certain way, not because it failed to address the problem of adverse selection.

Negotiators who are unable to fully investigate quality prior to reaching an agreement, and who lack the ability to require both lemons and peaches to participate in transactions, can use the tool of Deal Design to minimize the adverse-selection problem. A common approach is for the seller to add to the terms of the deal a *warranty* that the product or service will be of a certain level of quality. A used-car dealer might offer a 90-day warranty on any mechanical problems that occur, thus protecting the buyer against not knowing about a cracked engine block at the time of purchase. Mail-order companies typically add to their product a money-back guarantee if the buyer is unsatisfied with the product for any reason; if you are unhappy with the reception you get from your new headphones, you may return them to Amazon and obtain a refund. Prior to the passage of the Affordable Care Act, health insurance companies often required new customers to wait a specified amount of time before qualifying for coverage for any previously diagnosed maladies, effectively providing a warranty to the insurance company for costs that would otherwise be the responsibility of the insurer.

An alternative to warranties is for the party with more information to make legally binding *representations*—that is, factual statements that the negotiator warrants as being true—concerning the quality of goods or services. Whereas a used-car dealer is likely to provide a warranty as part of the deal, a private party selling his own used car would be more likely to represent that the car has had no major repairs and has not been in an accident. This representation gives some protection against adverse selection but not as much as the warranty, because the seller would have no liability to the buyer if the car broke down the following day, as long as the representation was accurate when made.

Complex contracts negotiated by lawyers typically include an entire section titled "Representations and Warranties," in which one or both

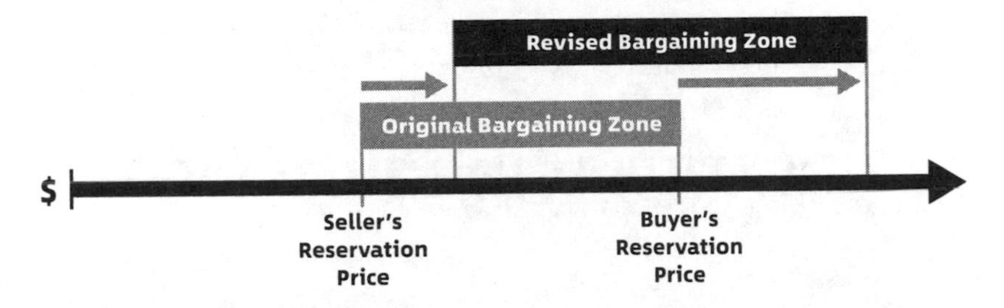

Assuming the seller knows that the car is a "peach" rather than a "lemon," adding a warranty to the deal can increase the buyer's reservation price more than the seller's reservation price, increasing the amount of cooperative surplus available.

parties represent facts of which they have knowledge but their counterpart does not and assume liability for risks of future harms that the counterpart could potentially suffer. For example, in a corporate merger, the target company might represent and warrant to the acquiring company that it had the legal licenses to use the intellectual property necessary to produce its products or services.

Legally actionable representations and warranties are useful tactics of Deal Design because they often benefit the recipient more than they cost the provider, thus expanding the bargaining zone and increasing cooperative surplus. In some cases, a seller's reputation for high quality or a preexisting relationship with the buyer will be enough to convince a buyer that she is not purchasing a lemon. But if not, a rational buyer will set a low reservation price to take this risk into account. A legally binding representation that a used car does not have any mechanical problems or a warranty that covers the cost of repairs in the near term protects the buyer from this risk and should cause her to increase her reservation price substantially. As long as the seller is not actually selling a lemon, the expected cost to him of providing representations or warranties should be modest, increasing his reservation price but by a smaller amount.

27

DISCOURAGING SHIRKING

A cartoon that I am fond of depicts a man, holding a letter in his hand, reporting to his wife that his life-insurance company has just offered to decrease his annual premium if he agrees to stop eating her cooking. The humor (if you find this funny) comes from the idea that a wife's meals could be so bad that they actually endanger her husband's life—and could therefore be costly to the insurer. While it is far-fetched that one's spouse's cooking could be so dangerous that it would generate the intervention of a life-insurance company, the cartoon illustrates a problem known as *moral hazard*—the reduced incentive to exercise care or exert effort when someone else bears the cost of a resulting harm—which is another obstacle to reaching negotiated agreements that can be addressed with the tool of Deal Design.

Let's stay with the sale of insurance for a simple example: Insurance companies fear that, once they enter into an agreement to take on a risk, the buyer of the insurance policy will no longer act as carefully as he otherwise would. If I buy theft insurance, and thus will not suffer financially if my possessions are stolen, I might be more likely to leave my house unlocked or leave my laptop unattended on the table at Starbucks while I run to the restroom. To be sure, there are some consequences of my behavior that insurance will not cover, which limits the extent of the moral hazard problem. My auto-insurance company will replace my car and pay my medical expenses in case of an accident, but I'm unlikely to drive like a maniac just because of this fact, because the reimbursement won't help me much if I'm dead. I might be more likely, however, to park in a tight parking space next to an already scratched-up car.

To reduce the risk that I might not behave as carefully as I should after someone else assumes responsibility for my carelessness, insurance agreements usually include deductibles, which effectively require me to retain at least a portion of any liability, or exclusions (such as for accidents caused by drunk driving), which require me to retain all liability for actions that are particularly dangerous or particularly likely to be the subject of moral hazard.

The problem of moral hazard arises in any situation in which the existence of an agreement changes the incentives of either party to put effort into his future performance. The problem is difficult to avoid entirely, but negotiators can use Deal Design to minimize its extent. One common approach is to structure the deal such that the value of one party's performance is determined after that performance is complete rather than at the time the agreement is reached, or such that the party is compensated based on the profits earned as a result of his efforts. A customer hiring a photographer to take his portrait might insist on a contract term that makes payment conditional on his satisfaction with the work, or the photographer might offer to take on the commission for a low fixed price plus an additional charge per photograph that the customer chooses to order after viewing the proofs. Either approach ensures that the photographer has an incentive to do her best possible work even after she is hired. Film distributors and movie theaters typically share profits from screening movies, rather than one paying the other a fixed fee and keeping all the profits, because the promotional efforts of both are integral to the success of the enterprise, and this arrangement gives both the incentive to put forth maximum effort.[1]

Another Deal Design technique is to provide one party with an opportunity to end a relationship if the other shirks. Corporate mergers almost always include what is known as a MAC clause, short for "material adverse change," which allows the purchaser to avoid closing the deal if the financial condition of the entity being sold substantially declines after the deal is reached but before the purchaser assumes operating control.[2] This Deal Design device incentivizes sellers to act as vigilantly in their day-to-day management of the company as they would if they intended to maintain control far into the future.

Negotiators typically add these terms to contracts because they are worth more to the party who is contracting to receive a service (i.e., the buyer) than they are costly to the provider—at least assuming that the provider has no intention of shirking—and thus they increase the total cooperative surplus created by deals.

It is worth noting that terms added to a deal in order to reduce moral hazard are often also desirable, independently, because they take advantage of the optimism bias (Chapter 15). Recall that people tend to be overly optimistic about their ability to perform at a certain level or to achieve desirable outcomes in a wide range of activities. The bias, like moral hazard, counsels in favor of structuring agreements so that compensation depends on the quality of performance. If a party tasked with delivering goods or providing services is optimistic about her ability to provide the highest quality, she will usually be pleased to have her compensation based on the outcome.

Consider again the negotiation between NBC and Paramount to extend the run of the television program *Frasier*, discussed in Chapter 5. No television show lasts forever. After eight successful seasons, *Frasier* was probably nearing the end of its run, meaning that the renewal agreement under negotiation would likely be the last one. NBC might have reasonably feared that, after locking in a new deal, Paramount, the creator and producer, would put less effort than before into making the show as entertaining as possible. That's the moral hazard problem. At the same time, if Paramount has no intention of shirking, it is likely to predict the show will earn higher ratings going forward than what NBC predicts. That's the consequence of the optimism bias. Both factors suggest that the bargaining zone will be larger if the agreement provides that the price NBC pays Paramount is based in part on the show's future ratings. The agreement that NBC and Paramount reached included precisely this feature.[3]

You don't need to be an entertainment-industry executive to benefit from the tool of Deal Design in the way that NBC and Paramount did. Let's say you are considering increasing your teenager's allowance by $10 per week in return for him performing certain household chores. Instead, consider proposing that he'll receive a $15 increase if the chores are performed to your complete satisfaction, and only a $5 increase otherwise. I guarantee that he'll earn more money and that you will receive better value.

SUMMARY OF KEY LESSONS FROM PART 3

- Deal Design changes the structure of an agreement, relative to what is customary for the particular type of deal, in a way that changes both negotiators' reservation points and increases the total amount of cooperative surplus.
- Adding issues to the customary structure increases cooperative surplus when the additional terms are more valuable to the benefiting party than they are costly to the providing party.
- Subtracting issues serves the same purpose when a customary or expected element of a transaction costs the providing party more than it benefits the receiving party.
- In complex negotiations with multiple issues, logrolling enables the negotiators to make concessions on issues they value less in return for concessions on issues they value more, increasing total cooperative surplus and making both parties better off.
- Deal Design principles can be used to reduce the risk of adverse selection (an information problem) and moral hazard (an incentive problem), which otherwise will routinely limit the value of negotiated agreements.

TOOL #4

POWER

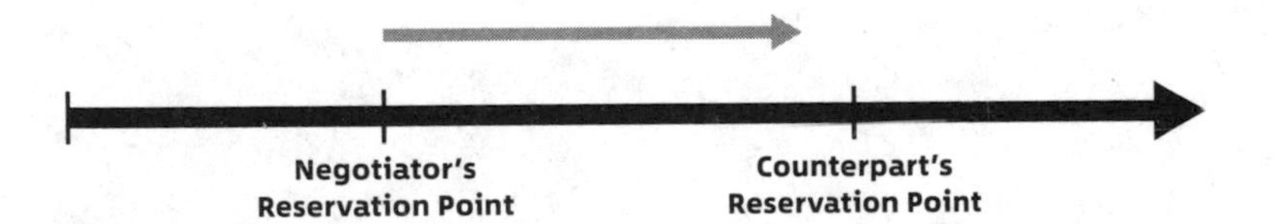
Negotiator's
Reservation Point
Counterpart's
Reservation Point

28

HARD BARGAINING AT THE OLYMPICS

As London prepared to host the 2012 summer Olympic Games, the city's 28,000 local bus drivers wanted a share of the increased transit revenues projected to accompany the two-week event. The drivers' union, Unite, demanded an "Olympic bonus" of £500 for each of its members, and threatened to strike during the games if their demands were not met by the local bus companies that directly employed them and the government transportation authority, Transport for London.[1]

As spring turned to summer, the issue remained unresolved. Transport for London promised some money to the bus companies to put toward driver bonuses, but not enough to satisfy the union, and the bus companies declined to supplement the public subsidy from their own coffers. On June 22, just over a month before the Olympics would begin, Unite staged a 24-hour strike, pulling 85 percent of London's drivers off the job and creating what one reporter called "travel misery" for the city's six million daily bus passengers.[2] Unite then scheduled another one-day work stoppage for July 24, only three days prior to the opening ceremonies. In mid-July, however, the bus companies agreed to the drivers' demands, the strike was averted, and London's transportation network operated smoothly through the Olympic fortnight.[3]

By shuttling workers around London during the Olympics, the bus drivers, the bus companies, and the local transportation authority collectively stood to generate a certain amount of income. The drivers wanted a larger cut of that money than they stood to receive under the terms of their standard contract; they wanted more of the cooperative surplus.

Power is the tool that negotiators use to force their counterparts to concede cooperative surplus even when they would rather capture it themselves. Unite began by making brutally explicit what is central to—but often is merely implicit in—the exercise of Power: the negotiator's threat to unilaterally force an impasse between the parties unless the counterpart satisfies its demand. If the bus companies did not meet the drivers' demands, in other words, there would be no deal during the Olympics, and thus no cooperative surplus for anyone to enjoy, even though, technically speaking, there was a wide bargaining zone. The drivers would destroy the golden goose rather than allow the bus companies to collect most of the golden eggs.

Anyone can bluster, of course, so simply threatening impasse does not alone translate into negotiating Power. To generate Power, the threat must be credible; that is, the counterpart must believe that if she refuses to accede to the threat and make the demanded concession, the negotiator actually will accept an impasse rather than make concessions himself in order to secure a deal. Unite's decision to stage the one-day demonstration strike well in advance of the Olympics was a masterstroke. By demonstrating their willingness to strike and sacrifice pay before the Olympics began, the drivers increased the credibility of their threat to do so during the games. Who on the other side of the negotiating table could confidently assume that the Olympic-strike threat was an empty bluff?

The success of Unite in winning concessions for the members of its blue-collar union illustrates an important principle of Power in negotiation: the ability to wring concessions from your counterpart does not depend directly on your general social power, as measured by things like wealth, brains, beauty, social status, or political connections. Negotiating Power is specific to the situation, and it depends on how desirable your plan B is or, more precisely, on *your counterpart's perception* of how desirable you find your plan B.

If you took a survey and asked who is more powerful, the London bus drivers who make up Unite's union membership or the bus companies, most would say the companies. But this is irrelevant to the question of which side can most successfully employ the tool of negotiation Power in any particular situation. Unite's plan B, should it have reached an impasse with London's bus companies and civic officials, was to strike during the Olympics, even at a substantial cost to workers who, although far from impoverished, almost certainly lacked fat bank accounts. It was able to use Power to force concessions by convincing its counterparts that its plan B of going on strike, although clearly not desirable, wasn't particularly undesirable either.

If your plan B isn't very good, convincing your counterpart that you are prepared to walk away from a potential agreement is going to be difficult. To remedy this problem, the place to start is to do whatever you can to generate a better plan B.

In the early 1990s, the Walt Disney Company licensed Pixar's computer-animation system, but Pixar's CEO, Steve Jobs, wanted to make a movie with Disney, not just supply tools to the Mouse. Disney's film-division head Jeffrey Katzenberg was interested, but when Jobs demanded part ownership of the movie, the characters, and the video rights, Katzenberg quickly rejected the proposal and threatened to walk away from the project. On the verge of bankruptcy, Pixar did not have a good plan B, and Jobs had virtually no Power in the negotiation. He ultimately agreed to a deal to create the original *Toy Story*, the first entirely computer-animated feature film, that gave Pixar only 12.5 percent of ticket revenues and no ownership or creative control.

Jobs recognized that if he wanted more of the cooperative surplus the next time, he needed a more desirable plan B. When *Toy Story* debuted, he moved to take Pixar public, against the advice of his lieutenant, John Lasseter, who thought the company would be in a better position to launch an initial public offering after it had made a second movie. The IPO provided Pixar with the financial wherewithal to finance its own movies, if need be, which gave Jobs the leverage he needed. He was then able to negotiate a deal with Disney CEO Michael Eisner to make five more movies together, with Pixar putting up half the funds and receiving half the proceeds, a share of secondary revenues from merchandise and advertising, and equal branding.[4]

It isn't just sophisticated union leaders or technology impresarios who understand the importance of having a good plan B. A few years ago, a student of mine who had just completed her first year at UCLA Law School told me that she was planning to apply to transfer to the law school at UC Berkeley, one of our rival schools. She asked me to write a letter of recommendation to try to help her gain admission. Berkeley is an excellent school, of course, but so is UCLA, so I asked why she was applying to transfer. I have had other students apply to transfer to Berkeley in the past. Most often, the reason is that they have family ties that make it more convenient for them to be attending school in the San Francisco Bay Area, 500 miles to the north. Sometimes the reason is that Berkeley usually ranks a bit higher in national rankings, so the student believes transferring will improve her career prospects.

This student was applying for a different reason: she was preparing for a negotiation by attempting to improve her plan B and thus create an opportunity to exercise more Power. A top student, she already had a partial scholarship that reduced the cost to her of attending law school at UCLA. But she wanted to negotiate with UCLA's director of financial aid to obtain an even larger scholarship. She understood that an offer to transfer to Berkeley would improve her ability to use the tool of Power in that negotiation. It would instantly make her threat to walk away if UCLA didn't give her what she demanded more credible.

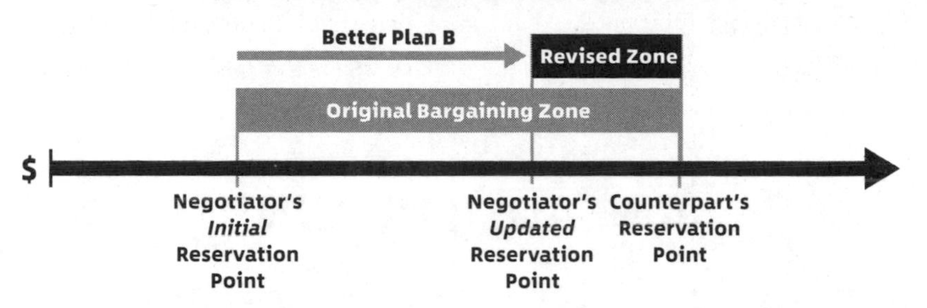

An improved plan B improves the negotiator's reservation point, limiting the bargaining zone to agreements that are relatively more desirable.

Unite, Steve Jobs, and my student all understood that negotiators can successfully demand more desirable terms if they have a good plan B, which implies a high reservation point. Experimental studies of negotiation behavior bear this out as well.[5] Identifying or developing a better plan B is the single most useful tactic for wielding the tool of Power. Before negotiating, five-tool negotiators always develop the best plan B possible.

29

A BEAUTIFUL MIND

A bit of economic game theory can help us to better understand the opportunities for using the tool of Power effectively by means other than identifying or creating a better plan B.

Let's assume that the average Unite member earned £25 per hour driving a London bus. If the union were to fail to reach an agreement with the bus companies, the plan B of the drivers was to strike for two weeks. This wasn't a very good option, of course, especially for a group of workers who, by and large, relied on their salaries to pay their bills. Let's assume that the reservation price of the drivers was also £25 per hour; for any amount less than that, they would prefer to sit home and enjoy the Olympics on television, and for that amount or more, they would prefer to work during the Olympics.

The bus companies and local London officials had a poor plan B as well. With no time to hire and train a fleet of replacement workers in time for the Olympics, in the event of a strike the companies would have to scramble to keep some buses operating—probably by putting some non-union members of management behind the wheels of buses—while desperately watching hundreds of thousands of visitors and ticket holders struggle to get to the Olympic venues for events. If the visitors and athletes were substantially inconvenienced, international humiliation would also be a likely consequence. Let's assume that the bus companies, wanting to avoid these consequences, had a reservation price of paying the drivers £45 per hour. Thus, the bargaining zone stretched from £25 to £45.

In the resulting negotiation, what agreement would we predict the union and the bus companies would reach? The answer isn't obvious. Any agreement within the bargaining zone would create £20 of cooperative surplus compared to an impasse, but this fact does not help us predict the precise outcome. The union would prefer a deal closer to £45 per hour, but it would prefer £25 to an impasse. The companies would prefer a deal closer to £25, but they would prefer to pay £45 than accept an impasse.

This puzzle of how to divide cooperative surplus fascinated Nobel Prize–winning economist John Nash, whose brilliance as a mathematician and struggle with paranoid schizophrenia were both portrayed in the Academy Award–winning movie *A Beautiful Mind*.[1] In the late 1940s, while a graduate student at Princeton, Nash used the newly developed tools of game theory to mathematically describe how self-interested negotiators should divide some fixed amount of cooperative surplus. The so-called "Nash bargaining solution" has served as a starting point for literally generations of game theorists dedicated to providing analytical solutions to negotiation problems.[2]

To simplify his analysis, Nash assumed two rational, equally skilled negotiators would be attempting to divide a fixed amount of cooperative surplus in a way that would maximize their individual allocations. He further assumed that both parties would have complete information about their counterparts—that is, that "each has full knowledge of the tastes and preferences of the other"—and that they would be able to compare their desires for various possible outcomes. For purposes of our example, assume that the union knows the bus companies' reservation price is £45, the bus companies know that the union's reservation price is £25, both sides value each incremental unit of money the same amount, and both know this about the other side. If they can't agree on a division of the surplus, each party, of course, would be presumed to pursue its plan B—in this case, the drivers would strike, and the companies would have to deal with the fallout.

Given this spare but strict set of assumptions, Nash concluded that rational negotiators would divide the cooperative surplus evenly. In our example, the parties would reach a deal for £35 per hour, the strike would be averted, and each side would enjoy £10 per hour of cooperative surplus.

Nash's proofs are mathematical and his work does not suggest any particular thought process on the part of the negotiators, but you might think about the situation this way: The higher the wage the union demands, the better off its members will be if an agreement is reached, but the greater the likelihood the companies will refuse. Demanding only £26 would be likely to leave money on the table, whereas demanding £44 would generate resistance. Presumed symmetry between the parties means the companies would employ the same reasoning from the opposite direction: Agreeing to pay £44 would provide them with less surplus than they might reasonably hope to capture, whereas offering only £26 could lead to no agreement and no surplus at all. These opposing but equal pressures will lead to the parties reaching agreement at £35 per hour.

In Nash's idealized world, negotiators never reach an impasse if there is a bargaining zone, and they always share the cooperative surplus equally, not because this is the *fair* thing to do (more on this in Part 5), but because it is the *rational* thing to do.

Anyone who has ever negotiated in the real world knows that cooperative surplus is not always divided evenly and that bargaining failures sometimes occur and impasses result, even when there is a bargaining zone. There are a number of explanations for this:

- The information that Nash assumes is shared between the parties often is not. Even 5TNs who are skilled at Bargaining Zone Analysis rarely know each other's reservation points, much less their tastes and preferences, with precision. This means both that negotiators can never be sure what their counterpart would be willing to accept and that the counterpart's lack of knowledge as to what the negotiator would be willing to accept can be a source of advantage.
- The structure of the negotiation process matters. Parties don't magically reach a cooperative solution; they usually exchange offers and counteroffers sequentially, in ways that can affect negotiated outcomes.
- Negotiators have different time constraints, different reputational concerns, and different tolerance for risk, all of which affect what proposals they are willing to accept.
- Negotiators don't always behave rationally. This fact can hurt them but, perhaps surprisingly, it can sometimes be a source of advantage.
- Finally, negotiators often have different amounts of bargaining skill.

For all of these reasons, 5TNs have an opportunity to use the tool of Power to capture the lion's share of the available cooperative surplus. The remainder of Part 4 explains how.

30

BLUFFING

In 1912, former president Theodore Roosevelt sought to regain the nation's highest office by running as a third-party candidate on the Bull Moose ticket against the Republican incumbent William Howard Taft and the Democratic standard-bearer Woodrow Wilson. Roosevelt's campaign staff designed a pamphlet that contained a transcript of a speech called "Confession of Faith" and featured a photograph of the candidate on the cover, taken by a Chicago photographer named Moffett. After printing three million copies of the brochure, the campaign staff realized it had overlooked the critical step of obtaining permission from the photographer to use the photo.

Unless it could obtain Moffett's permission, Roosevelt's campaign would have to either throw away three million brochures and print new ones or risk considerable legal liability. Either choice would be costly. As a consequence, the campaign certainly had a very high reservation price in its ensuing negotiation with Moffett for permission to use his photo.

Roosevelt's campaign manager, George Perkins, wrote to Moffett and explained that the campaign was planning to distribute millions of pamphlets with Roosevelt's picture on the cover. He pointed out that the brochure would provide excellent publicity for the photographer whose portrait was used. Perkins then asked how much Moffett would be willing to *pay* for his photo to be the chosen one. Moffett responded that he hadn't been in that situation before, but that he could offer to pay the campaign $250. Perkins quickly accepted.[1]

Moffett lacked a clear understanding of where his reservation price should be set. By explaining how an agreement would provide value for Moffett, Perkins used the tool of Persuasion, and he did so effectively. But this is only half of the story. The more interesting half is how Perkins manipulated Moffett's estimate of the campaign's reservation price by falsely implying that the campaign would not make a deal unless Moffett paid, a tactic often called *bluffing*.

If Moffett had known how bad the campaign's plan B actually was, and how high its reservation price was, he would have thought something like the following: "Sure, Perkins makes a good point that the publicity would be very valuable to me. But, on the other hand, my permission would be very valuable to Perkins, so he should be willing to pay me for the copyright, and quite a lot. Why should I pay him and let him capture more of the total cooperative surplus? I would prefer that the campaign pay me so that *I* will capture more of it."

The genius of Perkins asking Moffett how much he would be willing to pay was that it implied that the campaign had a very desirable plan B—selling the opportunity to some other photographer—and, therefore, a very low reservation price in its negotiation with Moffett. In fact, Perkins's question implied that the campaign's reservation price was *negative*; not only would it be unwilling to pay Moffett any money at all for use of his photo, as a publisher seeking a license to use copyrighted material would usually do, it would be willing to enter into an agreement only if Moffett would pay the campaign. Believing this to be true, Moffett made an offer to buy.

Assuming that the $250 Moffett paid was less than his reservation

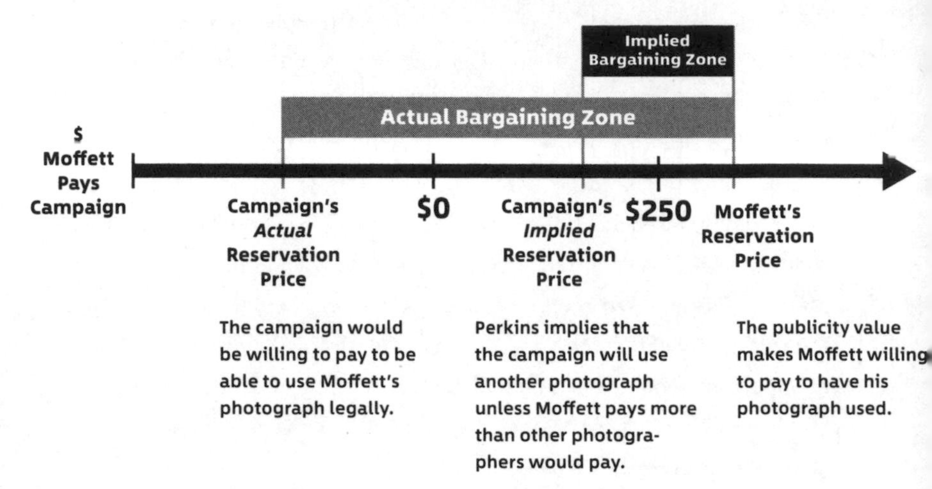

price—and there is no reason to suspect otherwise—the agreement fell within the bargaining zone. So, there is no reason to feel badly for Moffett, who, after all, obtained a lot of good publicity from the deal. In fact, Perkins's precarious position might have caused him to accept a lower price than he would have demanded had he been able to hold an auction among several photographers for the right to have their photo appear on the cover of millions of campaign pamphlets. From one perspective, then, the campaign's printing mistake probably saved Moffett money. But Perkins's deft move clearly enabled him to capture far more of the cooperative surplus than he was likely to obtain if Moffett had had an accurate estimate of the actual parameters of the bargaining zone.

Recall that, in our example based on the London bus strike, we hypothesized that the union's reservation price was £25 per hour and the companies' reservation price was £45 per hour, and we noted that Nash's bargaining theory would predict an agreement of £35 per hour. But what if the bus companies believed that the union's reservation price was actually £35 . . . or £40 . . . or even £45? As the bus companies' estimate of the union's reservation price went up, so would the hourly rate earned by the drivers, as the companies would have believed an impasse to be the likely result if they didn't concede further.

The successful use of Power depends on a complicated set of beliefs about beliefs: Specifically, a negotiator will find himself able to exercise Power *if his counterpart believes that he believes* that he has a strong plan B relative to reaching agreement in the focal negotiation. If a negotiator actually has a weaker plan B than he appears to have, or he believes his plan B is weak and thus desperately hopes not to have to pursue it, he will still have Power if his counterpart is unaware of his actual belief. Perception, not reality, provides the basis for negotiating Power. This fact makes bluffing a ruthlessly effective method of capturing cooperative surplus.

Negotiators can use bluffs to exercise Power by asserting that they have a better plan B than they actually have. Alternatively, they can claim that they like their *actual* plan B more, or the prospect of making a deal in the focal negotiation less, than they really do. Both variations on the concept of bluffing require deception to succeed. The first approach involves deception about objective facts, and the second, deception about the negotiator's subjective preferences.

As an example of deception about objective facts, my law student hoping to negotiate a larger scholarship could have falsely told the UCLA financial-aid director that she had received an offer of admission from UC Berkeley even if she had been rejected or not even applied. This would clearly be unethical, but from a strictly tactical point of view, it could be just as effective as actually having received admission to Berkeley, assuming that the lie is not discovered.

In addition to raising ethical concerns, a negotiator's claim that he has a better plan B than he actually has suffers from a second significant drawback: it can potentially be proved false, in which case the tactic would not only fail to capture cooperative surplus in the focal negotiation, it would almost certainly destroy any relationship of trust between the negotiators and risk broader reputational harm. Had my student falsely claimed to have been accepted at UC Berkeley, the financial-aid director would have asked to see the letter of acceptance, at which point the jig would have been up. And in many situations, the negotiator's plan B is well known to her counterpart, so trying to mislead a counterpart isn't even an option. Moffett did not know what the Roosevelt campaign's plan B was in his negotiation, but the London bus companies knew that Unite's plan B was to strike—the union could hardly have tried to contend that it had a "better" plan B of some sort.

Due to the practical and ethical problems with claiming to have a fabulous plan B that doesn't exist, the more typical bluffing tactic is to express exaggerated enthusiasm for one's actual plan B or to downplay interest in the focal deal. Because the counterpart cannot actually observe the negotiator's reservation point, this type of assertion, and the resulting threat to end the negotiation with an impasse if the counterpart does not make the demanded concession, can never be definitely proved to be a bluff. So real estate agents express more optimism than they actually feel that another potential buyer will offer the full listing price for their house, lawyers negotiating an out-of-court settlement claim they are more confident about winning their case than they actually are, and parents negotiating for their children to clean their rooms or do their homework feign indifference when they threaten to cancel the upcoming trip to the amusement park if kids don't do as they are told.

For a bluff to be successful, you usually have to convince your counterpart that you *will*, in fact, pursue your plan B if she will not make the concession that you are demanding. But this is not always a requirement. If the consequence of carrying out your threat would be sufficiently costly to your counterpart, a bluff can be successful even if she believes you *probably will not* carry out the threat, as long as there is at least some uncertainty about your true intentions. Consider this extreme example:

After Berlin was partitioned at the end of World War II and the western sector of the city incorporated into the new Federal Republic of Germany (i.e., West Germany), the Soviet Union considered the presence of this Western outpost deep inside the German Democratic Republic (i.e., East Germany) to be a serious provocation. In December 1958, at the height of the Cold War, Soviet premier Nikita Khrushchev issued a high-stakes ultimatum to the United States and its NATO allies: abandon West Berlin, or the East German army, with the backing of its Soviet patrons, would take control of the enclave by force.[2] The Western allies had no possibility of repelling an invasion of West Berlin with their conventional military forces, which were far outnumbered in Europe by those of the Soviet Bloc. Instead, deterrence of an attack of West Berlin relied on the threat that the United States would respond to an invasion of West Berlin with tactical nuclear weapons.

The NATO presence in Berlin annoyed Khrushchev—indeed, he was fond of referring to it as "a cancer" and a "bone in my throat."[3] But only a madman, which most American intelligence experts believed Khrushchev was not, would fight a nuclear war—putting the continued existence of the Soviet Union at risk—over West Berlin. The problem faced by President Dwight Eisenhower was how to make credible a threat to start a nuclear war to protect the freedom of a 185-square-mile enclave that had psychological but not strategic significance.

When Khrushchev's ultimatum expired without a negotiated agreement or a NATO surrender, the world held its collective breath, but Berlin was quiet, and a tense peace prevailed. The East German and Soviet militaries did not use their overwhelming advantage in conventional forces to invade West Berlin, as they undoubtedly could have. Khrushchev had conceded the cooperative surplus.

Did the Soviet leader believe that Eisenhower would have used nuclear weapons to repel an attack? In *Ike's Bluff: President Eisenhower's Secret Battle to Save the World*, author Evan Thomas exhaustively studied Eisenhower's foreign policy and concluded that the president probably had no intention of ever using nuclear weapons. This view was shared by Eisenhower's brother and his closest aide, although the president apparently never explicitly shared his true intention with anyone.[4] And while the historical record isn't clear, Khrushchev was probably not fooled into thinking that Ike would go nuclear. Fortunately, this wasn't necessary. Khrushchev caved to Eisenhower's threat because he could not be completely certain that Ike would allow West Berlin to fall. Given the potential calamitous cost of nuclear escalation, it was sensible for Khrushchev to back down if he determined that there was even the slightest possibility that Ike was not bluffing.

One more nuance of bluffing is important to mention: beginning a negotiation with an aggressive initial offer or demand can work exactly like a bluff, by implying that you will not be willing to reach agreement unless your counterpart agrees to terms close to that point.

In Chapter 13, I described how an aggressive first offer can establish an anchor value that affects your counterpart's determination of her reservation point. But even if your aggressive offer doesn't affect her view of how desirable a deal would be for *her*, it is likely to affect her estimation of *your* reservation point, causing her to believe that she needs to give up more of the cooperative surplus to strike a deal than she actually does.

In a simulation I use with my students, a buyer and a seller attempt to negotiate the sale of a piece of music memorabilia, a mint-condition version of the Beatles' *White Album* record cover autographed by band member John Lennon. The seller is in need of money, the buyer covets the item, and both have terrible plan Bs, which results in a very large bargaining zone; the buyer is willing to pay a high price, and the seller is willing to accept a low price.

The simulation's private instructions assign each party a reservation price (unknown to the counterpart) that cannot be adjusted. This point is important, because it means that attempts by either party to use the tool of Persuasion will be ineffective; neither party can expand the bargaining zone by convincing the counterpart that the deal would be more desirable than the counterpart initially believed. The participants are permitted to

THE EFFECT OF INITIAL OFFERS/DEMANDS ON PERCEPTIONS OF BARGAINING ZONE

HIGH INITIAL DEMAND BY SELLER

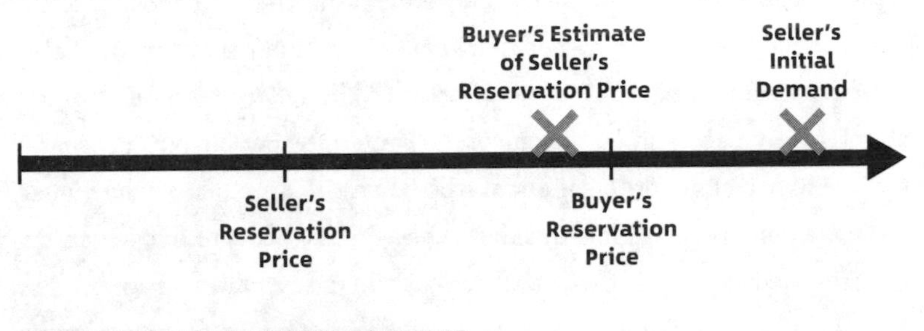

MODEST INITIAL DEMAND BY SELLER

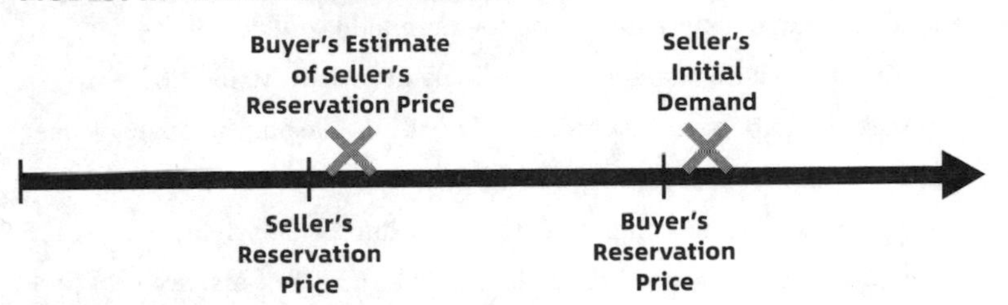

Because initial offers/demands are usually related to the offeror's reservation price, a higher initial demand made by the seller is likely to cause the buyer to believe that the seller has a higher reservation price.

negotiate only the issue of price, which means that they may not use the potent tool of Deal Design to try to increase cooperative surplus. Thus, the bargaining zone is fixed, and all that the parties can do is compete for the set amount of cooperative surplus.

The negotiated outcomes vary substantially, with some parties reaching deals at low prices, close to the seller's reservation price, and others agreeing on much higher prices, close to the buyer's reservation price. The single best predictor of the final sale price is the amount of the initial demand made by the seller: higher initial demands lead to higher final prices. Why would this be?

Although the seller can demand literally any amount of money for the album, buyers recognize from their life experience that sellers who ask for a high price tend to have a higher reservation price than sellers who ask for a low price, and they incorporate this understanding into their negotiation behavior. The buyers assume that the seller's initial offer, whatever it is, is higher than her reservation price, but they also assume that there is a relationship between the seller's reservation price and that first demand. At the end of the bargaining period, buyers usually agree to pay more for the album, rather than risk an impasse, the higher the amount of the original demand. The aggressiveness of the demand is interpreted as a signal that the seller has a high reservation price.

Bluffing is a dangerous tactic. The counterpart might refuse to make the concession demanded because the demand is outside of the bargaining zone or because he doesn't believe the negotiator will follow through with her threat to pursue her plan B. For either reason, the photographer Moffett might have told George Perkins that he would not pay to have his portrait appear on the campaign's brochure but would sell his permission for $1,000. Perkins would have then faced a choice between two poor alternatives: accept an impasse and pursue an inferior plan B (thus committing the second cardinal sin) or concede the cooperative surplus and tacitly admit to his attempt at deception. The former option is immediately costly. The latter option risks longer-term damage to the relationship and the negotiator's reputation for honesty. This means that bluffs should be used sparingly, carefully, and with due regard for the risks that they create. But the potential of bluffs to capture a significant amount of cooperative surplus makes them an essential tactic in the repertoire of a 5TN.

31

PLAYING "CHICKEN"

What if you lack a desirable plan B and your counterpart is well aware that your options are not good, so bluffing is impossible? Agreeing to a minimal offer from your counterpart would leave you better off than an impasse, and she knows it, or at least strongly suspects it. This significantly increases the difficulty of successfully employing the tool of Power, but there are still avenues to explore.

In the iconic scene in the 1955 film classic *Rebel without a Cause*, high school bullies challenge Jim Stark, portrayed by the actor James Dean, to a game of "chicken."[1] In the film's version of the game, two drivers point their cars toward a ravine and drive full speed ahead. The first driver who leaps from his car, to avoid crashing into the ravine and certain death, is deemed to be the "chicken," and loses the game. In the more typical version of the game, the two drivers point their cars at each other and accelerate, and the first to turn his steering wheel is the chicken.

Although it might seem that this game offers no good options for the participants, Thomas Schelling, another Nobel Prize–winning game theorist, identified one. If one driver can, in full view of the other, pull his steering wheel loose and throw it out the window of his car, Schelling contended, he can win the game. Before the steering wheel is dislodged, the other driver has hope that the first driver will swerve first to avoid an accident. But once the steering wheel is gone, the other driver knows that this is no longer a possibility. He now has only two options: he can swerve, and thus be the chicken, or crash headfirst into the car with no steering wheel, and thus die. Since being the chicken is surely the better option, the rational driver really has no choice. He has lost.[2]

Schelling's analysis of the game of chicken demonstrates that John Nash's bargaining theory doesn't apply if one party can make an offer before his counterpart does, as long as that offer cannot be modified or reconsidered. Instead, the party able to commit to an irrevocable, take-it-or-leave-it offer before the other can act has all the Power, which gives him the opportunity to capture most or all of the available cooperative surplus.

To see why, consider again the case of the London bus drivers, and assume that the drivers' union, Unite, has a reservation price of £25 per hour, and the bus companies have a reservation price of £45. If Unite can make a take-it-or-leave-it offer, assuming it knows the companies' reservation price, it can propose that its drivers work for just a fraction less than £45 per hour—let's say £44, or £44.99. This would put the companies in the position of having to choose between two poor options: accept the proposal and capture a tiny amount of cooperative surplus, or reject the proposal, suffer a strike, and thus receive no cooperative surplus at all. The rational negotiator, like the rational teenage daredevil, will choose the better of the two options; that is, he will concede the lion's share of the cooperative surplus to avoid the worse result of an impasse that would provide no cooperative surplus whatsoever.

A winning tactic, then, assuming your goal is to capture as much of the cooperative surplus as possible, is to make a final, take-it-or-leave-it offer backed up by the threat of impasse that will give you most of the cooperative surplus and your counterpart the smallest possible amount. But implementing this tactic, it turns out, is quite difficult. Any negotiator can *say* that she is making a final, take-it-or-leave-it offer, but in most situations, there is nothing that really stops her from making a further concession. If your metaphorical steering wheel can be reinstalled in the car, the other driver can reasonably expect you to swerve rather than crash. And if you can swerve, he might not.

Unite might claim that its demand for £44 per hour is a final, take-it-or-leave-it offer and that it will call a strike if the bus companies do not accept, but this is just bluster that cannot be expected to achieve the results of Schelling's chicken player. The problem is that if the bus companies' negotiator rejects the £44 demand and counters with an offer of £26 per hour, Unite would be better off accepting that offer and capturing £1 per hour worth of cooperative surplus than refusing the offer and launching a strike. How can Unite credibly commit to a strike if its demand is not met, when it would be in its best interest to behave otherwise and the bus companies know it (or at least strongly suspect it)?

The challenge people face in trying to make credible their commitments to take a certain action extends well beyond the bargaining context. Consider this example:

Dean Karlan was a graduate student with a familiar problem. He knew he was overweight and should shed some pounds, but he had a difficult time sticking to a diet and exercise regimen necessary to losing weight and keeping it off. Having a history of setting goals but failing to reach them, Karlan and a friend with the same problem promised each other that they would each donate half of their annual incomes to charity if they failed to reach a specified weight-loss goal by a given date. But this failed, too, because when the predetermined date approached and it became clear that Karlan and his friend were destined to fall short, they simply extended the deadline to avoid losing the money. Karlan made a commitment (in this case, to himself) to a certain course of action, but the commitment wasn't credible because it was more desirable to simply extend the time frame or renege on the commitment entirely than to forfeit such a hefty sum of money.

Realizing that he needed a way to credibly commit to suffering a real penalty should he fail to achieve his goals, Karlan then entered into a contract that would require him to pay a different friend, who was not trying to lose weight, half his annual income if he failed to meet his weight-loss goal. This time, Karlan succeeded in sticking to his commitment. Unlike Thomas Schelling's chicken player, it was still possible for Karlan to renege on his commitment; he remained perfectly capable of eating a slice of pie or skipping his morning workout. But by substantially increasing the cost of backsliding, Karlan changed the incentives so that it was now in his best interest, as he viewed it, to stick to his weight-loss plan, even though this required him to fight off powerful urges.[3]

Soon after, Karlan became a professor at Yale University and, with Ian Ayres and Jordan Goldberg, formed a company called stickK, which enables individuals to enter into similar contracts on the internet. Individuals who want to commit to a course of action, be it losing weight or anything else, provide their credit card number and authorize stickK to charge their card a specified amount of money if the commitment is broken. In that situation, stickK will send the money to an identified individual, to a charity, or—to make failure even more painful—to what stickK calls an "anti-charity" that has goals the individual opposes (such as the NRA Foundation for proponents of stricter gun-control laws or the NARAL Pro-Choice America Foundation for opponents of abortion rights).[4]

In theory, a negotiator could use a contract with a third party like stickK to lend credibility to a threat that otherwise would not be credible. A negotiation student of mine once used a stickK contract for this precise purpose: he contracted with stickK to pay $50 if he accepted any agreement in an upcoming classroom negotiation simulation that would be worse for him than a specified amount of (hypothetical) money. He then demanded that amount from his counterpart in the simulation, explaining that he would be better off with an impasse than he would be accepting any amount less than his demand because making a concession would cost him $50 of real money.

There was no way to cancel the stickK contract. The student had thrown his steering wheel out the window. His counterpart fumed and complained . . . and then agreed to the demand.

32

REPUTATION AND RATIONALITY ON THE HIGH SEAS

The potential for suffering reputational harm by making a concession can serve as a substitute for a severed steering wheel or a commitment contract with stickK.com.

In the late 1980s and early 1990s, as the country of Somalia descended into civil war, piracy emerged as a growth industry. At first, attacks on foreign ships were mostly aimed at relatively small fishing trawlers operating close to the Somali coast and were more like seaborne armed robberies than anything that would invoke the image of Blackbeard flying the Jolly Roger. Lightly organized bands of raiders would board a ship, take the possessions of its occupants, and move on. In those early days, there was at least a patina of a moral quid pro quo of these operations, as the victims were often illegally fishing in Somali waters and thus, at least in theory, cutting into the livelihood of Somali fishermen.[1]

By the early twenty-first century, Somali piracy had evolved into something entirely different. Well-organized armed bands ranging in size from 20 to 50 were regularly marauding in shipping lanes running from the Suez Canal through the Gulf of Aden on Somalia's north coast and around the Horn of Africa into the Indian Ocean. The targets were enormous frigates carrying huge amounts of oil, food, or other commodities through international waters.

As depicted in the Tom Hanks movie *Captain Phillips*, these modern pirates boarded their target ships, took control, held the crews hostage, and then demanded a ransom payment in return for releasing the ship and the crew.[2] Armed international patrols and onboard security eventually brought the problem under control, but between the years of 2005 and 2011, Somali pirates successfully hijacked more than 200 ships.[3]

Although the *Maersk Alabama*, depicted in *Captain Phillips*, and its crew were freed by an assault of U.S. Navy SEALs, this outcome was exceptional. In most cases, the pirates and the ships' owners were able to reach a negotiated agreement and end the standoffs without violence, with the owners or their insurance carriers paying ransom to the pirates. The money was transferred by chartered airplanes flying over the occupied vessels and literally dropping the pirates parachutes full of bundles of cash. In many cases, the ransom payments ran into the millions; at the high end, $13.5 million was paid in 2011 to ransom the supertanker *Irene SL*.[4]

These numbers suggest that the negotiations between the Somali pirates and the owners of their captured ships would be characterized by an extremely large bargaining zone. The ships and their cargo were themselves worth a large amount of money. Add to that the value of the lives of the dozens of crew members aboard the captured vessels, and it is clear why the owners and their insurers would be willing to pay millions.

But this describes only one end of the bargaining zone. The pirates should, by all rights, have had very low reservation prices. What was their plan B? The ships and their cargo were valuable to the owners, but the pirates could not sell the cargoes or rent out the ships for profit—no one would do business with such outlaws. The pirates threatened to sink the ships and kill the crews if their demands weren't met, but this would seem to be quite a poor plan B because the pirates had nothing tangible to gain by creating such mayhem. With such bad options, once in control of a hijacked vessel, the occupying pirates should have been willing to accept almost any offer of ransom at all, no matter how meager, rather than accepting an impasse. The riddle of the Somali-pirate experience is not why the shipping companies would be willing to pay millions of dollars to free their crews and cargo, but why they thought they had to do so.

Imagine a band of pirates threatening to destroy a ship's cargo and kill its crew members if the ship's owner did not pay a ransom of $5 million. Given that the pirates have nothing to gain from carrying out that threat, the owner might calculate that the threat lacks credibility and, consequently, that it would be in the pirates' best interest to free the ship and the crew in return for a token ransom payment—perhaps $5,000.

If the act of piracy were a one-time event, and the pirates were planning to return to a life of fishing afterward, this analysis would be sound. But these pirates were in the business of repeatedly ransoming ships, so a ship's owner could not be nearly so sanguine. The pirates' behavior in one negotiation would create a reputation that could help or hurt them in future transactions. Yes, the pirates would be better off accepting a token payment than destroying the ship. But once they threaten to burn the cargo and kill the crew if they are not paid a $5 million ransom, the incentives change. A failure to follow through would create the risk that shipowners would not take future demands seriously.

With reputational consequences at stake that extend beyond the focal negotiation, a threat that otherwise would not be credible can become credible. Rational shipowners might believe that they must parachute millions of dollars onto the decks of captured vessels to protect the ships from destruction and their crews from murder. And they often did just that.

There is a second explanation as well, and arguably a simpler one, for why Somali pirates armed with an objectively poor plan B proved able to convince sophisticated multinational corporations and their insurance companies to pay millions to ransom their captured ships. The strategic analysis presented by game theorists like John Nash and Thomas Schelling

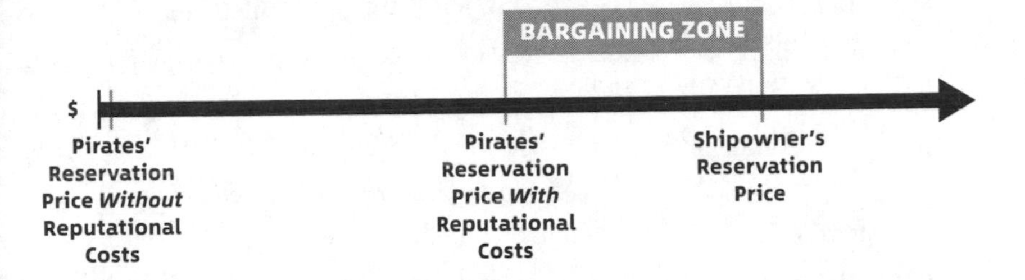

The reputational consequences that could affect future negotiations cause the pirates' reservation price in a ransom negotiation to be higher than it otherwise would be.

assumes rational behavior on the part of the actors being considered; that is, each person is assumed to make decisions that will maximize her expected utility. But not all negotiators follow the strict rationality assumptions of game theory when they decide how to act. The less likely a negotiator is to behave rationally, the more credible is his commitment to choosing impasse when doing so would seem less desirable than accepting a less generous offer.

Some elements of the Somali pirates' behavior echoed the organization and discipline of modern corporations. Pirate bands tended to be organized hierarchically, with clear lines of command and control and differentiated job assignments. In some cases, they even employed semiprofessional negotiators to handle the ransom discussions with Western shipowners. When the pirates who captured the *Maersk Alabama* demanded ransom, they assured Captain Phillips that the entire operation was "just business."

But the pirate bands also communicated a sense of desperation that could imply less-than-rational behavior. Pirate crews were often dispatched toward target vessels in small ships without enough fuel to make it back to shore should their attempt to board and capture the vessel fail. And when on the captured vessels, whiling away the days, weeks, and sometimes months that the negotiating process took, the pirates were known for consuming large quantities of khat, a plant with intoxicating leaves that can be chewed or boiled into tea. When consumed in small quantities, khat is a mild stimulant. But when consumed in large quantities, the plant can distort perceptions and make the user feel invincible.

In *The Pirates of Somalia: Inside Their Hidden World*, journalist Jay Bahadur described the 2009 hijacking and ransom of the German-owned freighter the *MV Victoria*, en route to Saudi Arabia with a cargo of rice. Bahadur characterized the nearly two and a half months that the freighter was held captive as a "khat-fueled vigil," during which supply vessels would make khat deliveries to the freighter several times a day and the bored and thoroughly inebriated pirates would often amuse themselves by firing their Russian-made Kalashnikov rifles into the air. All in all, this behavior would have reasonably caused already-jittery shipowners to wonder whether the pirates would behave rationally if their ransom demands were not satisfied. The owners eventually paid $1.8 million to free the ship and its crew—not as much as the $3 million the pirates originally demanded, but far more than would seem to be justified by the objective quality of the pirates' plan B.[5]

If the owners had refused to pay more than a token ransom—say, $10,000—would the pirates have taken the money or sunk the ship and shot the crew? Who could be sure?

Thomas Schelling observed that "if a man knocks at a door and says that he will stab himself on the porch unless given $10, he is more likely to get the $10 if his eyes are bloodshot."[6] In most aspects of life, being rational will usually work to your advantage; in negotiation, being irrational, or at least convincing your counterpart that you are irrational, can be a source of Power. It isn't fair, as my students often point out. But your mother told you long ago that life isn't always fair.

33

WARM LEMONADE AND THE POWER OF PATIENCE

Delays in reaching agreement can be costly. Somali pirates would rather collect their ransom now than in six months. Until the deal is struck, they can't buy anything, and they have to spend all of their time occupying the captured ships and guarding the kidnapped crew members. Unions and management would prefer to resolve strikes sooner rather than later, because each day of a work stoppage means employees lose their salaries and the company loses sales. And because negotiating usually involves some degree of unpleasant conflict, most negotiators would rather reach a deal today than tomorrow, even if only to minimize the time and stress of bargaining.

But while delay in reaching an agreement is usually undesirable for negotiators on both sides of the table, the costs are often greater for one party. As shorthand, think of a negotiator who is in relatively little hurry to reach an agreement as being *patient*. The patient negotiator has little to lose by waiting until tomorrow to conclude a negotiation rather than agreeing on terms today. In contrast, an *impatient* negotiator will suffer large out-of-pocket costs, opportunity costs, or even just personal psychological costs, if a negotiation that could be concluded with an agreement today carries over to tomorrow or the next day. When a patient negotiator squares off against an impatient negotiator, the former should be able to demand greater concessions by threatening a stalemate.

Here is an example: Imagine that two parties, Bonnie and Clyde, are negotiating the division of a cold pitcher of lemonade on a hot summer day. When the pitcher first emerges from the kitchen full of ice, both would obtain 10 utils worth of pleasure from drinking the entire pitcher and 5 utils of pleasure from drinking half. If Bonnie could credibly commit to making a final, take-it-or-leave-it offer, principles of game theory suggest she should be able to demand almost the entire pitcher (with Clyde receiving just a small sip), because Clyde should reason that a tiny bit is better than nothing. But if she cannot credibly commit to not considering a counteroffer, Clyde could respond to Bonnie's offer by turning the tables and pointing out that Bonnie, too, should prefer a small sip to nothing at all, and thus that she should agree to Clyde keeping nearly all the lemonade. A standoff would seem likely.

Now, imagine that there is one important difference between Bonnie and Clyde. Clyde detests warm lemonade. This means that each minute that the pitcher sits in the hot sunshine while the parties negotiate, the amount of utility Clyde would obtain from drinking it quickly decreases. At the end of the day, even the entire warm pitcher of lemonade would provide Clyde with no pleasure at all. Bonnie, on the other hand, enjoys lemonade exactly the same amount regardless of its temperature. A lukewarm pitcher quaffed at the end of the day would provide her with the same 10 utils of pleasure she would enjoy from drinking the ice-cold pitcher in the morning. If the two negotiators were to spend all day haggling over the division of the lemonade before reaching a deal, the patient Bonnie would not lose out on any value at all. For the impatient Clyde, though, the value of the lemonade would quickly decline and eventually reach zero.

Bonnie's patience provides her with a source of Power that stems not from her ability to credibly threaten impasse, which is the usual source of

Power, but from her credible threat to delay reaching agreement. Imagine that Bonnie begins the negotiation by proposing that Clyde receive one sip of the lemonade and she the rest, and that Clyde rejects the offer and proposes a more equal split. Bonnie refuses to make any concessions, and she says that she will sit and wait—all day if necessary—until Clyde decides he is willing to accept her proposal. Clyde knows that later in the day the lemonade will have no value to him at all. Even one small sip of cold lemonade in the morning would be more desirable for him than the entire pitcher in the late afternoon, so he is better off accepting Bonnie's offer now.

The story becomes only slightly more complicated if we assume, more realistically, that Bonnie also prefers her lemonade cold, but that she doesn't care nearly as much about its temperature as does Clyde. That is, Bonnie is not what we might think of as being *perfectly* patient, but she is *relatively* patient compared to Clyde. In this situation, Bonnie, like Clyde, should be willing to make some concessions in the morning.

Academic game theorists use complicated equations to show that rational negotiators should divide the cooperative surplus exactly according to their relative levels of impatience.[1] If the value of the lemonade declines while sitting in the sun exactly twice as much for Clyde as it does for Bonnie, the two should agree at the outset of the negotiation to a split that gives Bonnie two-thirds of the pitcher and Clyde one-third. This specific result depends on a series of strict assumptions that don't always apply, but the general point is this: the more impatient negotiator has an incentive to concede most of the cooperative surplus at the outset of the negotiation because this will tend to result in a better outcome for him than if he were to hold out for a larger share of a shrinking pie. The more patient negotiator might suffer some costs from delay, but her threat to hold out is made credible, notwithstanding these costs, by the fact that she knows that the impatient negotiator will ultimately have to make the larger concessions.

In an episode of the Netflix television series *Ozark*, ruthless protagonist Wendy Byrde, played by actress Laura Linney, owns a riverboat casino in Missouri and is trying to buy the adjacent hotel, which obtains nearly all of its business from tourists who have come to gamble. The owners, who also owned the casino before Byrde strong-armed them into selling it, don't want to part with the hotel.

Byrde announces that she is closing the casino for a month, depriving both parties of all their revenue. "You'll lose a fortune if you shut down, especially during the summer months," one of the shocked hoteliers observes. Byrde smiles and shrugs: "We can afford that. We are bigger than you and we are meaner, and we do not lose. So, why don't you just sell us the hotel?" Every day the casino stays shuttered is another costly self-inflicted wound, but the tactic is rational as long as Byrde believes that the hotel owners will become insolvent first. The angry hotel owners storm off—aggressive Power tactics are a poor way to make friends—but they soon come to their senses, and Byrde gets her hotel.[2]

The benefits of patience provide a third explanation for why the Somali pirates were able to negotiate many multimillion-dollar settlements from Western shipping companies, even though they had weak plan Bs. Piracy is a relatively low-volume business, all things considered. It is likely that a gang of pirates holding one ship hostage for weeks or months is not missing out on opportunities to hijack and ransom other ships within that same period of time. With a low value of time, waiting around for ransom negotiations to play out isn't very costly. In addition, informal financial markets existed in Somalia that enabled pirate gangs to borrow money against future proceeds expected from ransoms.[3] This suggests that, although the pirates were poor and no doubt preferred to receive ransom payments sooner rather than later, immediate cash flow was not necessary to finance the capital costs of their hijacking activities. They could wait.

For the shipowners, in contrast, the costs of a lengthy hijacking episode were substantial. While occupied by pirates, the expensive ships were producing no income, and with the cargoes stranded on the ships, the owners couldn't sell the merchandise and use the proceeds to purchase and transport more goods. Most importantly, the psychological costs suffered by the crew members and their families each day the ship was held hostage were enormous. The shipowners no doubt realized that agreeing to pay the relatively more patient pirates larger ransoms in order to quickly extricate their ships from captivity was a smarter strategy than suffering the considerable costs of ongoing delays in return for the possibility of saving some money in direct settlement payments down the road.

Patience is a virtue. For the 5TN, it is also a source of Power.

SUMMARY OF KEY LESSONS FROM PART 4

- Power forces the counterpart to agree to a deal that allocates most or all of the cooperative surplus to the negotiator.
- The ability to exercise Power stems from the negotiator's ability to credibly threaten an impasse if her demand is not met.
- Using Power depends on the negotiator's ability to convince her counterpart that the negotiator believes her plan B is desirable relative to reaching agreement in the focal negotiation. This can be accomplished by identifying or creating a better plan B, claiming that she has a better plan B than she does, or exaggerating her interest in pursuing her plan B or her lack of interest in the focal deal.
- The threat of impasse can be effective even if the counterpart believes only that the negotiator *might* actually pursue her plan B.
- Even if the counterpart knows that the negotiator would be materially better off reaching an agreement on less advantageous terms than pursuing her plan B, the negotiator can still exercise Power if she cannot accept a deal worse for her than her demand, if she would suffer sufficient reputational costs by accepting a deal that is worse for her than her demand, or if her counterpart believes that she might not determine her next move rationally.
- A negotiator who is more patient than her counterpart can exercise Power by threatening to delay reaching agreement, which would impose higher costs on the counterpart than the negotiator will suffer.

TOOL #5

FAIRNESS NORMS

34

ULTIMATUMS AND DICTATORS

In the fall of 1977, a young German economics professor named Werner Güth was offered some unexpected research funding, but only if he agreed to use the money to conduct laboratory experiments, a method of research that was uncommon in the field at the time. Güth devised an experiment that he called the "ultimatum game." His results, published in 1982,[1] launched decades of follow-up research and made the ultimatum game the most popular experimental bargaining game and probably the most popular experiment in the entire field of behavioral economics.[2]

The ultimatum game has generated so much attention because it simply and unequivocally demonstrates that people will act contrary to their economic interests in order to avoid being treated unfairly. The intense human desire for fair treatment makes the use of tool #5, **Fairness Norms**, critical for negotiating success.

Here's how the ultimatum game works: A researcher presents one experimental subject, called the "proposer," with a sum of money, called the "stake," which is traditionally $10. The proposer then must propose a division of the stake between himself and a second subject, called the "responder." The responder chooses to either accept or reject the pro-

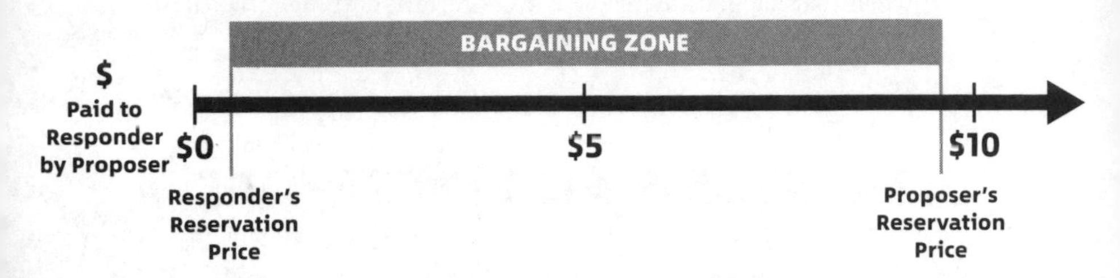

Game theorists say the proposers should offer to pay the smallest possible increment, but responders often reject offers much below $5.

posed division. If the responder accepts, the money is divided between the two in the manner the proposer described. If the responder rejects, both subjects receive nothing. The identities of the responder and proposer are unknown to each other.

The experiment creates a pure test of how real people act when two parties have perfect information about the other's reservation points and one of the parties can commit, with 100 percent credibility, to making a final, take-it-or-leave-it offer.

According to the reasoning of game theory, the responder in the ultimatum game should accept any amount of money that the proposer offers. The responder's plan B, rejecting the offer, will leave her with $0, and some money is obviously better than none. Because the proposer cannot revise his offer and the responder cannot make a counterproposal, the proposer is akin to Thomas Schelling's chicken player who throws his steering wheel out the car window. Unlike in most real-world negotiations, in which a negotiator cannot be certain whether her counterpart's so-called "final" offer is really final, the responder in the ultimatum game knows that the proposer is not bluffing.

But most experimental subjects don't play the way that game theory predicts. Many responders reject offers of less than 50 percent of the stake, and most reject offers of less than 20 percent.[3] Remember that rejecting any offer greater than $0 is the functional equivalent of burning money; when that happens, both the players receive nothing. The rules are crystal clear. There are no second chances.

The behavior of responders might be surprising to game theorists, but choices made by proposers demonstrate that they anticipate that responders might reject low offers. Relatively few proposers offer the smallest possible amount of money. In experiment after experiment, proposers usually offer responders between 40 percent and 50 percent of the stake, on average, and the most common offer is usually 50 percent. Patterns of responder and proposer behavior persist even when experiments are conducted in countries in which the size of the stake that researchers can afford to provide constitutes substantial income for the participants,[4] undermining the assumption of some economists that people will behave "rationally" if enough money is at stake.

The results of the ultimatum game lay bare the fact that negotiation is not merely a strategic interaction but also a social one. Most people value not only the material outcome that a negotiation can provide but also an agreement that they consider to be fair. And many people, it turns out, are willing to forfeit tangible rewards rather than willingly accept unfair treatment. Reaching agreement often requires not only the existence of cooperative surplus but also a mutual belief that a particular division of that surplus satisfies social standards of fairness under the circumstances.

It is common, in fact, for 5TNs to spend an inordinate amount of time and effort demonstrating that their proposal is "fair," even when they have a decisive power advantage that would seem to ensure their ability to demand the majority of the cooperative surplus by simply threatening impasse. There are several reasons for this.

First, a negotiator who uses Power, like the proposer in the ultimatum game who offers the responder just pennies, runs the risk that his counterpart will reject a deal she perceives to be unfair even if the resulting impasse leaves her materially worse off.[5] The choice between Power and Fairness Norms can be seen as one between force and finesse, with the latter often providing a smoother path to a desirable outcome.

Second, for many people, using Fairness Norms feels better as well. Some competitive negotiators love the rush of using Power to bend a counterpart to their will, but more negotiators go home feeling better about themselves when a counterpart who shakes hands on a deal proclaims "that's fair" than when the counterpart grimaces at that moment.

Third, a happy counterpart is more likely to return to do business in the future than a bitter one and is less likely to shirk on fulfilling her obligations under the agreement to which she reluctantly agreed.

Power and Fairness Norms are not mutually exclusive, however, and 5TNs often use both tools simultaneously. While the London bus drivers were threatening an Olympic strike—as clear an example of a Power tactic as there is—they were simultaneously buttressing their negotiating position by invoking Fairness Norms to justify higher pay.

In the media coverage leading up to the eventual settlement of the dispute, the two main arguments for the Olympic bonuses made by and on behalf of the drivers were that London Tube (subway) employees and other transportation workers had already been promised an Olympic bonus of a size similar to or greater than the amount the bus drivers were demanding, and that increased passenger traffic during the Olympics would increase the drivers' workload.[6] The first point relies for its rhetorical force on the principle of fairness that similarly situated people should be treated the same way; the second depends on the principle of fairness that compensation should reflect employee effort.

Commentators unsympathetic to the union demand accepted that fairness was relevant to the negotiation but contested what would be fair in the particular circumstance. They argued that more passengers during the Olympic fortnight did not necessarily translate into more work for drivers, that more work did not require higher pay because new fare-collection technology had recently lightened the workload of bus drivers but no pay cut had resulted, and that the union's insistence that all drivers receive bonuses—even those on routes that would not be burdened by increased traffic during the Olympics—was not justifiable in any event.[7]

This exchange demonstrates that what constitutes a fair agreement is usually contestable. No particular deal can be "fair" or "unfair" in any objective sense. Fairness is a social construct, and the outcome of any negotiation is fair only to the extent that the negotiators themselves or a broader social consensus deem it to be fair. Two negotiators might honestly and in good faith pledge to seek only a "fair" deal but still find themselves unable to agree to a set of terms, because each can defend very different proposals as consistent with a plausible (although different) conception of fairness.

The results of the ultimatum game suggest that some negotiators in some circumstances (but certainly not all negotiators in all circumstances) will reject a deal that is materially advantageous compared to their plan B if they perceive a proposal to be unfair. In this way, a negotiator's bargaining-table objection that she finds a proposed settlement "unfair" to her can work exactly like a claim that the proposed settlement is inferior to her reservation point; that is, it can buttress the credibility of a threat to end the negotiation in impasse.

For example, the London bus drivers might have had a reservation point of £25 per hour because they would prefer to work for £25 (but not for £24) than to strike, and yet they still might have rejected a final offer of £25 if they believed £32 was the fair wage, perhaps because that is what some other group of workers earned.[8] If they threatened to strike unless they received that "fair" amount, the bus companies would have to take that threat seriously.

A question that results of the ultimatum game do not answer is whether negotiators care only about avoiding *negative unfairness* (receiving less in a negotiation than what is fair) or whether they also value avoiding what can be called *positive unfairness* (reaching an agreement that is unfair to their counterpart and thus provides them with greater material benefit than fairness demands). The fact that proposers in the ultimatum game tend to make far more generous offers than game theory predicts might be because they intuit (correctly) that responders will often reject negatively unfair offers or, alternatively, because proposers wish to avoid positively unfair offers.

Another simple experimental game offers some insight into this question. The "dictator game" begins like the ultimatum game, with the proposer given a stake and asked to propose a division of it between himself and an anonymous responder. Unlike in the ultimatum game, however, the responder in the dictator game has no choice but to accept the proposed division (both players know in advance that the responder has no choice in the matter). The proposer dictates the result; hence the game's name. This means that an offer of more than $0 cannot be explained as the result of the proposer's fear that an unfair offer would be rejected.

Game theory predicts that the proposer in the dictator game will give nothing to the responder and keep everything for himself; there is no material benefit at all to be had from sharing. As is true of the ultimatum game, however, results from dictator game experiments, played for real money, routinely contradict this prediction. Approximately one-third of proposers do give the responder nothing, suggesting that they have no qualms about skewed distributions that favor themselves. But the majority of the proposers give something, suggesting at least some aversion to even positive unfairness, and about one-sixth give at least 50 percent of the stake.[9]

The difficult problem for 5TNs is to determine what conceptions of fairness their counterparts will find persuasive, or at least acceptable enough to justify reaching agreement on a particular set of terms. The following chapters describe the three conceptual approaches that negotiators use to justify the fairness of proposals:

- An agreement is fair if it embodies the principles of distributive justice between the negotiators.
- An agreement is fair if it treats negotiators the same as other negotiators in similar situations.
- An agreement is fair if it emerges from a fair negotiating process.

Negotiators disagree about what is fair because these approaches often point in different directions and are subject to different interpretations in particular situations. But 5TNs understand how to use this collection of concepts to produce deals that both parties are willing to accept.

35

DISTRIBUTIVE JUSTICE

During Barack Obama's presidency, Democrats and Republicans negotiated heatedly on several occasions about the marginal federal income-tax rate for high-earning individuals.[1] The Democrats demanded that the highest marginal tax rate, which had been reduced during the George W. Bush administration, be raised, while Republicans vehemently resisted any increase.[2] Senate Republicans reluctantly agreed to an increase in 2012 as part of a broader budget compromise, but House Republicans voted against the compromise rather than accept that outcome.[3] When Republicans took control of both houses of Congress and the presidency in 2016, they enacted a new tax bill that broadly reduced individual income taxes but provided the largest reductions, in percentage terms, to the highest income earners.[4] It was enacted without a single Democratic vote.[5]

The political parties' opposing positions on tax rates reflect a fundamental disagreement over the nature of *distributive justice*—that is, what allocation of resources among members of a group is most fair.

Social scientists identify three competing principles that animate people's views concerning distributive justice: equity, equality, and need.

- According to the *equity* principle, people are entitled to resources in accordance with their contribution to the creation of those resources. Individuals who produce more are entitled to larger shares.
- According to the *equality* principle, all members of a group should receive the same share of the benefits.
- According to the *need* principle, greater benefits should be allocated to group members with the greatest need.[6]

The Republican position on tax rates relies on the equity principle. Americans with high incomes earn their money in the marketplace, and high-income business owners, by virtue of being "job creators," also contribute substantially to the economic welfare of their employees and the nation. Consequently, their contribution makes it fair for them to keep a larger portion of the national income.

The Democratic position reflects a preference for the need principle over equity. To the extent taxes are necessary, Democrats think it is fair to require the wealthy to pay more because they can better afford to shoulder the costs of running the government than the poor or the middle class. Lower-income people need the money more.

Occasionally, support surfaces for a "flat tax," according to which all taxpayers would pay the same percentage of their income. Flat-tax rhetoric consciously invokes the equality principle: treat everyone the same. Although flat-tax proposals don't win a lot of popular support in the United States in the income-tax context, the equality principle provides the basis for the allocation of the sales-tax burden and seems to enjoy widespread support in that context, although it is often criticized as being unfairly "regressive" by proponents of the need principle.

As this example illustrates, negotiators often disagree over which distributive justice principle deserves primacy in a particular context. There is no commonly agreed-upon hierarchy among the principles (although there is some evidence that politically conservative individuals are, on average, more sympathetic to the equity principle than to equality or need), so even if negotiators on opposite sides of the table can agree that distributive justice should be the basis for an agreement, they will often fail to reach consensus.

Economic logic suggests that equity has a strong claim to primacy if the effort expended by the parties post-negotiation will affect the total amount of cooperative surplus. Assume, for example, that Aphrodite and Beacher are forming a business partnership, and they must negotiate whether to divide the future profits based on equity, equality, or need. In this case, an equitable division would minimize the moral hazard problem (discussed in Chapter 27) by giving both partners an incentive to work as hard as possible, whereas the equality and need principles could incentivize both to shirk and hope the other works hard. (Note that the equity principle would lack this advantage over equality and need if Aphrodite and Beacher were negotiating an agreement to dissolve an existing partnership, a situation in which the moral hazard concern would not exist because neither party would perform any services in the future.[7]) But economic logic is not necessarily consistent with social logic, so the equality and need principles often find strong advocates even in negotiations in which future effort is an important consideration.

When negotiators hope to build a long-term, cooperative relationship, and the focal negotiation represents only a small part of the value that they stand to achieve from working together in the future, a stronger argument might be made for equality. This principle, which implicitly suggests that all parties to a negotiated agreement have the same value, is more conducive to building strong social relationships than the equity principle, which by its very nature highlights differences in value between the negotiators. Again, however, since fairness is a social concept that, in the end, depends on what the negotiators perceive to be fair, there is no guarantee that equality will hold sway over equity or need even in this context.

While individual negotiators might tend to be more sympathetic to one distributive justice principle than to the others as a general matter, there is evidence that the views of most of us are at least somewhat sensitive to context. In a negotiation experiment conducted by psychologist Elizabeth Mannix and colleagues, business-school-student subjects were asked to play the role of one of three divisional vice presidents within a company that produces instructional videos and negotiate the responsibility for producing 12 new videos for a client. Each triad of negotiators was given one of three descriptions of the firm's culture. Negotiating groups told that the company's culture was economically oriented were more likely to emphasize the equity principle when allocating responsibilities among divisions; those told that the firm culture favored the development of personal relationships and respect were most likely to employ the equality norm; and those told the firm rewarded employee growth and development favored the need norm.[8]

In the standard version of the ultimatum game, the equality norm seems to dominate. Although the person in the role of the proposer has all the bargaining power, the results indicate that the majority of subjects believe the stakes should be divided based on simple equality. Offers of less than 50 percent of the stake are routinely rejected but offers of more than 50 percent are almost never rejected. In most published experiments, the most common offer made by proposers is precisely 50 percent.[9]

Results often differ, however, when experimenters provide context that implies there might be an equitable basis for unequal outcomes. Economists Werner Güth and Reinhard Tietz auctioned subjects the right to play the proposer role and found that the winning bidders rarely offered 50 percent of the stake to responders and responders usually accepted one-sided proposals.[10] Economist Elizabeth Hoffman and colleagues gave subjects a trivia quiz and then assigned subjects who achieved higher scores the role of proposer and the subjects who earned lower scores the role of responder. In this situation, too, responders were willing to accept smaller shares of the stake. Both experiments suggest that subjects were sympathetic to an equity norm, as opposed to pure equality, and the second suggests subjects believed that a higher quiz score gave subjects an equitable claim to an unequal allocation of the cooperative surplus even though the relevance of the quiz to the monetary rewards was not obvious.[11]

Other research suggests that the relationship between the negotiators can affect preferences between justice norms. Psychologist Harris Sondak gave subjects a test and then, regardless of their actual answers, told subjects that they either scored 30 points and their assigned partner 70 points or the opposite, giving each group a total of 100 points. The subjects were then tasked with negotiating with their partners on how to divide the 100 points awarded to their group, which the individuals could then redeem for lottery tickets and other benefits. In half of the negotiations, subjects were partnered with their roommate, and in the other half they were partnered with complete strangers. Consistent with the theory that equality is more desirable when long-term relationships are at issue, subjects partnered with strangers were more likely than those paired with roommates to distribute the points based on the equity norm (i.e., based on who supposedly scored higher on the test that generated the points), and the roommate pairs were more likely than the stranger pairs to distribute the points based on the equality principle (i.e., 50-50).[12]

Even if negotiators can agree on one of the distributive justice principles to serve as the basis for their agreement, they might disagree on how that principle applies in a particular case. For example, does equity require that resources be allocated between the parties in proportion to their *effort* or their actual *accomplishments*? If Aphrodite works twice as many hours as Beacher, but Beacher invents the most profitable product or closes the most sales, who is entitled to a larger share of the cooperative surplus? Does equality require that each claimant receive precisely the same share of whatever particular resource is being allocated, or should shares of the resource in question be adjusted so that each person receives the same share of overall resources, taking into account that other resources might have previously been distributed unequally? Does the need principle permit, require, or even prohibit taking into account whether claimants have taken all possible actions to minimize their need? None of these questions has an obvious answer.

Although the Democratic position on income tax usually privileges the need norm, Democratic leaders sometimes challenge the standard Republican claim that the equity principle favors lower tax rates for the wealthy. If high incomes are (predominantly) a consequence of luck or privilege rather than effort and skill, the claim that equity requires allowing high earners to keep more of their income loses force. When the left tries to contest the right's equity claim, the right pushes back. President Obama was pilloried by his Republican adversaries when, pointing out that publicly financed infrastructure, such as roads and bridges, enables business owners to earn more money, he observed that "you [individual business owners] didn't build that."[13]

When negotiators convince their counterparts that a particular division of benefits or burdens is just, a deal usually isn't far away. But as this last example demonstrates, achieving this goal is no easy task.

36

CONVENTION

In the early 1980s, legal scholar Robert Ellickson decamped from Stanford Law School to rural Shasta County, California, to study how the residents resolved disputes that occurred when one rancher's cattle would trespass on a neighboring farmer's land and damage his crops. In these situations, it was far from obvious which party was to blame. It was usually the case that the rancher could have prevented the damage by doing a better job fencing in her livestock, but it was also true that the farmer could have avoided the harm by doing a better job fencing in his crops. Ellickson assumed that the terms of negotiated resolutions of these disputes would depend on whether or not the ranchers were legally liable for the damage. Both parties' plan B was taking the dispute to court, which meant that whoever the law favored would have been in an excellent position to use Power.

Ellickson knew that in some circumstances the relevant law in Shasta County favored the rancher, and in others it favored the farmer, so he was surprised to discover that, in these negotiations, custom trumped legal entitlement. The disputes were routinely settled with the rancher paying for all the damage, even when the rancher had the law on her side.[1]

Ellickson's negotiators relied on a different category of Fairness Norm than those discussed in the previous chapter. When perceptions of fairness are based on distributive justice principles, fairness depends on how the cooperative surplus is shared between the parties to the negotiation. A responder in the ultimatum game who rejects an offer of less than 50 percent of the stake does so because the equality principle implies that it is unfair for her to receive a smaller payoff than the proposer, the person with whom she must divide the surplus. In Shasta County, the fair allocation of the cost of cattle trampling crops was understood to depend not on the allocation of the burden between a rancher and a farmer, but on farmers being treated like other farmers and ranchers being treated like other ranchers. Fairness claims that appeal to such horizontal social comparisons are what I call appeals to *convention*. From this perspective, fairness means that the negotiator (or the group he represents) is treated in the same way that similarly situated parties are (or have been) treated in similar situations.

This is not to say that ultimatum game players do not care about convention. When they are able to compare themselves with other players who have the same role, they do take this into account. Economists Iris Bohnet and Richard Zeckhauser compared the decisions of ultimatum game responders who received the standard information (the amount of the stake and the amount offered to them by their individual proposer) to those of responders who were told the average amount of the offers made by proposers. Responders in the second group, who could compare themselves to other responders, were more likely to reject their proposal, demonstrating the importance they placed on that comparison.[2] Interestingly, proposers clearly understood the importance of this horizontal social comparison as well; when they knew that responders would be told the average offer amount, proposers made higher offers.

The concern with being treated no worse than others who are similarly situated, and the willingness to reject mutually beneficial transactions in protest when this form of fairness is violated, is not, by the way, a characteristic unique to humans. Primatologists Frans de Waal and Sarah Brosnan trained capuchin monkeys to "pay" experimenters stones for slices of cucumber, which they enjoyed doing. But when they watched other monkeys receive more desirable grapes in return for stones, many of the cucumber monkeys refused to trade their stones and refused to accept cucumbers.[3]

To generalize the lesson, terms of an agreement that are typical are often presumed to be fair because this ensures that similarly situated negotiators are treated the same. 5TNs understand that, as a result, their counterpart is far more likely to accept an agreement if it appears to follow convention, regardless of how the convention divides the cooperative surplus between the negotiators in the particular situation. No one likes to be treated worse than the next monkey!

37

THE ROLE OF MARKET PRICE

If local gardeners normally charge $100 to trim a tree, a potential customer will likely perceive a price quote of $125 to be unfair, even if the customer has an extremely high reservation price. If a company pays its entry-level employees in a particular department $70,000 per year, a job applicant is likely to find the company's offer to him of $59,000 to be unfair, even if it so happens that his next-best alternative would be much worse and the employer has many good candidates. If a house sold last month for $600,000, a buyer will probably believe the listing price of $700,000 for a similar house on the same block is unfair, even if she desperately wants the house and it is the only one in the neighborhood for sale.

For convention to serve as the indicator of a fair agreement, negotiators need a basis for determining what the applicable convention is. I call previous deals, usually entered into by unrelated parties, that the negotiators look to for guidance *reference transactions*. In commercial negotiations, negotiators often judge the fairness of a price by looking at the price paid in reference transactions, which they will commonly refer to as the *market price*. The market price of goods or services can affect the course of a negotiation in two very different ways, one economic and one social. In order to appreciate the important of market price and use it effectively in negotiations, it is important to understand the difference.

When many buyers and many sellers are transacting for goods or services with exact or close substitutes, the market price affects the bargaining zone, because the parties' plan Bs involve buying or selling for that market price.

Let's assume that Aphrodite is shopping in a busy farmers' market in which a dozen local farmers are offering nearly identical ears of corn for $1 each, and many shoppers are excited to purchase corn. She steps up to Beacher's stall to negotiate the purchase of one ear. Aphrodite's plan B is to purchase an identical ear of corn from another farmer for $1. Since those farmers are literally steps away, her reservation price in the focal negotiation will likely be $1. Beacher's plan B is to sell that ear of corn for $1 to another customer in the line, so $1 is also his reservation price.

In this situation, the market price directly affects the bargaining zone and limits the range of potential agreements. This is what I mean when I say that the market price has an economic effect on the negotiation. In this situation, we can predict that Aphrodite and Beacher will agree to a price of $1. No other agreements are possible.

Now consider the role played by market price in another situation with a slight but important difference. Assume that Aphrodite doesn't like the appearance of any other farmer's corn, so her plan B is to leave the market without any produce. Given that she is hungry, she much prefers to reach an agreement with Beacher than to pursue her plan B, and she determines that her reservation price for an ear of Beacher's corn is $3. Beacher has a lot of corn and there are not many shoppers in the market, so he realizes that if he does not reach an agreement with Aphrodite, his plan B is to take that ear of corn to a different farmers' market the next day and sell it there. This would be a hassle that he would rather avoid, so he determines that his reservation price is 75 cents.

We still might say that the "market price" for an ear of corn is $1,

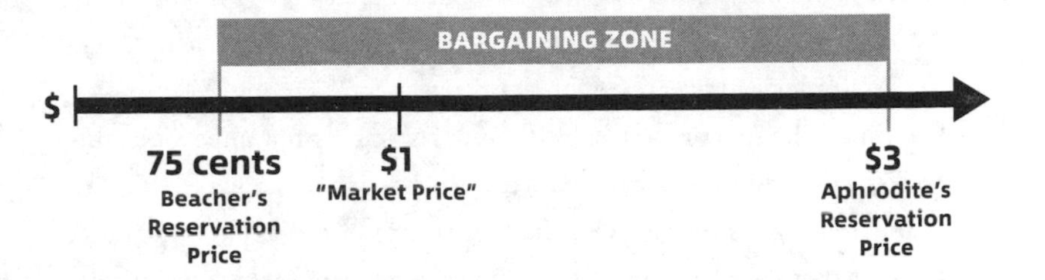

Negotiators will often believe that the typical market price is fair, even if the parties' plan Bs are *not* to buy and sell at the market price.

but this statement has a different meaning in this situation. The fact that $1 is the customary price in this market does not make it either party's reservation price because neither's plan B is to make a deal with another participant in that market, but the parties will still consider all of those other $1 sales as appropriate reference transactions. It is likely that Aphrodite and Beacher will both believe that $1 is a fair price, because similar customers pay $1 and similar sellers receive $1. This is what I mean when I say that market price has a *social* meaning. As in our first hypothetical case, we can predict Aphrodite and Beacher will agree on a price of $1, even though in this case 80 cents, $1.10, $1.40, and $2.95 all also fall within the bargaining zone.

The importance of market price as convention, even when it lacks economic relevance, is nicely illustrated in a story told by law professor Steven Lubet about his visit to the ancient Jordanian city of Petra. The ancient city can be accessed only by traveling for over a mile through a narrow gorge carved into steep mountains. No motorized vehicles are permitted in or out of Petra, so the only two ways to traverse the gorge are to walk or to hire a Bedouin guide to transport you by horseback. At the time of Lubet's visit, round-trip tickets were sold for seven Jordanian dinars at the entrance to the gorge. Rather than purchase a round-trip ticket, tourists could walk into Petra and then at the end of the day attempt to negotiate with individual guides for a one-way ride out (the more uphill direction) of the city.

By speaking with a number of Bedouin guides, Lubet learned that the established market price for the one-way journey out of Petra was four dinars. Lubet assumed, however, that bargaining power between the horse guides and the tourists would change along with market conditions as the evening approached and the tourist area of the city was about to close. If there were few guides remaining and many tired tourists, the plan B of a guide negotiating with a tourist—waiting for another, more desperate tourist willing to pay a higher price—would seem strong, causing guides to set a high reservation price and enabling them to extract higher fares from tourists who also had high reservation prices. But if there were many guides and few tourists, as Lubet suspected, each guide's plan B would be weak, causing him to lower his reservation price below four dinars. After all, for an idle guide, just like a responder in the ultimatum game, some income is better than none.

At the end of a long, hot day of hiking through Petra, Lubet preferred to ride out of the city, but he didn't mind his plan B of walking. Accordingly, he set his reservation price for hiring a horse at three dinars. When he observed that a large collection of idle Bedouin guides but only a handful of tourists remained as darkness approached, he assumed that the guides would realize they had a weak plan B and reduce their reservation prices, and that he would be able to procure a ride out of town for three dinars or even less. No dice. No matter how clear it became that the Bedouins' plan B was quite poor, they refused to accept less than the conventional price of four dinars.

Perhaps the guides believed that the tired American tourist would eventually relent and pay four dinars; that is, maybe they were trying to exercise Power through patience. But Lubet makes a strong case for rejecting this hypothesis. After emphasizing that he would pay no more than three dinars, Lubet started walking out of Petra, didn't turn back, and continued all the way until he reached the end of the gorge. And he did exactly the same thing three days in a row. At no point did a single horse guide stop him and agree to accept his three-dinar offer.

The better explanation seems to be that the guides believed that the price of four dinars was fair because it was the convention and believed that any lesser amount would be unfair. The negative utility of accepting an unfair price—Lubet aptly called this "pride"—outweighed the utility of the three dinars being offered. The result was that the horses were underutilized and a tired Lubet, who was quite willing to pay three dinars for a ride, walked.[1]

38

POINTS OF COMPARISON

According to the logic of convention, the terms of a proposed deal are fair if they match the terms in reference transactions. Since fairness claims rely on social understandings, however, there is never a "correct" or "incorrect" reference transaction; what matters is whether the negotiator can convince her counterpart that the similarity of a past transaction makes it an appropriate basis for comparison. For this reason, negotiations frequently devolve into debates about which of several possible reference transactions is most appropriate.

Imagine, for example, that Aphrodite has offered Beacher the position of director of marketing for her small e-commerce company. Beacher is Aphrodite's favorite candidate—in fact, she doesn't like any of the others very much—so she has a high reservation price. Beacher thinks the job is a much better fit for his skill set than his current position and is enthusiastic about the offer, so he has a low reservation price. What would be a fair salary?

As is true of many jobs, this one isn't exactly like any other. Beacher might invoke salaries paid to employees with the same title at other companies as the appropriate reference transactions, but Aphrodite could point out that her company is quite small and that Beacher would be managing a smaller budget and supervising fewer people than most marketing directors. Aphrodite might suggest the more appropriate reference transaction is the salary she agreed to pay the company's director of operations, but Beacher could contend that he has more experience and education than that colleague so the comparison would not be appropriate.

Because the negotiating context lacks a perfect analog, agreement is likely to require the parties to implicitly select a reference transaction that is *reasonably* similar and then adjust from that baseline using other conventions. For example, Aphrodite might suggest that she pay Beacher some amount *less* than what marketing directors at larger firms earn, in order to take account of the convention that managerial salaries are based in part on the size of the budget and the number of employees to be supervised. Or Beacher might propose a salary somewhat higher than what the director of operations is paid in recognition of the convention that employees with more experience and advanced degrees are typically paid higher salaries, all other things being equal.

In noncommercial settings, negotiations are just as likely to become debates over the appropriate reference transactions, as anyone with children will recognize. If your six-year-old's usual bedtime is 8 p.m., he is likely to try to negotiate a later bedtime when his grandparents come to visit. You have a plausible argument that it is fair for you to require him to hit the sack at 8 p.m., because that is the standard bedtime in your house. But if you allowed him to stay up until 9 p.m. last week to watch a special program on television, you can be sure that he is going to claim that agreement is the more appropriate reference transaction—it may not have involved grandparents, but it was also a special occasion. Whoever is able to convince the other that his preferred reference transaction is more analogous to the circumstances surrounding Grandma and Grandpa's visit is going to control bedtime.

The appropriateness of a reference transaction is not always debatable, of course. In many negotiations, a reference transaction is so similar to the focal negotiation that most or all fair-minded observers will agree that fairness requires replication of its terms. Negotiated agreements will usually be very easy to reach in such circumstances. Consider a letter to Slate.com's advice column, "Dear Prudence." The advice seeker was a woman who had attended a professional conference and, at the request of her employer's human resources department, agreed to share a hotel room (and even a bed) with other female colleagues whom she did not know well. The writer found the experience uncomfortable. After the conference, she learned that two male colleagues who also attended were not asked to share a room and were provided with private accommodations. She sought advice on how to approach the issue as preparations for another conference were underway.

Advice columnist Emily Yoffe advised the writer to assert that the agreement between the company and the male conferees was the appropriate reference transaction: "Tell HR that given the fact that the men in the company are given separate rooms, and that you need privacy during the hours you are off, you also would like this (very basic) courtesy."[1] The company would find it impossible, I think, to articulate a reason why the treatment of the male employees was not an appropriate reference transaction in a negotiation over the accommodations provided to female employees attending exactly the same conference. I would wager that the letter writer's negotiation for a private room for her next conference was one of the quickest and most successful negotiations in which she had ever participated!

Compare the situation in the Dear Prudence letter to an attempt to invoke a reference transaction that intuitively seems implausible. During its 10-year run beginning in 1994, the sitcom *Friends* grew into one of the most popular television shows of its era. In 1998 it became the anchor show of the NBC network's Thursday night ratings juggernaut, known at the time as "Must See TV," when the popular *Seinfeld* ended its run. As an ensemble program with six main characters who shared close-to-equal amounts of screen time, the stars found themselves able to exercise a great deal of Power in their salary negotiations with NBC after *Friends* became prime-time television's highest-rated program in its eighth season. Having originally been paid $22,500 each per episode in the show's first year, the actors negotiated staggering salaries of $1 million each, per episode, for the final two years of its run.[2]

Midway through its final season, 2003–04, *Friends* was joined on NBC's Thursday night lineup by a new reality program called *The Apprentice*, starring a brash New York real estate mogul named Donald Trump. Contestants on the program competed in various tasks similar to business-school projects, vying to be chosen by Trump to serve as his actual apprentice for one year. An instant hit, *The Apprentice* was promoted to take over *Friends*' role as NBC's Thursday anchor program.[3]

Whatever your opinion of Trump as a president, his popularity as an entertainer earned a lot of money for NBC, so distributive justice (specifically, the equity principle) suggested that it would be fair for him to receive a raise from the $50,000 per episode he was paid during the show's first season. But how much of a raise? According to a report in the *Wall Street Journal*, Trump had heard (incorrectly) that the six *Friends* stars earned $1.5 million per episode each, for a total payroll of $9 million per episode. There was only one of him, and the hour-long episodes of *The Apprentice* were twice as long as the episodes of *Friends*, so Trump claimed he was due $18 million per episode. "That seemed fair," he said.[4]

The producers of *The Apprentice* were not convinced, presumably because *Friends* had a track record of 10 years rather than three months and was destined to earn billions in syndication, among other reasons. Trump received a raise in the second season of *The Apprentice* to $100,000 per episode.[5] That's real money to most of us but a far cry from $18 million.

It is worth noting that the importance of convention to the perception of fairness can create barriers to using the tool of Deal Design. Recall that Deal Design requires negotiators to identify circumstances in which agreeing to noncustomary terms will increase the cooperative surplus created by an agreement. When terms are perceived as fair because they are customary, one negotiator's proposal to alter the structure of the deal will often meet resistance on fairness grounds. For example, a lengthy warranty might maximize the value of a transaction if the buyer is particularly risk averse and the seller is especially confident in the quality of her product. But if a shorter warranty is the industry standard term, a proposal to structure a deal to include a lengthy one is likely to be a difficult sell. One way to overcome the objection is to logroll a concession on a different issue in return for the longer warranty: "If you will lengthen the warranty, I'll make payment today rather than in three months." This tactic can succeed because trading one concession for another satisfies the principle of procedural fairness, described in the next chapter.

39

DANCING THROUGH THE BAZAAR

In the classic movie farce *Monty Python's Life of Brian*, the title character finds himself being chased through the marketplace in biblical-era Jerusalem by Roman soldiers who mistake him for Jesus and plan to crucify him. In desperate need of a disguise in order to escape, Brian spots a merchant selling an absurd-looking fake beard and stops to ask how much it would cost.

When the merchant responds that the price is 20 shekels, Brian immediately agrees and attempts to hand the merchant a coin. But rather than take the money, the outraged merchant objects to Brian's failure to haggle over the price. When Brian says he doesn't have time to negotiate, the merchant becomes more incensed and protests Brian's obvious violation of the rules of the bazaar to others in the vicinity. He then turns back to Brian and explains, "Now, I want 20 for that. Now, are you telling me it's not worth 20 shekels? Look at it, feel the quality."

Still in a hurry, for obvious reasons, a confused Brian offers 19 shekels. This, unfortunately, fails to satisfy the merchant, who chastises Brian to "haggle properly!" Belatedly catching on, Brian offers to pay 10 shekels. The lowball offer, ironically, makes the merchant happy. "That's more like

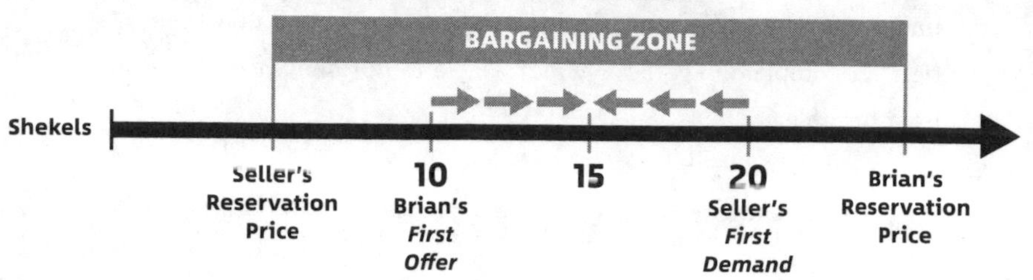

A series of reciprocal concessions often enables negotiators to converge on a particular agreement within a larger bargaining zone, helping to avoid an impasse.

it," he says encouragingly, before switching gears and loudly protesting so that everyone in the vicinity can hear, "Ten? Are you trying to insult me?"

Further back-and-forth ensues, after which the merchant instructs Brian to offer 14 shekels. When the increasingly desperate fugitive does as he's told, the merchant responds, "Seventeen, my last word, and I won't take a penny less or strike me dead!" Before a bewildered Brian can respond, the merchant announces that he will accept 15 shekels, and the deal is done.[1]

The shtick is funny because nearly every viewer, no matter how naïve to the ways of negotiation, has participated in a less exaggerated version of this type of bargaining interaction at some point. The negotiation proceeds like this: First, the parties trade sometimes absurd, usually extreme, and always aggressive initial demands and offers. Then both make attempts, sometimes perfunctorily and sometimes with great fanfare, to assert that their aggressive demands are at or near their reservation points, so very little movement can reasonably be expected. These half-hearted bluffs are quickly abandoned, and, over time, the negotiators grudgingly moderate their demands, the distance between them gradually narrows, and offers and counteroffers are batted back and forth like ping-pong balls. Finally, an agreement is reached somewhere between the two original positions.

Decision theorist Howard Raiffa appropriately labeled this pas de deux the *negotiation dance.*[2] For many people, this interchange is the first image that comes to mind when they think about the subject "negotiation." A complete negotiator must be able to do the dance, because, at least in some contexts, an agreement that arises from the haggling process seems fair.

But why should this be so? As the *Life of Brian* sketch highlights, the negotiation dance is a tremendous waste of time and effort. Why can't the negotiators cut to the chase and home in on the terms of agreement straightaway?

The answer lies in the tremendous social power of *reciprocity*—the principle of human interaction that says we should repay gifts or kindnesses provided by others—as a Fairness Norm. A birthday gift or a dinner invitation provokes a response in kind from most people, and there are few trivial things that can cause such deep pain as receiving a holiday card from someone who you left off your list. In the 1930s, the Fuller Brush company's door-to-door salespeople gave away millions of vegetable-cleaning "Handy Brushes" as a way to get housewives to agree to listen to their sales pitches.[3] Today, charities of all kinds send small gifts in the mail, often mailing labels or other trinkets, in an effort to exploit the norm by making the recipients feel obligated to donate in return. According to sociologists, the reciprocity norm is well ingrained in most if not all cultures, suggesting that it probably provided people who abided by it throughout evolutionary history, in which social cooperation has usually been necessary to ward off starvation, a survival advantage over those who took without giving back.[4]

What makes the reciprocity norm so important in negotiation is that it can provide a purely procedural justification for agreeing to a particular division of the cooperative surplus. That is, if both parties make reciprocal concessions until their offers converge and agreement is reached, the resulting agreement will often seem fair even without the parties agreeing that the end point satisfies some criterion of substantive fairness, such as distributive justice or convention.

Reciprocity can help break stalemates in distributive negotiations over a single issue. This can be the price of some good or service, as in *Life of Brian*: when Brian, after finally learning how to play the game, increased his offer, the merchant reduced his demand and a deal was quickly closed.

Alternatively, the issue can be a mustache. In 1978, the Warner Brothers movie version of *Superman* was in production. The movie launched the career of a little-known actor named Christopher Reeve, who played the title role, but also featured Hollywood icons Marlon Brando as Superman's father and Gene Hackman as Superman's evil nemesis, Lex Luther. Hackman's million-dollar contract failed to specify any changes he would have to make to his appearance to play Luther, and when director Richard Donner explained that Luther must be bald and clean shaven, Hackman resolutely refused to shave either his head or his mustache for the filming.

Donner addressed the first problem by having Hackman's hair styled differently in different scenes, which, along with the use in one scene of a skullcap to simulate baldness, portrayed Luther as wearing a variety of wigs. But the director continued to insist that Hackman shave his mustache, and the actor just as insistently resisted. Donner had his makeup staff create as realistic-looking a mustache as possible for himself to wear the day filming was set to begin. With the faux facial hair applied to his upper lip, Donner visited Hackman in the makeup room and renewed his request that Hackman shave off his mustache. When Hackman again refused, Donner offered to remove his own (fake) mustache in return for Hackman shaving off his, and the actor finally, if reluctantly, agreed. After the production staff shaved Hackman's mustache, Donner, to the actor's surprise, peeled off his.[5]

Even though Gene Hackman was unmoved by Donner's insistence that the movie would be best served by Luther appearing clean shaven, he found it impossible to refuse to give up his mustache when the director promised to do the same in return.

The reciprocity norm doesn't necessarily require the quid pro quo for a concession to be a concession of the same type. In one experiment, psychologist Dennis Regan organized groups of two "students" each and had each pair participate together in a task, but, unbeknownst to the actual subjects, each pair included "Joe," a paid actor working for the experimenter. During a so-called break in the experiment, Joe left the room. Half of the time he came back with nothing. The other half of the time he returned with two bottles of Coca-Cola, drank one himself, and gave the other one to the real subject. Later, during another "break," Joe explained to the real subject that he was selling raffle tickets and could win a prize if he sold the most, and then requested that the subject buy some tickets, which cost more than the bottle of Coke. Subjects who had previously been given the Coke bought more than twice as many tickets as did subjects in the control group.[6] A recent, similar experiment found that when an associate of the experimenter, pretending to be a subject, brought back a bottle of water for real subjects during a "break" in the experiment, the subjects were three times as likely to later agree to fill out an unrelated survey at the request of the associate.[7]

Reciprocal concessions do not necessarily need to be equivalent in terms of value in order to be perceived as satisfying the fairness requirement. Imagine that Aphrodite is leaving town for the weekend and wishes to hire Beacher to dogsit her hound, Hermione, while she is away. The service is worth $60 to Aphrodite, and Beacher would do it for $35. Beacher routinely hosts dogs for weekend visits and customarily charges $50, so the parties agree this is a fair price. Aphrodite knows she will be rushing to leave town, so she asks if Beacher might pick up Hermione from her house on Saturday morning. This is worth $25 to Aphrodite and is easy for Beacher to do because he has errands to run nearby. Beacher asks if, in return, Aphrodite would bathe Hermione in advance. A clean pet makes the job slightly more pleasant, reducing Beacher's reservation price from $35 to $30. Aphrodite agrees.

The reciprocal concessions benefit Aphrodite more than Beacher: her reservation price increases from $60 to $85, while Beacher's reservation price decreases from $35 to $30. Beacher could ask for a side payment to equalize the value of the concessions. Specifically, he could ask Aphrodite to wash Hermione and also pay an extra $10, so that both would enjoy an extra $15 of cooperative surplus compared to the baseline deal. Adding a side payment in order to equalize the value of the benefits sometimes occurs, but in my experience, as long as one concession is reciprocated in some form, the parties are more likely to ignore the difference in value and consider the account settled. That is, with logrolling, negotiators usually allow the gains to lie where they naturally fall, although if the benefits are too uneven, the party with less to gain might ask for two concessions in return for her one.

How reciprocity can be most effectively used as a Fairness Norm depends, not surprisingly, on social context. In the United States, the vast majority of lawsuits seeking monetary compensation settle out of court by negotiation rather than through adjudication by a judge or jury, and nearly all of these involve a negotiation dance. The dominant custom is for the parties to start out with initial offers that are far apart, meaning that concessions by one or both parties have to be substantial in order for agreement to eventually be reached.

Attorney Lisa Klerman, who works as a mediator in employment-dispute cases (meaning she is paid to help facilitate the settlement negotiations between the parties and their lawyers), along with coauthor Daniel Klerman, analyzed all of the cases she had mediated over a four-year period. She found that the first demand made by the plaintiff was, on average, 68 times the size of the first offer made by the defendant. In other words, a typical plaintiff might begin the dance by asking for $680,000 to settle the case, to which a typical defendant would respond by offering to pay only $10,000. Amazingly, in light of this enormous disparity, nearly all of Klerman's cases eventually managed to settle out of court.[8]

When employment lawyers stake out opening positions that are different from each other by a factor of 68, this is a signal to start the negotiation dance. But if you entered a car dealership and offered to pay 1/68th of the sticker price on the car's window—say, $500 for a car with a list price of $34,000—it is highly unlikely that you would even receive a counteroffer, much less eventually reach an agreement. You could probably start the negotiation dance, however, by offering 5 or 10 percent less than the sticker price. To successfully execute the dance, negotiators must understand not only that reciprocity operates as a Fairness Norm, but also the relevant social conventions about how to begin the dance, how long to dance, and how many steps to take.

In some contexts, the social consensus concerning fairness will operate against the negotiation dance even taking place. Haggling is still the norm in the stalls of the old city of Jerusalem today, not unlike the way that environment is depicted in *Life of Brian*. But in the supermarkets of the industrialized world, the negotiation dance gives way to the norm that the store offers a price and the customer either accepts or rejects it. You might think that the price of milk at the supermarket is too high, and you might decide not to purchase any if you do, but I can safely predict that you will not try to haggle with the checkout clerk. More to the point, you would probably not believe that you were being treated unfairly if you were to offer a lower price only to find the clerk staring at you quizzically and refusing to participate in the negotiation dance, as he most certainly would.

In the negotiation literature, the strategy of making such take-it-or-leave-it, nonnegotiable demands is called *Boulwarism*, so named after a famous management-side labor negotiator named Lemuel Boulware, who is reputed to have used this approach with his labor union adversaries.[9] But while Boulwarism has a bad reputation in the context of labor-management negotiations, where it not only will ruffle feathers but quite possibly run afoul of federal labor laws, it is clearly the standard method of negotiating in many other types of situations, including in the American supermarket. 5TNs will recognize Boulwarism as a commitment tactic appropriately classified as a use of Power. Whether it will be accepted with a shrug or angrily rejected as a violation of Fairness Norms depends on whether the context calls for the negotiation dance or not.

Since context is so important to the question of whether the negotiation dance is appropriate, it should come as little surprise that disputes can arise when negotiators have different social expectations. The advice columnist Judith Martin, known as "Miss Manners," once received a letter from an antiques dealer who was annoyed by customers who tried to initiate a negotiation dance rather than pay the prices marked on the goods. "People keep trying to haggle with us, asking 'What is the best you can do?' or 'What would you really take?' after we have told them the price," the frustrated dealer wrote. "Once we had an Italian customer who said, 'What is your final word?' and I said, 'It's *arrivederci.*' "

Hard feelings arose because the seller was negotiating according to the social customs of an American supermarket, while the customers believed that the type of merchandise at issue made the norms of the Jerusalem bazaar more appropriate. Neither the merchant nor her customers were right or wrong in any objective sense; they simply approached the negotiation with different Fairness Norms in mind. Unless the letter writer or her customers could convince the other that their preferred procedural norm was fair in that particular context, they were unlikely to strike a bargain, even when doing so could have generated cooperative surplus and made both sides materially better off.

40

WHERE YOU STAND DEPENDS (SOMETIMES) ON WHERE YOU SIT

The role of fairness in negotiation is complicated by the variety of conflicting norms that can appear relevant in any particular setting. A further complication is that we humans tend to think that the terms that favor us happen to be the ones that are fair.

Research indicates that our perceptions of fairness are subject to a *self-serving bias*, closely related to the optimism bias (discussed in Chapter 15) that causes most of us to overestimate both our abilities and our future prospects. This means that, on average, we tend to honestly believe that agreement terms that would work to our benefit are more objectively fair than terms that would result in more disadvantageous outcomes.[1]

Consider this simple example of the bias at work: Pairs of experimental subjects were given a pot of money to divide, the size of which was based on how well each subject performed individually on a task. Higher-performing subjects were more likely to invoke the equity principle, proposing that the money be divided based on each participant's performance and thus contribution to the pot. Lower-performing subjects were more likely to propose an equal division of the money.[2]

It is similarly predictable that sellers are more likely than buyers to think that it is fair to increase the nominal price of goods to reflect inflation, that workers are more likely than their bosses to think the salary of a higher-paid colleague is a more fair reference transaction than the salary of a lower-paid colleague, and that teenagers will think fairness requires that they be accorded the privileges enjoyed by their friends with the most permissive parents. The old adage of politics that "where you stand depends on where you sit"[3] often applies to fairness claims in negotiation.

The difficulty in reaching agreements caused by such predictable differences in perceptions of fairness can be exacerbated when negotiators believe that their counterparts are disingenuously using the language of "fairness" for strategic advantage. Negotiations between Republicans and Democrats over tax rates, for example, are particularly fraught when Democrats assume Republicans use fairness arguments as a smoke screen for self-interest and Republicans assume Democrats want to opportunistically soak the rich, rather than both sides assuming that their counterparts' positions are (often, at least) rooted in sincerely held, if conflicting, views about distributive justice.

When negotiators assume that their counterpart's fairness claims are not made in good faith, they are unlikely to respond effectively. For example, if Aphrodite attempts to exercise Power ("I refuse to sell for a penny less than $100"), a response in kind might be Beacher's best tactic ("I won't pay a penny more than $25"). In contrast, if Aphrodite justifies her demand with a Fairness Norm ("I am demanding $100 because that is the amount commonly charged for this type of item"), Beacher is better off contesting Aphrodite's proposed reference transaction ("Those that sell for $100 are made of higher-quality materials") or proposing an alternative Fairness Norm ("I cannot afford to pay more than $50"). But if Beacher wrongly thinks that Aphrodite doesn't really believe that $100 is a fair price, he is likely to respond with a threat ("I won't pay a penny more than $25"), which in turn will seem unfair to Aphrodite, and could eventually result in an impasse that was avoidable.

An important principle for preventing inevitable disagreements over fairness from devolving into intractable conflict is to not equate self-serving bias with dishonesty.

SUMMARY OF KEY LESSONS FROM PART 5

- Negotiators use Fairness Norms to justify particular agreements when multiple different agreements would fall within the bargaining zone.
- Because negotiation is a social as well as strategic interaction, negotiators will often choose impasse over an agreement that falls within the bargaining zone when they believe that the deal would be unfair.
- The Fairness Norm of distributive justice—with its competing principles of equity, equality, and need—is used to justify agreements based on the allocation of benefits or burdens between the negotiators.
- The Fairness Norm of convention is used to justify agreements based on comparisons between the negotiators and similarly situated third parties—usually parties who have reached agreements in the past. Successful appeals to convention require consensus concerning which reference transactions are most analogous to the focal negotiation.
- The Fairness Norm of reciprocity, commonly demonstrated by the "negotiation dance," is used to justify agreements based on the procedure, avoiding the need for the parties to reach consensus concerning substantive fairness.
- Negotiators tend to perceive agreements that benefit themselves, relative to other potential deals, as fairer, which can make it difficult to determine whether a counterpart is using Fairness Norms in good faith or merely strategically.

USING THE TOOLKIT

41

A COMPLETE SET OF TOOLS

From one perspective, negotiation is an almost infinitely complex activity. The subject matter of what we negotiate is as varied as human experience itself, the circumstances surrounding negotiations are never precisely the same, and the most effective strategy for a negotiator to pursue depends on choices made by her counterpart.

But structurally, negotiation is simple: identify the parameters of the bargaining zone, expand the bargaining zone, and divide the cooperative surplus. There are five tools that can help you do this and obtain the best possible outcome given the constraints of the situation.

Tool #1, Bargaining Zone Analysis, enables the negotiator to identify the range of potential agreements that would make both parties better off than an impasse. By setting her own reservation point appropriately, the negotiator ensures that the decision of whether to enter into an agreement is made correctly and thus avoids committing either of the two cardinal sins of negotiation: agreeing to a deal that makes her worse off than an impasse or failing to make a deal that would make her better off than an impasse. By estimating the counterpart's reservation point as accurately as possible, the negotiator can make wiser judgments about whether and how to use the other tools. If there is no bargaining zone initially, Persuasion and Deal Design might help to create one. If there is a large bargaining zone, Power and Fairness Norms can be used more aggressively to attempt to capture as much cooperative surplus as possible.

Tool #2, Persuasion, enables the negotiator to convince her counterpart that reaching agreement would be more desirable than the counterpart previously realized. This has the effect of shifting the counterpart's reservation point, creating a bargaining zone when otherwise there would not have been one and making agreement possible, or expanding an existing bargaining zone and creating more cooperative surplus than would otherwise be available.

Tool #3, Deal Design, allows the negotiator to structure an agreement to maximize the amount of total cooperative surplus it will produce. Whereas Persuasion expands the size of the bargaining zone by changing perceptions of value, Deal Design creates additional value by structuring the agreement in a mutually profitable way. By adding issues, subtracting issues, or logrolling, the reservation points of both negotiators change to reflect what is fundamentally a different agreement with a larger bargaining zone.

The first three tools enable the negotiator to identify, shift, and reposition the bargaining zone in ways that both increase the likelihood of agreement and pave the way for the negotiator to capture the most cooperative surplus possible. But none of these tools by itself will guarantee that the negotiator will capture any particular amount of the available cooperative surplus. Reaching an agreement that falls within the bargaining zone requires that the negotiator convince her counterpart not only that there is a bargaining zone but also that he should be willing to accept a particular division of the cooperative surplus.

Tool #4, Power, enables the negotiator to capture cooperative surplus by using a threat, either implicit or explicit, that she will not accept an agreement unless the counterpart makes the concessions demanded. The negotiator can make the threat credible by improving her plan B, by convincing the counterpart that her plan B is more desirable than it actually is, or by convincing her counterpart that she is unable or unwilling to accept less cooperative surplus, even though doing so would seem to be in her interest.

Tool #5, Fairness Norms, allows the negotiator to justify a particular agreement based on social understandings of fairness, which has the effect of dividing available cooperative surplus between the parties. Competing norms—based on fairness between the negotiators, fairness in comparison to other similar negotiating parties, or fairness in the bargaining process—have different implications for the allocation of cooperative surplus, so success depends on convincing one's counterpart that a particular principle is most appropriate in the particular circumstance.

Every tactic that can help a negotiator to obtain the best possible deal uses one of these five tools.

- Understand the negotiation landscape.
- Promote the value of what you have to offer.
- Design the most valuable deal possible.
- Force your counterpart to concede to you most of that value.
- Use finesse to divide the benefits amicably.

These are *all* the tools of successful negotiation. 5TNs have the complete toolbox at their disposal.

42

USING THE FIVE TOOLS TOGETHER

AN EXAMPLE

Suppose that you are considering selling your nearly five-year-old Toyota Prius. It is reliable transportation, and its hybrid engine is environmentally friendly, but you've been thinking it might be time for a vehicle that goes from zero to 60 in less than five minutes. Maybe something with a bit more style wouldn't be the worst thing in the world either. In fact, you've been eyeing a new convertible sitting on the lot of a local car dealer that you pass by most days.

Last week, you placed a sign in the passenger-side window with the words "For Sale by Owner" and your phone number. A couple of days later, while you were parked at a 7-Eleven to pick up a Slurpee, a neighbor filling up her hulking black SUV noticed the sign in your window. As the dial on the gas pump spun north of $90 with no signs of slowing down, the woman said hello, introduced herself as Sheila, and told you that she might be interested in the Prius. Later that day, she left you a voicemail. It turned out she lives only a few blocks away from you, and you agreed to meet Thursday evening at the local Starbucks to see if you could negotiate a deal.

As you prepare for the meeting, you begin with Bargaining Zone

Analysis. The first step is to identify your plan B, which could be to sell the car to a dealer (the easiest option) or to place an ad on the internet and try to sell directly to a private buyer (which is likely to yield a higher price). Since you're a cheapskate, like me, you decide that you would rather sell it yourself.

With the internet at your fingertips, you can obtain a great deal of information that is helpful in setting your reservation price with a fairly small investment of time. Several websites provide estimates of both the value you are likely to receive from a car dealer and the private-party value. By entering the car's mileage and condition, one of these websites spits out an estimated private-party value of $12,000.

Since used cars are usually purchased locally, you can improve the accuracy of this prediction by looking for sales information in your city. By checking the want ads on various internet sites, in 30 minutes' time you learn that only a few similar cars are for sale, and the asking prices range from $12,200 to $12,800. This is encouraging, but you recognize that some of these cars might be priced unreasonably high, and even the lower prices might be subject to some haggling. With this information, you decide that your best prediction of what you would earn by pursuing your plan B is $12,200. This number serves as the baseline for your reservation price calculation.

The more difficult question is how much you should adjust from that baseline to set your reservation price. The first issue is that, although $12,200 might be the best estimate of a sales price you can make, it could be wrong. Perhaps there are no buyers willing to pay that price at the moment, regardless of what sellers might be asking in their ads. It's probably worth sacrificing $300 to have the certainty of a sale.

Selling to Sheila would also save you transaction costs, in terms of both time and money. With a few more clicks on the computer, you determine that placing ads on two websites would cost $200. How much is it worth to you not to have to deal with the hassle of placing the ad, scheduling appointments, and dealing with (perhaps) multiple, (perhaps) flaky potential buyers? This is obviously a subjective question, but after thinking through the likely series of events, you decide avoiding the aggravation would be worth an additional $500.

The last important question is how much would it be worth to you to sell to a neighbor, albeit one you haven't met before, rather than a complete stranger, and help her to get out of that horrible SUV? You decide that this isn't worth a lot in this circumstance but that you would be willing to sacrifice $50 to do a solid for someone you might see at a PTA or neighborhood-council meeting. Combining these benefits of reaching an agreement compared to pursuing your plan B, you set your reservation price at $11,250. For that amount or more, you'll hand over your key fob. For any less, you'll decline to make a deal and can maintain your good standing with the folks at Greenpeace and the Sierra Club instead, at least for the time being.

What is your estimate of Sheila's reservation price? She has the options of purchasing a fuel-efficient car from a dealer or a private seller, along with the option of keeping her SUV. You can't know for sure which of these alternatives is her plan B, but you can make some tentative assumptions now and try to verify when you meet her to negotiate. If she were interested in purchasing a used Prius from a dealer, she probably would have already done so, so that is not likely her plan B. If her plan B is to keep her current vehicle, it is very hard to estimate her reservation price for purchasing yours. It could be very low and there might well be no bargaining zone, or it could be very high if she is particularly enthusiastic about a more environmentally friendly driving experience. If she does not demonstrate any knowledge of the used-car market when you negotiate, you might conclude that doing nothing at all is her plan B, and you will need to try to obtain more information about her preferences in order to estimate her reservation price at that time.

If Sheila is knowledgeable about the used-car market, her plan is most likely to purchase a similar vehicle from another seller. If this is the case, she will probably estimate that she would have to pay $12,200 for a similar car. You should not assume that she would value buying from you more than from another private seller, but it would probably be worth some amount of money to her to not have to find strangers with Priuses for sale, crisscross the city to test-drive the cars, and negotiate with those owners. Without specific information, you might reasonably estimate this would be worth $500, which would suggest a reservation price for Sheila of $12,700. Combining both estimates yields a prediction of a bargaining zone that extends from $11,250 to $12,700.

When you meet with Sheila on Thursday, you should begin the negotiation by asking questions designed to elicit information about how she thinks about her alternatives, which will help you to hone your estimate of her reservation price. You start by asking how long she's been considering purchasing a Prius. She tells you that the idea has been floating in the back of her mind for a while, but she hadn't been actively investigating the possibility. When she saw your "for sale" sign, she decided maybe this was the time to take the plunge. She also mentions that this morning she quickly did an internet search of local used-car dealerships to get a general idea of the price of a used Prius.

This information tells you that, although it is possible that Sheila will not purchase any car if she doesn't purchase yours, you should now assume that Sheila's plan B is to purchase a used Prius from a dealer. This calls for a reevaluation of her reservation price. You know from your research that the typical "dealer price" for a Prius similar to yours is around $13,000, so assume this is her baseline. Purchasing a used car from a dealer is less hassle than buying from a private seller, so you estimate that avoiding that inconvenience by buying from you is only likely to be worth a $250 premium to Sheila (as opposed to your original estimate of $500). In addition, dealers usually include a warranty with their used cars, which you estimate would provide $750 worth of value compared to purchasing from you. So, based on the new information, you revise your estimate of Sheila's likely reservation price to $12,500 ($13,000 plus $250 minus $750).

A better understanding of what Sheila's interests are in purchasing a Prius will facilitate a more effective use of both Persuasion and Deal Design, so you begin your discussion by asking her why she has decided she would like to own a Prius. She tells you that she's sick and tired of paying more than $100 at least once a week to fill up her SUV, and she doesn't really need the extra space or horsepower that it gives her. In this simple negotiation, your counterpart's interests might seem obvious: there are only so many reasons why someone would be interested in buying a gas-electric hybrid car. But some Prius admirers are more concerned with their fuel costs, while others are more concerned with their contribution to global warming. Taking the time to discover that Sheila falls into the former category is helpful to crafting a Persuasion strategy.

You follow up by asking Sheila how many miles she typically drives in a year and what type of driving she does, and you learn that her son, who has just completed college, is moving to a city that is 300 miles away, and she anticipates making that drive fairly frequently. She tells you that, in fact, she will be driving there this Saturday morning for a quick weekend trip to help him shop for an apartment. This information will help you to effectively use the tool of Deal Design to your mutual advantage.

To attempt to increase Sheila's reservation price, your most straightforward Persuasion tactic is to convey all the information that you have and she does not have that would suggest purchasing your Prius would be better for her than pursuing her plan B. You begin by explaining that your Prius has relatively low mileage (only 54,000) for a five-year-old car, that it has never been in an accident, and that you have performed all factory-recommended maintenance and oil changes (and have the records to demonstrate this). In addition, since your car is a few months short of being five years old, its five-year manufacturer's power-train warranty is still in force, which should give her peace of mind in case it has any serious problems now or in the near future. Since you don't have any particular knowledge or insight about purchasing from dealers, you decide not to offer any negative comments about her plan B.

You also want to establish reference points that will make the Prius appear desirable by comparison—even if those reference points are not related to Sheila's plan B. You start by comparing the $100 she spends every week to fill up her car to the $40 that you spend every other week, then ask her what gas mileage she typically gets in her SUV, and let her know that your car gets 50 miles per gallon on the highway.

You then let Sheila test-drive the car, not only so she can see for herself that it is in good condition, but to encourage her to start thinking of it as her car, rather than merely one of many possible futures. Hand her the keys before you walk out of Starbucks and ask her what her favorite radio station is so that you can set the dial there. During the drive, point out that the Prius has more power than most people would anticipate, and tell her that you always feel good about yourself when you drive it because of its environmental friendliness. At the end of the test drive, Sheila seems pleased with the car, and you estimate that her reservation price—whether or not she has actually focused on a precise value—is probably around $13,000 at this point.

You suggest returning to Starbucks to talk further (you buy the coffee—a small gesture that might trigger the reciprocity norm, or at least increase the amount that Sheila likes you). You then ask Sheila if she is interested in the car. She says that she is and asks you how much money you are asking for it. Social norms suggest that in an automobile-sale transaction, the seller customarily makes the opening offer in the form of an asking price, so it would be awkward for you to suggest that Sheila make the first offer. In any event, because you have a good estimate of Sheila's reservation price, it is to your advantage to make the first offer in this situation.

You respond by saying that you are "asking $13,000." You explain that similar cars are being advertised for anywhere between $12,500 and $12,800 but that you noticed that most have somewhat higher mileage than your car, plus you believe that they are not likely in the pristine condition yours is in. You tell Sheila that you just recently put the for-sale sign in your window and you have not advertised the car yet, but, before she called, you were planning on advertising it on the internet this weekend.

This proposal makes use of three tools. First, it uses Persuasion by setting a high anchor value of $13,000, which is likely to subtly affect how much Sheila thinks the car should be worth to her. By indicating your plan to advertise the car far more widely in the near future if she doesn't purchase it right away, you also hope to use the principle of reactance to increase the car's desirability in her eyes: if she doesn't act quickly, it might be sold.

Second, to exercise Power, you would like Sheila to believe that your reservation price is high—closer to $13,000 than to $11,000. You do not want to claim that you have a more desirable plan B than you really do, which in this case would probably mean asserting that you have a firm offer in hand for a high price. There is an obvious ethical problem with telling Sheila such a bald-faced lie, but making a false claim would have practical downsides as well. First, Sheila might not believe you, which could weaken the credibility of other claims you have made, such as those concerning the quality of your car. If someone had in fact made a firm offer at a price that a dealer would charge for the car, you probably would have accepted it and you wouldn't be spending your evening negotiating with her. Second, if Sheila did believe you had a firm offer of $13,000 and that amount is higher than her reservation price—which it might be—she could conclude there is no bargaining zone and end the negotiation.

Making a high opening offer, however, is likely to generate at least some power without these risks. When you ask for $13,000, Sheila might infer that your reservation price is not quite as high as $13,000, but she is likely to believe it is substantially higher than $11,250. Indicating optimism that you could obtain $13,000 by pursuing your plan B and demonstrating enthusiasm for the process are also likely to convince Sheila that your reservation price is somewhat higher than it actually is.

Third, your approach attempts to invoke both substantive and procedural Fairness Norms to your advantage. By referencing the advertised prices of similar cars, you use the convention of "market value" to justify your demand and provide a neutral basis for Sheila to accept it. In a negotiation between people who neither have a preexisting relationship nor routinely participate in this particular type of negotiation, the relevant norms of procedural fairness are likely to be ambiguous. Specifically, it is uncertain whether Sheila will assume that proper etiquette requires her to choose between accepting and rejecting your offer or whether she will think it appropriate for her to respond with a counteroffer. That is, you don't know if Sheila will assume that the rules of the bazaar or the rules of the supermarket apply. If she follows the latter, she might accept your initial offer rather than attempt to claim more of the cooperative surplus.

Sheila considers your proposal and then tells you that $13,000 is more than she had planned to pay. Invoking the convention that used cars sold by private parties are priced lower than those sold by dealers, she points out that $13,000 is roughly dealer price, and although your car still has its power-train warranty in effect, car dealers usually provide more extensive warranties for at least 90 days. Sheila also says that she would have difficulty coming up with that amount of cash before she sells her SUV, especially given that she is going to have to make a deposit on an apartment for her son—a statement that could be interpreted as using Power (she does not have enough money to pay your price, so she will not) or invoking the need principle of distributive justice (you should make a concession because she needs the money).

Her response, which is not an unambiguous rejection, leads you to believe that your offer was either below her reservation price or only slightly above it. If you hold firm, she might ultimately agree to pay $13,000. On the other hand, impasse is definitely possible; your offer might be outside of the bargaining zone. Sheila made a good point, which you hadn't adequately considered, that even though your car is still under its basic warranty, her plan B of purchasing from a dealer could come with a better warranty that would provide better protection against the adverse-selection risk that car buyers face. She might value that difference enough that her reservation price is lower than $13,000. An additional concern is that even if your offer falls just inside the bargaining zone, now that Sheila has voiced an objection, she might think that a failure on your part to make some concession in response violates a procedural Fairness Norm, which could cause her to walk away from the deal. There is almost certainly a bargaining zone here, and you do not want to risk committing the second cardinal sin of negotiation, so this situation presents a good opportunity to use Deal Design tactics to expand the bargaining zone and make sure that you can strike an agreement.

Taking all of this into account, you make the following proposal: You reiterate your offer of $13,000, but you will turn over the Prius to Sheila right away so that she can drive it on her road trip this weekend. You will also give her the right to rescind the deal and return the car at the end of the weekend if she is unhappy with it for any reason, in which case you will refund all but $100. Finally, you will accept a payment of $10,000 now, and defer the remaining $3,000 for one month.

These three changes to the terms of the deal, compared to what Sheila was likely anticipating, should substantially increase the bargaining zone. The ability to drive the Prius on her upcoming trip provides a benefit she would not be able to obtain if she decided to pursue her plan B (since she has yet to seriously shop elsewhere) and will save her approximately $100 in gasoline costs. The ability to spend the entire weekend verifying the quality of the car substantially reduces the adverse-selection risk that she would otherwise face, which should be worth at least a couple of hundred dollars to her. And if her short-term cash-flow concerns are real, deferring a portion of the payment should also provide substantial value.

All of these alterations to the structure of the agreement would impose some costs on you, so your reservation price for the redesigned deal would be higher than your original reservation price. But the costs are modest. You have no important plans this weekend, and you can easily get by without a car for two days. At worst, you might spend $50 in Uber trips. Allowing Sheila to drive the car all weekend with the option to return it creates a moral hazard concern in theory (what if, knowing she can return the car, she doesn't drive it carefully?), but Sheila is a middle-aged neighbor who seems responsible, so this risk seems very small. She is unlikely to return the car after paying you and driving it away, but if she does you are no worse off than you are now. And deferring $3,000 for one month creates no problems for you. In theory, you could have problems collecting, but again, the risk seems small in this case.

Your calculation is that your reservation price for the redesigned deal is $11,500 (a $250 increase) and that the changes should increase the value of the deal to Sheila by a minimum of $500, which should ensure that her reservation price is comfortably over the $13,000 mark. Your proposal would net you $1,500 of cooperative surplus, while still providing Sheila with at least several hundred dollars of cooperative surplus and perhaps more. In addition, the series of concessions that you offered should satisfy any hesitation on Sheila's part that is caused by procedural fairness concerns, and the reciprocity norm provides pressure for her to now make a concession.

Sheila accepts your proposal, and you make arrangements to meet tomorrow, at which time she will bring you a cashier's check for $10,000 and you will exchange the keys and the pink slip.

43

THE ORIENTATION DECISION

The five tools of negotiation are universal; there are opportunities to employ each of them in any negotiation, whether you are negotiating a corporate merger, the settlement of a lawsuit, an international treaty, the location of a family vacation, or the sale of your five-year-old Toyota Prius. But this does not mean that a 5TN should always use the tools in the same way or rely on each to the same extent. When it comes to using the tools wisely, context matters.

How to deploy the five tools depends fundamentally on whether you decide to adopt a *self-interested* or *other-regarding* approach to a negotiating situation. I call this the *orientation* decision. A negotiator who adopts a self-interested orientation focuses entirely on obtaining the most advantageous deal for himself, with no concern at all for his counterpart. A negotiator who chooses an other-regarding orientation, in contrast, seeks a beneficial outcome for herself but provides equal concern for her counterpart. You can think of an other-regarding orientation as exemplifying the Golden Rule, treating others as you would like to be treated.

Here is how the orientation decision should affect how you deploy the five tools:

Bargaining Zone Analysis

Self-interested and other-regarding negotiators use the same analytical approach to estimate the bargaining zone, but they have different purposes in mind when estimating their counterpart's reservation point.

The self-interested negotiator endeavors to reach agreement as close to that point as possible, capturing as much of the cooperative surplus as he can, through the strategic use of Power or Fairness Norms. He even endeavors to coax a counterpart into committing the first cardinal sin of negotiation: agreeing to a deal that makes her worse off than pursuing her plan B. Mistakes made by the other party are welcome.

The other-regarding negotiator, in contrast, wants to estimate the bargaining zone accurately so that she can propose agreements that fall comfortably inside the zone and benefit both sides. She does not wish for her counterpart to commit the first cardinal sin, even though this would benefit her, and she helps him to avoid doing so to the extent that she is able.

Persuasion

The self-interested negotiator strives to convince his counterpart to place the highest possible value on reaching an agreement. He will use every tactic of Persuasion available, without regard to whether he himself believes an agreement would actually benefit his counterpart to the extent that he asserts or implies.

The other-regarding negotiator uses Persuasion to ensure that the counterpart understands and appreciates the value that the negotiator believes a deal with her will provide, so that an agreement can be reached that will make the counterpart better off than an impasse would. Unlike her self-interested colleague, she will not attempt to persuade her counterpart of any point that she herself does not believe. If the counterpart is well informed about both the features and benefits of what the negotiator has to offer, the other-regarding negotiator will often decide that the use of Persuasion is superfluous.

Deal Design

The self-interested negotiator views Deal Design as a means to the end of capturing more cooperative surplus for himself. He proposes altering a deal's structure in a way that will create more cooperative surplus when he believes he can then use Power or Fairness Norms to capture that increase in value.

The other-regarding negotiator views her counterpart as a partner in a problem-solving exercise, rather than as a competitor in a pitched battle for the cooperative surplus. She advances proposals for structuring a deal that will maximize the total cooperative surplus available, without regard to how that surplus will be distributed between the two parties, and she is pleased if both sides can benefit from a more optimal Deal Design.

Power

The self-interested negotiator uses any Power tactic available to convince his counterpart to concede cooperative surplus right up to (or even beyond) the counterpart's reservation point. He hopes that his counterpart will believe that his plan B is better than it actually is and that his enthusiasm for reaching an agreement is less than it actually is, and he will seize any opportunity to encourage such a misperception that is not legally or ethically prohibited. He avoids using Power only when he believes it will unduly damage his relationship with his counterpart or his reputation.

The other-regarding negotiator uses Power only to keep an impasse from occurring when a bargaining zone exists but the counterpart misestimates the negotiator's reservation point. She will disclose her plan B, even if it is not very desirable, and she will threaten to walk away from the bargaining table and pursue that option, but only when it would actually be in her interest to do so and her counterpart fails to realize this. She will not try to capture additional cooperative surplus by exaggerating her desire to pursue her plan B, minimizing her interest in reaching an agreement, threatening impasse when she does not have a plan B that would be more desirable than reaching agreement, or otherwise attempting to force concessions by imposing costs on her counterpart.

Fairness Norms

The self-interested negotiator uses Fairness Norms strategically. When different norms point toward different terms of a deal, he first determines which principles suggest that he is entitled to the greatest possible share of the cooperative surplus, and then provides the strongest available arguments for why those are the fairest under the circumstances. He will try to use Fairness Norms as sources of Power by threatening impasse if his counterpart will not agree to terms that he identifies as fair, even when his plan B is inferior to reaching agreement on less desirable terms.

The other-regarding negotiator attempts to judge the fairness of any particular agreement from a neutral perspective. Her fairness judgments might be colored by an unconscious self-serving bias, but she proposes agreements that she honestly believes are the fairest under the circumstances, whether it is she herself or her counterpart who is favored by the division of the resulting cooperative surplus.

Personal temperament certainly affects a negotiator's choice of orientation—some people are more self-interested in general; some are more other-regarding—but the nature of the negotiator's relationship with his counterpart is the most critical variable. Most of us adopt an other-regarding orientation when negotiating with family or friends, and perhaps with close colleagues in our organizations. Your marriage wouldn't last long if you announced to your spouse, "Either we're going to the movie theater to see *X-Men* on Saturday night, or I will refuse to spend the evening with you. Take it or leave it!" But in the workaday world of business, law, or politics, the proper balance between attentiveness to one's own interests and concern for the interests of others can be far from obvious, and the choice between the two basic orientations is difficult. Making the right choice will enable you to get the maximum possible benefit from the five tools.

44

NEGOTIATION AS A PRISONER'S DILEMMA

The "prisoner's dilemma" is the most famous problem in the field of game theory,[1] and it provides a useful metaphor for the orientation decision that negotiators must make.

Two suspected criminals are arrested on private property following a burglary and placed in separate prison cells, making communication between them impossible. The police interrogate the prisoners separately, and each must choose between remaining silent or providing evidence that will incriminate the other prisoner in the burglary. The police currently have enough evidence to convict both prisoners of trespass and send each to jail for one year. If either prisoner incriminates the other, the police can convict the incriminated colleague of burglary and send that person to jail for five years. The police offer both prisoners a one-year reduction in their own sentence if they will incriminate the other. Each prisoner must choose independently whether to "cooperate" (with the other prisoner) by keeping mum or "defect" by ratting the other out.[2]

With two prisoners both choosing between two options, there are four possible outcomes. If Prisoner 1 cooperates and remains silent, she will be sentenced to one year for trespass if Prisoner 2 also remains silent and five

THE PRISONER'S DILEMMA

		Prisoner 2 Choice	
		Cooperate	Defect
Prisoner 1 Choice	Cooperate	1 year / 1 year	0 years / 5 years
	Defect	5 years / 0 years	4 years / 4 years

The prisoners will serve less time if both choose to cooperate than if both choose to defect, but each one will serve less time by choosing to defect regardless of the choice the other makes.

years for burglary if Prisoner 2 squeals. If Prisoner 1 defects, she will go free if Prisoner 2 remains silent and will serve four years if Prisoner 2 also squeals.

What makes the choice interesting, and earns it the label of a "dilemma," is that each prisoner will serve a shorter sentence by ratting out her colleague, no matter which choice the other prisoner makes, yet both prisoners will be better off if they both choose to cooperate than if they both choose to defect. This makes cooperation the other-regarding strategy and defection the self-interested strategy.

Which option would you choose? Any game theorist will tell you that a rational prisoner will always opt for self-interest and choose to defect. Defection guarantees you the shortest possible prison sentence, whichever choice the other prisoner makes.

Would your decision be different if you knew you were going to be engaged in the same interaction with the same colleague again in the future? If you are going to play a prisoner's dilemma–type game with the same person multiple times, wouldn't it then make sense to cooperate, in order to encourage your counterpart to also act cooperatively? Not if you know how many times you will play the game. Imagine that you are going to play the prisoner's dilemma game 10 times in a row with the same counterpart. You might think that it would be wise to cooperate in the first round to encourage your counterpart to be other-regarding in the following 9 rounds, but the logic of game theory suggests that you would be wrong.

The reasoning process known in game theory as "backward induction" demonstrates why. Before the first round of the game, think ahead to the 10th and final round. If the other player is rational, she is going to defect in that round, for the same reason she would defect if the game were played only once. Your behavior in round 9 will not affect her choice in round 10, so you should defect in round 9 in order to optimize your outcome. Your counterpart knows that you will defect in round 10 as well, so she should also defect in round 9—she has nothing to lose. Knowing that she will defect in round 9 no matter what you do, you should defect in round 8. And so on. Follow this logic for seven more iterations and you will conclude that you should defect in all rounds, including the very first (as should your counterpart).

The logic of game theory is compelling, but it is at odds with how experimental subjects play the prisoner's dilemma and other "social dilemma" games with similar structures and incentives, even when real money is at stake. Across hundreds of published experiments, roughly half of all subjects choose to cooperate.[3] If you participated in these experiments and always chose to defect, your overall results wouldn't have been very good, at least in multiround games, because players who were inclined to be other-regarding and cooperate would become upset and start defecting. On the other hand, many players defect, so if you always cooperated, you would find yourself with the worst possible result—which game theorists call "the sucker's payoff"—quite frequently.

So, what should determine whether you adopt an other-regarding orientation and cooperate or a self-interested orientation and defect? The answer is *trust*, or lack thereof.

There are two distinct questions that you should ask before deciding whether to cooperate or defect. First, do you trust your counterpart to be other-regarding—in this case, to spend an extra year in prison rather than ratting you out? Are you confident that she will give your interests due concern along with her own? Are you brave enough to take the chance? Trust is costly if it is misplaced. If you trust her and she is not trustworthy, you will serve five years rather than four, while she walks free.

Second, are you willing to be trustworthy, even though it will cost you? Are you generous enough to sacrifice your own well-being for her and spend an entire extra year in prison? Are you sure?

Negotiators face a situation similar to the one faced by the players in the prisoner's dilemma. Authors David Lax and James Sebenius have called it, appropriately enough, the *negotiator's dilemma*.[4]

Approaching a bargaining encounter with a self-interested orientation is likely to produce a better material outcome if your counterpart chooses his strategy independently of your choice. An other-regarding counterpart will honestly reveal information known only to him about his preferences, costs, and resources, in order to better determine whether there is a bargaining zone and help to structure the terms of an agreement that creates the most cooperative surplus. By acting self-interestedly, you can exploit that strategy by creating cooperative surplus and then capturing most or all of it. If your counterpart is self-interested, your decision to pursue self-interest enables you to avoid being exploited.

On the other hand, a partnership between two other-regarding negotiators will usually produce better results for both than a competition between two self-interested parties. Two other-regarding negotiators honestly exchange information, together determine the scope of the bargaining zone, structure a deal that maximizes the total amount of cooperative surplus, and divide the surplus in a way both parties view as fair under the circumstances. Two self-interested negotiators might be perfectly polite and exceedingly professional, but they will withhold information, obfuscate, deceive, and misdirect. This behavior will often cause them to commit the second cardinal sin of negotiation: reaching an impasse even though agreements that would have made both better off were available. Even when they are able to avoid this fate and do manage to strike a bargain, it is often not as mutually profitable as it could have been, and it almost always requires more time, effort, and expense than is necessary.

In 2004, famed investor Warren Buffett's Berkshire Hathaway acquired a business unit called McLane Distribution from Walmart for $23 million. Finalizing a deal of this magnitude would usually require Berkshire Hathaway's lawyers to spend months verifying the financial condition of McLane. The parties' other-regarding orientation saved those costs, leaving more cooperative surplus for the parties. Buffett wrote to his shareholders afterward that "we did no due diligence. We knew everything would be exactly as Walmart said it would be—and it was."[5]

If you are tempted to defect, it might be out of fear (lack of trust) or greed (lack of trustworthiness). You might be afraid of being exploited by a self-interested counterpart and left with the sucker's payoff, or you might be eager to take advantage of a naïve patsy in the other cell.

The robust data from prisoner's dilemma experiments do not tell us whether self-interested behavior is caused by fear or greed, because either could explain the decision to defect. But a slightly different social dilemma, called the "trust game," separates the motivations. In the trust game, subjects make their choices sequentially, rather than simultaneously. The first player, the "trustor," is given some amount of money (often $10) and the option to keep it all or transfer some or all of it to the second player, the "trustee." Any amount transferred to the trustee is tripled by the experimenter. The trustee then has the option of keeping all of that (now tripled) amount or transferring some or all of it back to the trustor. The game then ends.[6]

An other-regarding trustor will transfer all or most of the stake to the trustee, because this maximizes the total pot of money. An other-regarding trustee returns to the trustor more than the amount originally transferred, ensuring that both players profit from the interaction. A

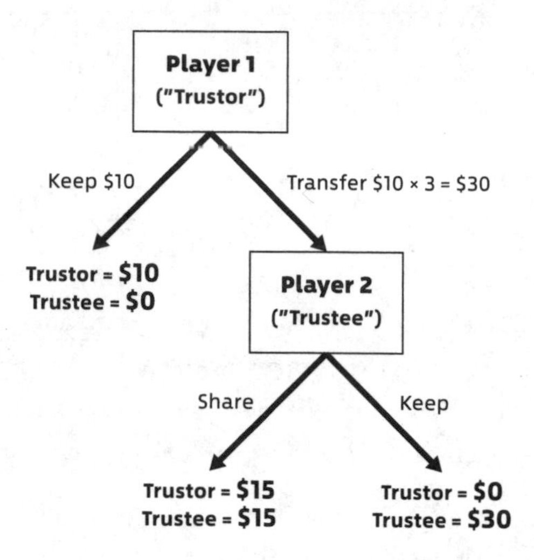

A trustor who keeps can be motivated only by fear; a trustee who keeps can be motivated only by greed.

self-interested trustor gives nothing to the trustee, and a self-interested trustee keeps all of whatever amount she receives.

The trustor cannot exploit his counterpart, so if he chooses not to transfer money to the trustee, his motivation can only be fear that the trustee will keep all of the proceeds and return none to him—this would be the equivalent of receiving the sucker's payoff in the prisoner's dilemma. The trustee, on the other hand, has no reason to fear exploitation, because the game ends as soon as she makes her decision. If the trustee keeps all of the money she receives and transfers little or none back to the trustor, her motivation can only be greed.

Results of the trust game demonstrate that self-interested behavior is motivated in part by fear and in part by greed. Some trustors don't trust, and a healthy number of trustees who are trusted do not vindicate that trust with trustworthy behavior. Both fear and greed, it seems, can obstruct mutually profitable cooperation.

45

WHO AND WHEN TO TRUST

The extent to which you trust your counterpart has two very different implications, and it is important to understand each.

The first question is whether you trust your counterpart to fulfill her obligations if and when you reach a negotiated agreement. The answer to this question will affect the bargaining zone. If you don't trust that the other party will abide by the terms of the deal, there will usually be no bargaining zone, because your plan B will be desirable compared to agreeing to a deal in the focal negotiation that will not, or might not, be honored. A buyer, for example, will not be willing to pay very much for goods that she fears won't be delivered or services that she suspects won't be performed.

When trust in performance is lacking, it is often possible for negotiators to use the tool of Deal Design to structure agreements in ways that solve the problem. In meetings with Soviet leader Mikhail Gorbachev, President Ronald Reagan proclaimed his principle of "Trust, but verify" (which is actually a Russian proverb) on several occasions. His point was that, in the waning days of the Cold War, the United States was prepared to limit its production of nuclear weapons in return for the Soviet

Union doing the same, but he didn't trust the Soviets to abide by their commitments. There would be a bargaining zone only for arms-control agreements that were designed with mechanisms that would enable both nations to verify the other's performance.

When verification of performance is possible, the threat of reputational harm or legal sanctions for nonperformance is often sufficient for the negotiators to trust one another to satisfy their obligations. If you sell your Toyota Prius to your neighbor Sheila with the provision that she can delay payment of the final $3,000 of the purchase price, you are likely to trust her to pony up the cash for two reasons, even if you don't know her well enough to feel certain about her integrity: First, if you were to report her failure to pay to your mutual neighbors, this would likely harm her reputation. Second, you could sue her for the money in small-claims court. In larger, more significant deals, the backstop provided by the legal system to ensure the performance of contracts is crucial. Indeed, research has demonstrated that nations that reliably protect property rights and enforce contracts enjoy more trade and greater economic growth than countries without strong legal institutions.[1]

If neither reputational concern nor law is sufficient to ensure performance, the threat of retaliation for a failure to comply with obligations can sometimes fill the void. As long as the United States could verify whether the Soviets were abiding by their arms-control commitments, Reagan was willing to trust Gorbachev, because the United States would stop abiding by its treaty commitments if the Soviets proved untrustworthy and would potentially withhold future cooperation in other areas as well.

When experimental subjects play a multiround version of the prisoner's dilemma game, most intuitively realize that it is sensible to choose to cooperate in the first round because defecting, though it will earn you a better immediate result, will lead to retaliation (and worse results) in the subsequent rounds. In fact, in prisoner's dilemma tournaments, in which each contestant submitted a computer program that played a multiround game against every other program, an entrant called Tit-for-Tat, which cooperated unless and until the counterpart defected, and then retaliated for defection in the following round before returning to cooperation, performed better than self-interested strategies.[2] Retaliation is possible, however, only because defection can be verified. A prisoner's dilemma player always knows, with certainty, when the other has defected. Things are not always so clear in real life.

The second question is whether you trust your counterpart in her conduct of the negotiation itself, as opposed to in performance of the terms of agreement. Most violations of trust in the negotiation process cannot be redressed through the legal system (an important exception to this rule is when a negotiator lies about the quality of products or services, which can give rise to civil or criminal legal sanctions for fraud). Even more importantly, it is often difficult to verify whether your counterpart's behavior is honestly other-regarding or is instead deceptively self-interested.

When a seller uses the tool of Persuasion by praising the value of her product, is she providing her honest appraisal in order to educate you, or is she trying to convince you to pay more than she actually believes it is worth? When she invokes a Fairness Norm in an attempt to reach agreement, does it represent her sincere belief about what is objectively fair in that situation, or is she defending a particular division of the cooperative surplus because it is to her advantage? When she uses Power by threatening an impasse unless you agree to pay more, would the current offer really be worse for her than pursuing her plan B, or is she bluffing to grab more of the cooperative surplus?

In some cases, the answers to these questions might be apparent, and the risk of harming the relationship or her reputation will dampen your counterpart's incentive to adopt a self-interested orientation. More often, however, it is difficult to distinguish between a counterpart who is other-regarding and one who is secretly self-interested and skilled at subtle exploitation. The difficulty in verifying other-regarding behavior makes it dangerous to trust.

Yet even when self-interested behavior cannot be deterred with the threat of reputational, relational, or legal sanction, negotiators often do trust their counterparts and adopt an other-regarding orientation. When deciding whether trusting your counterpart is worth the risk, three factors should inform your judgment:

- Social distance
- Contextual cues
- Prosocial tendencies of your counterpart

Social Distance

In the American Civil War, 45,000 Union soldiers unfortunate enough to be captured by the Confederacy were interred in the infamous Andersonville camp in south-central Georgia. The conditions and deprivations faced by these prisoners, especially as the war neared its conclusion, almost defy belief. Built to hold 10,000 soldiers, the population grew to more than 30,000 at a time, with no fixed structures to provide shelter. Daily rations were mostly limited to cornbread and cornmeal, which caused widespread scurvy in addition to extreme hunger. Diarrhea and dysentery were ubiquitous. Marauding prisoner gangs known as "Raiders" stole from their own comrades. Forty percent of the Union soldiers who reached the gates of Andersonville died there, half within three months of their arrival.[3]

In these extreme conditions, cooperation was no luxury—it was critical to survival. The prisoners of war needed to work together to create shelter and procure rations, they needed to rely on others for care if they fell ill, and they needed to band together to protect themselves from bandits. The difference between life and death could be whether a POW, facing extreme vulnerability, chose to trust fellow prisoners, and whether the recipients of that trust were trustworthy.

In *Heroes and Cowards: The Social Face of War*, economists Dora Costa and Matthew Kahn studied the records of Andersonville and uncovered the importance of social distance (the psychological kind, not the physical kind that became part of public discourse during the COVID-19 pandemic) to other-regarding behavior. A POW imprisoned with family members (in the Civil War, soldiers often served alongside sons, fathers, brothers, and cousins) was more likely to survive. Not everyone was fortunate enough to have kin to rely on, of course; the next best thing was the presence of soldiers from one's own unit. A Union soldier who was captured and imprisoned in Andersonville with 10 or more members of his company had a 90 percent chance of being alive after four months, whereas a soldier imprisoned with fewer than 10 comrades had only a 75 percent chance.[4]

This is hardly surprising. Throughout most of human history, we roamed the land in small bands of hunter-gatherers. People survived and prospered by forming small, tight-knit social groups built largely on kinship networks. You cooperated with members of your group to ensure safety and sustenance, while mostly competing with outsiders for resources that were in short supply (and maybe occasionally trading shells with them). It wasn't until the agricultural revolution that began roughly 10,000 years ago, quite recently in evolutionary terms, that people began to live in somewhat larger villages and towns, and it was thousands of years later still that large cities first appeared, making interaction with complete strangers a routine event.[5]

This long history has hard-wired into the human psyche a sharp distinction between others we recognize as members of our *in-group* and those we do not. We tend to adopt an other-regarding orientation in our dealings with the former and assume they will do the same. In earlier days, selfishness within the in-group would have risked ostracism or expulsion, with those who unsuccessfully attempted to cheat or exploit the group unlikely to pass on their genes to subsequent generations. We are instinctively inclined to trust and be trustworthy toward in-group members because we have always had to do so in order to survive.

In contrast, we tend toward suspicion and distrust of others, the *out-group*. For most of our history, out-group members would have attempted to take our resources and exploit our vulnerabilities. In the twenty-first century, we don't expect out-group members to rob or murder us but we often presume, or at least fear, that they will pursue their self-interest in their dealings with us. We don't even usually think that their self-interested behavior constitutes a social norm violation.[6]

Contextual Cues

It is often difficult to decide whether to adopt an other-regarding or self-interested orientation toward others, so it should come as no surprise that we humans like to search for external cues that indicate how we should choose to relate to others, in much the same way that we search for external cues to help evaluate how valuable a potential deal would be. The social distance between us and our counterpart is one powerful cue of the appropriate orientation to adopt, but it is not the only one. The context surrounding the interaction can provide another cue.

Of the hundreds of prisoner's dilemma game results published by social scientists, one of the more interesting explores how the name of the game affects subjects' behavior. Psychologist Lee Ross and colleagues provided subjects with the usual payoff matrix, which, of course, indicates that they could earn more money by defecting than by cooperating but that mutual cooperation would be more profitable than mutual defection. They then told half of the student participants that they were playing the "community game" and the other half that they were playing the "Wall Street game." Twice as many subjects randomly assigned to the former group chose cooperation compared to subjects assigned to the latter treatment (60 percent versus 30 percent).[7] A similar experiment found that trustors in the trust game transferred twice as much money if the researchers referred to the trustee as a "partner" as opposed to an "opponent."[8]

The label *community game* and the term *partner* imply that generosity and cooperation are appropriate behaviors and greediness is not. If the other player receives the same cue, this is a reason, holding everything else equal, to think that he is likely to adopt an other-regarding orientation, which reduces the chance that his counterpart will be exploited if she adopts an other-regarding orientation. A general research finding, and one that is hardly surprising, is that subjects playing social dilemma games are more likely to adopt an other-regarding approach when they believe their counterparts are likely to do the same.[9] There is no doubt that many negotiators are greedy and look to exploit every advantage, but many others adopt a self-interested orientation because they fear that their counterpart is not trustworthy.

Approximately two-thirds of my law students will become litigators after they graduate and pass the bar exam. In that role, a routine part of their job will be to negotiate settlements of lawsuits. Most of the rest of my law students will become transactional lawyers, whose day-to-day work will be negotiating business deals of various types. In which of these roles do you think the very same student would be more likely to adopt a self-interested orientation when deploying the five tools of negotiation?

Litigation is viewed as a blood sport. Clients engaged in legal disputes expect their attorneys to be their gladiators, fighting tooth and nail for every possible advantage. And there are scant reputational or relational costs to being known for taking a self-interested approach on behalf of one's client. Referrals from satisfied clients will generate future business. And while a self-interested and uncooperative litigator might not make a lot of friends with the lawyers on the other side of the table, once she sues someone (or once her client is sued) those displeased lawyers won't be able to avoid interacting with her, in the way that business lawyers or executives can often avoid negotiators with reputations for extreme self-interest.

All of the social cues in settlement negotiations suggest that a self-interested orientation is expected. I have never seen a litigator make an initial offer to settle a lawsuit that honestly reflected the merits of the case as he viewed them, even accounting for an optimism bias. Every offer is designed to suggest that the offeror's case (and, thus, his plan B of going to court) is stronger than it really is, or designed to set a favorable starting point for a likely negotiation dance, or both. This is why Lisa Klerman found that the average plaintiff's demand in employment-law disputes that she mediated was *68 times* the amount of the average defendant's initial settlement offer.[10] If you are uncomfortable with approaching negotiation with a self-interested orientation to using the five tools of negotiation, you should definitely not become a litigator! My law students instinctively understand this, even though they are not yet lawyers. They tend to adopt a much more self-interested orientation to using the five tools when I have them engage in classroom simulations that require them to negotiate litigation settlements than they do when the subject of a simulation is a business deal.

When contextual cues are ambiguous, another tactic is to seek a commitment from your counterpart to approach the negotiation with an other-regarding orientation. Research has demonstrated that people are more likely to exploit others for their selfish benefit than they are to lie,[11] so, at least statistically speaking, it does make sense to be more willing to trust someone who promises to be open, honest, and truthful, even though this obviously does not eliminate the risk of receiving the sucker's payoff. Negotiators seem to sense this. Psychologist Maurice Schweitzer and economist Rachel Croson have demonstrated that subjects playing social dilemma games are more likely to trust a counterpart who pledges to adopt an other-regarding strategy, even when such promises are completely unenforceable.[12]

When I have my students play a multiround prisoner's dilemma game without communicating, more than half will typically defect at some point in the game, although not necessarily in the very first round, in order to gain an advantage or to protect against exploitation. I then have them replay the game with an opportunity for oral communication, during which most seek (and obtain) promises that their counterpart will not defect. It turns out that very few students promise that they won't defect and then break that promise, even though there is no rule that prevents them from doing just that.

Prosocial Tendencies

In the prisoner's dilemma experiment that tested the effect of describing the interaction as either the "Wall Street game" or the "community game," the label used was far more predictive of the student participants' behavior than whether the subjects' dormitory advisers described them as having either cooperative or competitive personalities.[13] But there is little doubt that some people are simply more other-regarding, and some naturally more self-interested, than others. The same can be said of businesses, which have different cultures.

In their extensive study of social dilemma games played for multiple rounds, Ernst Fehr and Herbert Gintis found that they could categorize experimental subjects into two basic types.[14] One type is thoroughly self-interested. Subjects in this category nearly always defect. The other type is cautiously other-regarding. Subjects in this category cooperate at first, assuming that others will do the same, but they will switch to defection if their cooperative behavior is not reciprocated.

We can call individuals in the second category, who tend to approach new interactions with an other-regarding mindset, *prosocial*. You can trust anyone to act in an other-regarding way if selfishness would get her sued or severely damage her reputation. But in the absence of these incentives for good behavior, the best way to ensure that you can safely adopt an other-regarding approach without being exploited is to select prosocial counterparts with whom to negotiate.

Well, sure. If life were only so simple. The problem, of course, is that self-interested negotiators have every incentive to act *as if* they are prosocial. How can you identify a *truly* prosocial counterpart? Interestingly, one signal of prosocial tendency that researchers have identified is a willingness to trust others. Absent evidence to the contrary, we humans tend to assume other people will see the world much like we do. Trustworthy people usually assume others will be similarly trustworthy, while people looking for an opportunity to exploit others will tend to fear others are as self-interested. So, a counterpart willing to trust you—perhaps by disclosing private information about his interests or weaknesses with his plan B—is more likely to be trustworthy himself.[15]

46

TRUST-BUILDING STRATEGIES

You might or might not trust your negotiation counterpart, but either way you will want that person to trust you. Generating trust paves the way to successfully deploying all five tools of negotiation.

In the Andersonville prison, Union soldiers learned that it was best to have relatives or friends in camp with whom to cooperate. But in the absence of those relationships, an ethnic or even geographical bond could provide a basis for trust. Prisoners of Irish, French, and German extraction were more likely to survive if the other prisoners in their company were of the same group. For soldiers hailing from small towns, the presence of other prisoners from the same town also increased the odds of survival in the camp.[1] In social dilemma games played in laboratory settings by college students, subjects demonstrate more other-regarding behavior when counterparts are identified as students from the same university than as students from a different university.[2]

What's the lesson? People are remarkably flexible about whether to classify others as in-group or out-group members.[3] Strangers have the ability to form bonds of collegiality based on a wide range of factors. If you want to be trusted, join the in-group!

Social contact has the potential to reduce social distance, and often remarkably quickly. In social dilemma games, experimental subjects become substantially more other-regarding when they are allowed to see or speak to their counterpart prior to engaging, even if they have never met that person before, than when their counterpart is an anonymous player connected through the internet.[4] This explains why savvy businesspeople invest time and energy in building personal relationships with their contracting partners, reducing social distance in order to create a basis for trust.

Many years ago, I was a management consultant for Bain & Company. Fresh out of college and with little real-world experience, I was suspicious of my clients who seemed to spend an undue amount of time (and their company's money) playing golf and dining with their customers or suppliers. I understood why they would enjoy a first-class Super Bowl junket, but was it really worth the cost to the shareholders? Today I understand that, while executives certainly can and do overinvest in social activities at work because they are enjoyable, breaking bread together can help create a mutually other-regarding orientation when it comes time to negotiate important corporate deals.

The instinct to trust those with whom we form social bonds is reinforced, if not driven, by our body's chemistry. Social contact generates the production of the molecule oxytocin, which in turn causes the brain to release the pleasurable chemicals dopamine and serotonin. Sometimes called the "cuddle hormone," oxytocin is best known for causing people to fall in love and mothers to bond deeply with their infants, but it also promotes empathy and attachment in a much broader set of social situations.[5] This chemical change causes people to both care for others and trust them, which, of course, promotes cooperation and other-regarding behavior more generally. Neuroscientist Paul Zak has demonstrated, for example, that treating trustors playing the trust game with an oxytocin-laced nasal spray makes them twice as likely to transfer their entire stake to the trustee as trustors who are treated with a placebo spray.[6]

Face-to-face interaction is best—one study found trust in a prisoner's dilemma game played face-to-face was three times as high as when the game was played over the telephone.[7] Touching another person gently on the arm or shoulder appears to help as well.[8] But even technology-mediated interaction can have the same effect. One study found that photographs and introductory emails increased trust between student subjects participating in a negotiation with students from other universities,[9] and Zak has found that even connecting with others digitally, through social media, for 15 minutes can trigger increases in oxytocin.[10]

When you are interacting with a negotiating counterpart, the best way to reduce perceived social distance and trigger trust is to demonstrate empathy, the ability to truly understand the other person's perspective and feelings, whether or not you agree with her. Hostage-negotiator-turned-negotiation-professor Chris Voss teaches that his starting point in negotiating with really bad people is to recognize that everyone wants to be understood. He observes from his experience that the tenor of any negotiation changes when he can display sufficient empathy for his counterpart's point of view that the counterpart says two critical words in response: "That's right."[11]

Another tactic Voss recommends to build trust is mirroring his counterparts—their words, mannerisms, facial expressions, tone of voice, and tempo of speech.[12] The benefits of this tactic have been scientifically validated. Psychologist William Maddux and colleagues had subjects participate in a negotiation between a job candidate and a recruiter involving eight different issues, with the candidate subject, the recruiter subject, or neither instructed to subtly mimic the counterpart's mannerisms during the interaction. When one subject mimicked, the pair designed more mutually profitable deals, on average, than if neither mimicked. Both parties obtained more cooperative surplus in the process (although the subjects doing the mimicking captured more of the additional surplus).[13] Even mimicking a counterpart's use of jargon and emoticons in negotiations via email has been shown to lead to more profitable deals.[14]

Displaying generosity when it is not required is another fundamental tactic for creating conditions of trust, as this can identify you as someone who is prosocial. In 1999, the online auction site eBay was the darling of the tech world, with a stock price that had nearly tripled on the day of its initial public offering the prior fall. But on June 10, its website suddenly went dark for nearly 24 hours—a serious problem for a company whose entire business model was based on real-time transactions over the internet. To make matters worse, during the outage the company promised several times that it would restore service quickly, only to fail to do so.

Though eBay's contracts with its online sellers required the company only to extend any auctions that were underway at the time of the outage, CEO Meg Whitman instead decided to refund all fees collected by eBay for all of the more than two million auctions that were disrupted. Although the decision cost the company about $5 million and caused it to miss its quarterly revenue projections, of keen interest to stock market investors, Whitman said that it became the obvious course of action as soon as she asked her senior advisers the question "What is the right thing to do here?"[15]

Doing right by business partners, rather than doing what is immediately profitable, is classic prosocial behavior. Generosity in the course of the negotiation process is as well, such as making a concession or offering some additional form of compensation without asking for anything in return. So is being transparent. Author Stephen M. R. Covey tells a good story about how a counterpart immediately established his trustworthiness by sending Covey the markups of a draft contract prepared by his department heads, without first editing or censoring the comments.[16] It's a bit of a cliché, but doing something that is good for your counterpart at some cost to yourself, whether the cost is large or small, is the best way to engender trust. Walk the walk.

In high-conflict negotiations, such as attempts to resolve a dispute or allocate resources under conditions of scarcity, an apology is often an invaluable tool for generating trust. Saying "I'm sorry" is a nearly foolproof way to change a counterpart's perception of you from an opponent who must be vanquished to a partner who can be trusted to prioritize his interests and concerns.

An experiment conducted by economist Johannes Abeler and colleagues (also relating, coincidentally, to eBay) provides an impressive example of an apology's power. eBay customers who posted negative feedback about sellers were sent either five euros or a pro forma message saying that the seller was "sorry" that the customer was not satisfied and that the seller wanted "to apologize." Either way, the message requested that the customer take down the negative report. Nearly half of the recipients given the very generic apology complied with the request, willing to let bygones be bygones, which was nearly twice the rate as those who were given cold, hard cash.[17]

Apologies have also been shown to pay impressive dividends in a far more high-stakes and emotionally fraught negotiation context: medical malpractice lawsuits. Traditionally, when trying to negotiate out-of-court settlements, defense lawyers have been reluctant to allow their clients to apologize to the injured plaintiffs, either for mistakes or even merely for poor outcomes, out of fear that these statements could be used to help prove liability if the cases were to proceed to court. In recent years, a number of states have enacted new "I'm Sorry" laws that explicitly protect apologies in these negotiations from being used as evidence. Studies have found that these have resulted in fewer lawsuits and reductions in settlement payments.[18]

Another way to demonstrative prosociality, although a risky one, is to make a leap of faith and extend trust to the other party, at least in modest increments. Prosocial individuals who will adopt a self-interested negotiation orientation out of fear of being exploited will respond to demonstrations of trust with enthusiastic other-regarding behavior. In the trust game, the more trust displayed by trustors (i.e., the more money transferred), the more money returned by trustees on average.

One interesting study compared the behavior of trustees who were told that the trustor chose to transfer money to them to the behavior of trustees who received the same amount of money but were told the amount was determined randomly. The trustees in the former group returned twice as much money to their trustor as did those in the latter group. This experiment was conducted by Paul Zak, who, not surprisingly, also found that the trustees who thought they had been trusted by their counterpart enjoyed a boost in oxytocin not experienced by the trustees who thought their payment resulted from chance.[19]

If trust begets trust, a noticeable lack of trust can have the opposite effect. In Zak's experiments, male (but not female) trustees who received a transfer from the trustor of less than 30 percent of the stake experienced a sharp spike in testosterone (which promotes aggressive and self-interested behavior) and tended to return almost nothing.[20]

When you fear that your counterpart might not trust you, find a way to either reduce social distance or demonstrate, with your actions, that you are prosocial. The first approach signals that you will behave in a trustworthy manner toward your particular counterpart; the second signals that you are trustworthy to everyone.

47

THE IMPORTANCE OF THE STAKES

Unsurprisingly, in social dilemma experiments, as the amount of the payments that subjects can earn increases, so does self-interested behavior (although, happily, other-regarding behavior does not disappear entirely).[1] When the stakes are high, the temptation to exploit increases, even when reputational or relational damage is certain to result.

An example from a British game show called *Golden Balls*, which aired from 2007 to 2009, illustrates this point. At the end of each episode, two contestants play a game called "split or steal," which is similar in structure (but not identical) to the prisoner's dilemma. The players must allocate a pot of money that they have built up until that point. Each contestant has two gold orbs that open and close, one with the word *steal* lodged inside and the other with the word *split*. Each player selects one of his two balls. Then, on the command of the show's host, the players simultaneously open the balls they have chosen and reveal their contents.

If both players choose split, they divide the money evenly. If one player chooses steal and the other chooses split, the player who steals wins the entire pot. But if both choose steal, they both lose and neither receives a penny. Before making their choices, the players have an opportunity to negotiate. Most of the time is typically spent by both players promising that they will choose split and exhorting the other to trust them.

In one memorable episode of the show, an unusually large pot of more than £100,000 was at stake. During the negotiation interlude, Steven and Sarah repeatedly pledge to each other that they will choose split, and both go to great lengths to claim that the reputational cost of stealing should make their counterpart comfortable trusting them. Steven says that if he were to steal, members of the studio audience would come down to the stage and lynch him. Sarah responds that if she were to steal, "everyone I know would be absolutely disgusted."

When the moment of truth arrives, Steven chooses split, but Sarah chooses steal. Steven places his face in his hands and his head on the table, in obvious anguish over his misplaced trust. Sarah doesn't look much happier. Her lips appear to curl involuntarily. She turns her head, places one hand in front of her face, and then looks down, as if she is trying desperately to hide from the camera. But then, of course, she leaves with £101,500.[2]

In the brief postgame wrap-up interview that concludes the episode, Steven says the lesson he learned from appearing on *Golden Balls* is that "greed has no bounds." Sarah tries to attribute her behavior to fear rather than greed, saying that she worried about being "stabbed in the back." But this explanation, while it could explain defection in the prisoner's dilemma game, doesn't wash in *Golden Balls*, which has a slightly different incentive structure. If Steven were to have betrayed her by choosing steal, Sarah would have received nothing, regardless of her choice. Unlike in the prisoner's dilemma, there was no worse outcome—no sucker's payoff—that Sarah could protect herself from by choosing to steal. Her choice could be explained only by greed.

So much for the general finding that even people who are willing to exploit others are unlikely to do so after promising that they will not. As Steven learned, high stakes can make trust especially risky. In the first three seasons that the show aired, exactly 50 percent of the contestants chose split and 50 percent chose steal but, as the size of the pot increased, so did the propensity of the players to choose steal.[3]

Compare Steven's approach to that of another contestant, Nick, on a different episode of *Golden Balls*. Ibrahim promises to split the £13,600 pot with Nick. He explains that he learned to be trustworthy from his father, who had taught him in boyhood that a man who fails to keep his word "is not a man—he's worth nothing." Nick is willing to share the pot but doesn't trust Ibrahim, so he vows that he will choose steal and then divide the money with Ibrahim after the show, assuming Ibrahim chooses split. The show's host, Jasper Carrott, is flustered by Nick's unusual tactic—*everyone* promises to split; no one vows to steal!—and clarifies to a visibly agitated Ibrahim that Nick's promise to share the money later is not legally binding.

"Why don't we both just choose 'split?'" Ibrahim asks. Nick doesn't come right out and say that he doesn't trust Ibrahim, but he holds firm and reiterates, over and over, that he is "definitely" going to choose steal. An angry Ibrahim threatens to also choose steal so that both will go home empty-handed, and he blames this potential outcome on Nick being "an idiot." When the moment of truth comes, though, Ibrahim succumbs to Nick's use of Power and chooses split, rationally concluding that choosing split and hoping Nick will keep his promise is a better option than choosing steal and definitely receiving nothing. (As matters turned out, Nick proved to be so trustworthy that he actually chose split, meaning that Ibrahim received his half of the money without having to meet Nick in the parking lot after the show with his fingers crossed!)

Nick's unwillingness to trust Ibrahim proved to be a wise decision. In the interview after the dramatic finish, Ibrahim admitted that had Nick agreed to his proposal that both men split, he (Ibrahim) would have chosen to steal and walked off with all the money.[4]

The decision to trust a negotiation counterpart always entails some risk. But high stakes and the potential for your counterpart to enjoy outsize gains by being untrustworthy require particular caution. To make matters worse, high stakes are also likely to make your counterpart fear that you will exploit him, which increases the likelihood that he will adopt a self-interested orientation as a means of self-protection, thus making trust doubly dangerous!

CODA

48

HOW TO CONTINUALLY IMPROVE YOUR SKILLS

Phil Ivey is one of the most successful professional poker players in history, having won more World Series of Poker tournaments (10) than all but one other player. In 2017 he was inducted into the Poker Hall of Fame, an exclusive club that, as of this writing, has only 58 members.[1] Fellow poker professional and author Annie Duke tells a story about Ivey that provides an important insight into his success.

In 2004, Duke's brother, Howard Lederer, also a poker pro, provided television commentary for a tournament that Ivey won. Afterward, the two went out for a celebratory dinner. But rather than bask in his triumph or celebrate his half-million-dollar payday, Ivey spent the evening critically assessing how he had played each hand and seeking Lederer's evaluation about where he might have erred and how he could have done better.[2]

Ivey understood something important about mastering any complex skill. Sure, he is blessed with a great deal of natural ability. And yes, he has logged tens of thousands, if not hundreds of thousands, of hours sitting at poker tables, playing hand after hand after hand and gaining valuable experience. But talent and experience alone were not enough for Ivey to reach his true potential. He knew that being the best also required him to learn from his experience and constantly incorporate those lessons in order to improve his game.

As members of a highly social species, we constantly enlist the help of others to achieve our goals, and they seek our assistance in achieving their goals. This means we spend a healthy chunk of our waking hours negotiating. At work, many of us negotiate with clients or customers, and we all negotiate with bosses, employees, and co-workers. Outside of the office, we negotiate with salespeople, service providers, family members, friends, and acquaintances. But, as is true of poker, all of that experience will not help us to achieve our potential unless we learn from it.

The fundamental challenge for any negotiator is not how to *do it*, but how to learn from our experience in order to do it *better*. As you negotiate both formally and informally day in and day out, you may breeze through each interaction in an ad hoc, seat-of-the-pants fashion, relying on the intuition and instinct provided by the System 1 mind. This is the path taken by most negotiators. If you choose this course, you might achieve good results; at worst, you will muddle through and live to negotiate another day. Alternatively, you can approach negotiation the way Phil Ivey approaches poker.

It has long been understood that, as a general matter, the human brain can keep between 5 and 10 pieces of data in short-term, working memory.[3] This is why it is easy to recall telephone numbers that you use frequently (at least it used to be, before smartphones eliminated the need to know them) but quite difficult to remember a 16-digit credit card number, even if you provide it often to merchants on the internet or over the phone. The 5TN approach allows you to carefully plan for your negotiations in advance, and then critically evaluate your performance after the fact, by committing to memory just five pieces of information—the labels I've given to each of the five tools.

These tools are the only sources of advantage in negotiation. Depending on the context, you will choose to focus on some tools more than others. Persuasion is relatively less important with more sophisticated counterparts, who will have carefully analyzed the value to them of reaching an agreement. Deal Design is more useful in negotiations with many issues than in those with just one (such as price). Power is more appropriate in high-stakes or one-time negotiations than in less important negotiations or repeat interactions. Fairness Norms are likely to be more central when ongoing relationships are involved. But there is a role for each of the five tools in any negotiation.

My parting advice is this: Prior to engaging in your next negotiation, think carefully about how you can use Bargaining Zone Analysis, Persuasion, Deal Design, Power, and Fairness Norms to negotiate the best possible deal. Take out a sheet of paper, divide it into five columns, and make notes in each one as to how, specifically, you can best use the tool. After the negotiation, whether it ends with agreement or impasse, return to that same document and critically evaluate how successful you were in using each tool to your advantage, and determine what you could have done better. Then incorporate those insights into your preparation for your next negotiation.

Vow to be the Phil Ivey of negotiation. I can't promise that you will earn $500,000 in one sitting or be voted into the Hall of Fame, but I can promise that you will enjoy significantly better negotiation outcomes.

ACKNOWLEDGMENTS

This book is the culmination of nearly three decades of my thinking about how to best understand and explain the complex human interaction that we call "negotiation," so it is impossible for me to acknowledge all of the intellectual influences.

The first thanks go to Bob Mnookin, who taught me negotiation and encouraged my academic career in the field, and to Tom Ulen, my longtime mentor and friend, who gave me my first faculty position and encouraged my study of behavioral economics.

The many colleagues from whom I have learned so much of what I know about negotiation, some of whom also provided specific advice and comments on the book, are too numerous to mention, but they include most prominently Richard Birke, Jonathan Greenberg, Chris Guthrie, Carrie Menkel-Meadow, Woody Mosten, Barry O'Neill, Andrea Schneider, Jean Sternlight, and Paul Zak. The fabulous UCLA law students who have served as my research assistants and worked over the years on concepts that eventually made their way into the book include Emily Bisnestt, Nicholas Celletti-Nissinbaum, George Chapman, Armound Ghoorchian, Maxwell Harwitt, Jordan Jeffery, Parker Johnson, Connor

Kampff, Michael LaPlante, Andrew Lux, Margaret Lynch, Erin Malone, Grace Meador, Nicholas Palatucci, Daniel Peikes, Jonathon Townsend, Luke Ward, and the incomparable Sam Pierce, who insisted on continuing to help after he graduated.

The project would have never gotten off the ground without the confidence, support, and encouragement of my agent, Rafe Sagalyn of ICM, and of Phil Marino, formerly of Liveright. The editing I received, both at a conceptual level and line by line, paragraph by paragraph, from Bill Rusin and Gina Iaquinta of Liveright and copyeditor Sarah Johnson, was extraordinary. I cannot believe how much their work improved the quality of what you now see.

The UCLA School of Law and deans Jon Varat, Michael Schill, Rachel Moran, and Jennifer Mnookin have supported, unwaveringly, not just this project, but my study and teaching of negotiation since 2000. Jennifer also deserves a separate thanks for encouraging me to step away from my administrative duties, at least temporarily, in order to finish the manuscript. Thanks also to Susan Akens, David Babbe, Diane Birnholz, Robert Feldman, Genevieve Helleringer, Megan Hutchinson, Eileen Scallen, Cambra Sklarz, Elizabeth Scully, and Barbara Spellman for coteaching my UCLA negotiation course, which has been a constant source of personal and professional fulfillment, and to my colleagues and friends Michael Dorff, Doug Lichtman, Jason Oh, and Adam Winkler, who gently nudged me toward the finish line with this project.

Finally, thanks to my wife, Sarah, for her encouragement, support, and patience, and to my daughter, Jessica, for the inspiration she gives me to be the best person I can be.

NOTES

1. A Tale of Two Pitchers

1. Amy K. Nelson, "Dream on a Shelf," Outside the Lines, ESPN, April 23, 2009, http://www.espn.com/espn/eticket/story?page=090423/harrington.
2. Bob Nightengale, "Content with Less, Weaver Still Dealing," *USA Today*, July 13, 2012, 4C.

2. Decision Analysis 101

1. For a detailed discussion of decision analysis for purposes of negotiation, see Howard Raiffa, John Richardson, and David Metcalfe, *Negotiation Analysis: The Science and Art of Collaborative Decision Making* (Cambridge, MA: Belknap Press of Harvard University Press, 2002), 14–32.
2. I am far from the only negotiation professor to use the term *plan B* as shorthand for the course of action the negotiator will pursue if he reaches impasse in the focal negotiation. For a recent example, see Michael Wheeler, *The Art of Negotiation: How to Improvise Agreement in a Chaotic World* (New York: Simon and Schuster, 2013), 57. In *Getting to Yes*, Roger Fisher and William Ury labeled the negotiator's plan B his "BATNA," an acronym for "best alternative to a negotiated agreement." Roger Fisher, William Ury, and Bruce Patton, *Getting to Yes: Negotiating Agreement without Giving In* (New York: Penguin Books, 1991). The popularity of that book has made this funny word common in negotiation circles ever since. I find, however, that negotiators often confuse the term *BATNA* with the concept of the reservation point.

4. Advanced Decision Analysis II: Comparing the Differences

1. For similar descriptions of differences to evaluate, see Robert H. Mnookin, Scott R. Peppet, and Andrew S. Tulumello, *Beyond Winning: Negotiating to Create Value in Deals and Disputes* (Cambridge, MA: Belknap Press of Harvard University Press, 2000), 14–17; David A. Lax and James K. Sebenius, *The Manager as Negotiator: Bargaining for Cooperation and Competitive Gain* (New York: Free Press, 1986), 90–102.
2. Joe Halverson, "Why the MLB Draft Is the Best Bargain in the Game," Bleacher Report, February 2, 2011, http://bleacherreport.com/articles/593565-why-the-mlb-draft-is-the-best-bargain-in-the-game; "Baseball Signing Bonuses," Baseball Almanac, accessed April 3, 2020, http://www.baseball-almanac.com/players/baseball_signing_bonus.shtml; Steve Henson, "Borchard Signs for Record Bonus," *Los Angeles Times*, July 29, 2000.

5. The Other Side of the Bargaining Zone

1. Guhan Subramanian, *Negotiauctions: New Dealmaking Strategies for a Competitive Marketplace* (New York: W. W. Norton, 2010), 3–4.
2. Subramanian, *Negotiauctions*, 8–9.
3. Richard P. Larrick and George Wu, "Claiming a Large Slice of a Small Pie: Asymmetric Disconfirmation in Negotiation," *Journal of Personality and Social Psychology* 93, no. 2 (2007): 212–33.
4. See Subramanian, *Negotiauctions*, 94–95; James Surowiecki, "The Agony of Victory and the Thrill of Defeat," *New Yorker*, January 8, 2001, 31.

7. Who Goes First?

1. Binion told this story during a panel discussion on poker and negotiation. See "How to Play Your Hand: Lessons for Negotiators from Poker," *UNLV Gaming Law Journal* 2 (2011): 231, 234.

8. We Are All Salespeople

1. Joshua William Busby, "Bono Made Jesse Helms Cry: Jubilee 2000, Debt Relief, and Moral Action in International Politics," *International Studies Quarterly* 51, no. 2 (2007): 247, 266–67; Lisa Ann Richey and Stefano Ponte, "Better (Red)™ Than Dead? Celebrities, Consumption and International Aid," *Third World Quarterly* 29, no. 4 (2008): 711; James Traub, "The Statesman," *New York Times Magazine*, September 18, 2005.
2. Traub, "The Statesman."
3. Busby, "Bono Made Jesse Helms Cry," 247–48, 266.
4. Daniel Pink, *To Sell Is Human: The Surprising Truth about Moving Others* (New York: Riverhead Books, 2012), 22.

9. Thinking Fast

1. This question is part of the Cognitive Reflection Test, developed by Shane Frederick to test individuals' propensity to override System 1 intuitions with System 2 analysis. Shane Frederick, "Cognitive Reflection and Decision Making," *Journal of Economic Perspectives* 19, no. 4 (2005): 25–42.
2. Daniel Kahneman, "Maps of Bounded Rationality: Psychology for Behavioral Economics," *American Economic Review* 93, no. 5 (2003): 1449–75.
3. See Peter Railton, "Intuitive Guidance: Emotion, Information, and Experience," in *Homo Prospectus*, ed. Martin E. P. Seligman et al. (New York: Oxford University Press, 2016), 33–75.
4. Christopher D. Fiorillo, Philippe N. Tobler, and Wolfram Schultz, "Discrete Coding of Reward Probability and Uncertainty by Dopamine Neurons," *Science*, March 21, 2003, 1898–1902.
5. Paul Slovic et al., "The Affect Heuristic," *European Journal of Operational Research* 177, no. 3 (2007): 1333–52; Robert Zajonc, "Feeling and Thinking: Preferences Need No Inferences," *American Psychologist* 35, no. 2 (1980): 151; Robert Zajonc, "On the Primacy of Affect," *American Psychologist* 39, no. 2 (1984): 117–23; Luiz Pessoa, "On the Relationship between Emotion and Cognition," *Nature Reviews Neuroscience* 9, no. 2 (2008): 148.
6. Daniel Kahneman, *Thinking, Fast and Slow* (New York: Farrar, Straus and Giroux, 2011), 12.

10. Two Sides of the Same Coin

1. Scott Rothman and Rajiv Joseph, *Draft Day*, directed by Ivan Reitman (Lionsgate, 2014), DVD.

11. One Size Doesn't Fit All

1. Neil Rackham, *SPIN Selling* (New York: McGraw-Hill Education, 2017), 3, 14.
2. It is likely that Epictetus is not actually the source of this proverb. "'Two Ears, One Mouth': Hunting a Proverb from Zeno to Paul's Mom," Sententiae Antiquae, May 15, 2016.
3. Rackham relates that in most successful sales the customer describes the benefit in response to the salesperson's questions. Rackham, *SPIN Selling*, 17, 81–88. Academic research suggests that asking whether a speaker's position is convincing leads to higher levels of agreement than asserting the position. Robert E. Burnkrant and Daniel J. Howard, "Effects of the Use of Introductory Rhetorical Questions versus Statements on Information Processing," *Journal of Personality and Social Psychology* 47, no. 6 (1984): 1218–30.

12. Compared to What?

1. Dan Ariely, *Predictably Irrational: The Hidden Forces That Shape Our Decisions* (New York: HarperCollins, 2009), 1–6.
2. Christopher K. Hsee, "The Evaluability Hypothesis: An Explanation for Preference Reversals between Joint and Separate Evaluations of Alternatives," *Organizational Behavior and Human Decision Processes* 67, no. 3 (1996): 247–57.
3. Amos Tversky and Itamar Simonson, "Context-Dependent Preferences," *Management Science* 39, no. 10 (1993): 1179–89.
4. William Poundstone, *Priceless: The Myth of Fair Value (and How to Take Advantage of It)* (New York: Hill and Wang, 2010), 158.
5. Robert B. Cialdini et al., "Reciprocal Concessions Procedure for Inducing Compliance: The Door-in-the-Face Technique," *Journal of Personality and Social Psychology* 31, no. 2 (1975): 206–15.

13. Dropping Anchor

1. Edward J. Joyce and Gary C. Biddle, "Anchoring and Adjustment in Probabilistic Inference in Auditing," *Journal of Accounting Research* 19, no. 1 (1981): 120–45.
2. Amos Tversky and Daniel Kahneman, "Judgment under Uncertainty: Heuristics and Biases," *Science*, September 27, 1974, 1124–31.
3. Brandon M. Turner and Dan R. Schley, "The Anchor Integration Model: A Descriptive Model of Anchoring Effects," *Cognitive Psychology* 90 (2016): 1–47.
4. Margaret Ann Neale and Max H. Bazerman, *Cognition and Rationality in Negotiation* (New York: Free Press, 1991); Gregory B. Northcraft and Margaret A. Neale, "Experts, Amateurs, and Real Estate: An Anchoring-and-Adjustment Perspective on Property Pricing Decisions," *Organizational Behavior and Human Decision Processes* 39, no. 1 (1987): 84, 87–91.
5. Russell Korobkin and Chris Guthrie, "Psychological Barriers to Litigation Settlement: An Experimental Approach," *Michigan Law Review* 93, no. 1 (1994): 107.
6. Adam Galinsky and Maurice Schweitzer, *Friend and Foe: When to Cooperate, When to Compete, and How to Succeed at Both* (London: Random House Business Books, 2015), 258.

14. Losses versus Gains

1. Daniel Kahneman and Amos Tversky, "Choices, Values, and Frames," *American Psychologist* 39, no. 4 (1984): 341–50.
2. William Samuelson and Richard Zeckhauser, "Status Quo Bias in Decision Making," *Journal of Risk and Uncertainty* 1, no. 1 (1988): 7–59.
3. *Popov v. Hayashi*, No. 400545, 2002 WL 31833731 (Ca. Sup. Ct. 2002).
4. Peter Adomeit, "The Barry Bonds Baseball Case—An Empirical Approach—Is Fleeting Possession Five Tenths of the Ball?," *Saint Louis University Law Review* 48, no. 2 (2004): 475.

15. Rose-Colored Glasses

1. George Loewenstein et al., "Self-Serving Assessments of Fairness and Pretrial Bargaining," *Journal of Legal Studies* 22, no. 1 (1993): 135, 145–55.
2. Jane Goodman-Delahunty et al., "Insightful or Wishful: Lawyers' Ability to Predict Case Outcomes," *Psychology, Public Policy and Law* 16, no. 2 (2010): 133.
3. Tali Sharot, "The Optimism Bias," *Current Biology* 21 (2011): R941, R942–44.
4. Garrison Keillor, "The Lake Wobegon Effect," A Prairie Home Companion, April 1, 2013, https://web.archive.org/web/20170902094711/https://www.prairiehome.org/story/2013/04/01/the-lake-wobegon-effect. (Actually, according to Keillor, what has become known as the "Lake Wobegon effect" is really a misunderstanding of the sentiment he expressed in the conclusion of every edition of *A Prairie Home Companion*. In response to a listener's question, Keillor explained that the notion that "all the children are above average" expresses a distaste of trying to stand out: the phrase means that in Lake Wobegon things like test scores don't count for much. "The 'Lake Wobegon effect' is a bunch of hogwash, as far as Lake Wobegon is concerned.")
5. Stephen J. Hoch, "Counterfactual Reasoning and Accuracy in Predicting Personal Events," *Journal of Experimental Psychology* 11, no. 4 (1985): 719, 725; James R. Dalziel and Raymond F. Soames Job, "Motor Vehicle Accidents, Fatigue and Optimism Bias in Taxi Drivers," *Accident Analysis and Prevention* 29, no. 4 (1997): 489, 493; Kathryn Patricia Cross, "Not Can, but Will College Teaching Be Improved?," *New Directions for Higher Education* 1977, no. 17 (1977): 1, 10.
6. Lisa Bortolotti and Magdalena Antrobus, "Costs and Benefits of Realism and Optimism," *Current Opinion in Psychiatry* 28, no. 2 (2015): 194–98.
7. Cameron Anderson et al., "A Status-Enhancement Account of Overconfidence," *Journal of Personality and Social Psychology* 103, no. 4 (2012): 718–35; Jerry Useem, "Why It Pays to Be a Jerk," *The Atlantic*, June 2015.
8. Albert H. Hastorf and Hadley Cantril, "They Saw a Game: A Case Study," *Journal of Abnormal and Social Psychology* 49, no. 1 (1954): 129–34.
9. Richard Roll, "The Hubris Hypothesis of Corporate Takeovers," *Journal of Business* 59, no. 2 (1986): 197–216. Suggesting overconfidence by individual decision makers explains why businesses overbid and overpay for acquisitions when recent ones have done well. That is, decision makers believe their prior success and ability to control the outcome will mean continuing success.
10. Don A. Moore, "Not So Above Average After All: When People Believe They Are Worse Than Average and Its Implications for Theories of Bias in Social Comparison," *Organizational Behavior and Human Decision Processes* 102, no. 1 (2007): 42–58.

16. Prominence and Probability

1. Malcolm Gladwell, "The Engineer's Lament: Two Ways of Thinking about Automotive Safety," *New Yorker*, May 4, 2015.
2. Paul J. Becker, Arthur J. Jipson, and Alan S. Bruce, "State of Indiana v. Ford Motor Company Revisited," *American Journal of Criminal Justice* 26, no. 2 (2002): 181–202.

3. Amos Tversky and Daniel Kahneman, "Availability: A Heuristic for Judging Frequency and Probability," *Cognitive Psychology* 5, no. 2 (1973): 207–32.
4. For an excellent analysis of this, see Gary T. Schwartz, "The Myth of the Ford Pinto Case," *Rutgers Law Review* 43, no. 4 (1991): 1013–68.

17. Following the Crowd

1. Solomon E. Asch, "Effects of Group Pressure upon the Modification and Distortion of Judgments," in *Groups, Leadership and Men: Research in Human Relations*, ed. Harold Guetzkow (Oxford, UK: Carnegie Press, 1951), 177–90.
2. Stanley Milgram, "Behavioral Study of Obedience," *Journal of Abnormal and Social Psychology* 67, no. 4 (1963): 371–78.
3. Noah J. Goldstein, Vladas Griskevicius, and Robert B. Cialdini, "Invoking Social Norms: A Social Psychology Perspective on Improving Hotels' Linen-Reuse Programs," *Cornell Hospitality Quarterly* 48, no. 2 (2007): 145–50.
4. James Surowiecki, *The Wisdom of Crowds* (New York: Anchor Books, 2004), 4.
5. Trident Gum, "Four out of Five Dentists Recommend Trident Sugarless Gum," video, posted by MondelezSalesPortal April 21, 2014, https://www.youtube.com/watch?v=tXqAyMhgc7I.
6. Hershey H. Friedman and Linda Friedman, "Endorser Effectiveness by Product Type," *Journal of Advertising Research* 19, no. 5 (1979): 63–71.

18. Wanting What We Can't Have

1. "Home" page, Colleen Szot: Wonderful Writer, accessed April 3, 2020, http://wonderfulwriter.com/.
2. Steve Martin, "98% of HBR Readers Love This Article," *Harvard Business Review*, October 2012.
3. Jack W. Brehm, "Postdecision Changes in the Desirability of Alternatives," *Journal of Abnormal and Social Psychology* 52, no. 3 (1956): 384–89.
4. *Modern Family*, "Aunt Mommy" episode, directed by Michael A. Spiller, written by Abraham Higginbotham and Dan O'Shannon, aired February 15, 2012, on ABC.
5. *Silicon Valley*, "Runaway Devaluation" episode, directed by Mike Judge, written by Ron Weiner, aired April 19, 2015, on HBO.
6. Elizabeth Weintraub, "Why Average Days on Market Matter to Home Buyers," The Balance, July 26, 2016, https://www.thebalance.com/why-days-on-market-matter-to-home-buyers-1798769.
7. Lee Ross and Andrew Ward, "Psychological Barriers to Dispute Resolution," *Advances in Experimental Social Psychology* 27 (1995): 255–304; Lee Ross and Constance Stillinger, "Barriers to Conflict Resolution," *Negotiation Journal* 7, no. 4 (1991): 389–404.
8. Ifat Maoz et al., "Reactive Devaluation of an 'Israeli' vs. 'Palestinian' Peace Proposal," *Journal of Conflict Resolution* 46, no. 4 (2002): 515–46.

9. Lee Ross, "Reactive Devaluation in Negotiation and Conflict Resolution," in *Barriers to Conflict Resolution*, ed. Kenneth J. Arrow et al. (New York: W. W. Norton, 1995), 27–42.

19. Preferences about Preferences

1. Ron Grossman, "Unlikely Civil Rights Hero: Illinois' Everett Dirksen Rose to the Occasion 50 Years Ago to Get Civil Rights Act Passed," *Chicago Tribune*, June 28, 2014.
2. Adam M. Grant and David A. Hofmann, "It's Not All about Me: Motivating Hand Hygiene among Health Care Professionals by Focusing on Patients," *Psychological Science* 22 (2011): 1494–99.
3. Philip H. Dougherty, "Advertising: Michelin's Broader Approach," *New York Times*, January 10, 1985.

20. The Likability Bonus

1. *Veep*, "Frozen Yoghurt" episode, directed by Armando Iannucci, written by Simon Blackwell and Armando Iannucci, aired April 29, 2012, on HBO.

21. Creativity in Negotiation

1. Frank Partnoy, *The Match King: Ivar Kreuger, the Financial Genius behind a Century of Wall Street Scandals* (New York: PublicAffairs, 2009), 23–25, 226.
2. Partnoy, *The Match King*, 22–23.

22. Wine, Wool, and the Wealth of Nations

1. Howard Raiffa, *The Art and Science of Negotiation* (Cambridge, MA: Belknap Press of Harvard University Press, 1982), 131; M. P. Follett, "Constructive Conflict," in *Dynamic Administration: The Collected Papers of Mary Parker Follett*, ed. H. C. Metcalf and L. Urwick (New York: Harper, 1940), 30–49; Richard E. Walton and Robert B. McKersie, *A Behavioral Theory of Labor Negotiations* (New York: McGraw-Hill, 1965), xii.
2. Adam Smith, *The Wealth of Nations* (New York: Modern Library, 1994), 399.
3. David Ricardo, *On Principles of Political Economy and Taxation* (Amherst, NY: Prometheus Books, 1996), 27–29.
4. Economists call this standard "Kaldor-Hicks efficiency." Antony W. Dnes, *Principles of Law and Economics*, 3rd ed. (Northampton, MA: Edward Elgar Publishing, 2018), 9–11, 149–50.
5. Economists call this standard "Pareto efficiency," after the economist Vilfredo

Pareto. Technically, a transaction is Pareto efficient if at least one party is made better off and no party is made worse off. Thomas M. Tripp and Harris Sondak, "An Evaluation of Dependent Variables in Experimental Negotiation Studies: Impasse Rates and Pareto Efficiency," *Organizational Behavior and Human Decision Processes* 51, no. 2 (1992): 279–80.

23. *Roulez les Bon Temps*

1. Arnold Whitridge, "The Louisiana Purchase, 1803: America Moves West," *History Today* 3, no. 7 (1953): 476–83.
2. Farhad Manjoo, "The Rise of the Fat Start-Up," *New York Times*, May 24, 2017; Opendoor, "Our Pricing," accessed April 3, 2020, https://www.opendoor.com/pricing.
3. According to lore, the violinist was Fritz Kreisler.

24. Divide and Subtract

1. Shirley A. Kan et al., *China-U.S. Aircraft Collision Incident of April 2001: Assessments and Policy Implications*, CRS Report for Congress RL30946, October 10, 2001; Hang Zhang, "Culture and Apology: The Hainan Island Incident," *World Englishes* 20, no. 3 (2003): 383–91.
2. Michael B. Oren, *Six Days of War: June 1967 and the Making of the Modern Middle East* (New York: Oxford University Press, 2002), 170–73, 305–9.
3. Shibley Telhami, "The Camp David Accords: A Case of International Bargaining," *Pew Case Studies in International Affairs, Case 445* (Washington, DC: Institute for the Study of Diplomacy, 1992).
4. Fisher, Ury, and Patton, *Getting to Yes*, 24.

25. Logrolling

1. Davy Crockett, *An Account of Col. Crockett's Tour to the North and Down East* (Philadelphia: Carey and Hart, 1835), 120; Nicholas R. Miller, "Logrolling, Vote Trading, and the Paradox of Voting: A Game-Theoretical Overview," *Public Choice* 30 (1977): 51–75.
2. Martin Tolchin, "Social Security: Compromise at Long Last," *New York Times*, January 20, 1983, sec. B; Robert A. Rosenblatt, "Social Security Accord Reached: Presidential Panel Agrees on Plan; Reagan, O'Neill Support Proposals," *Los Angeles Times*, January 16, 1983, sec. A.
3. David E. Rosenbaum, "The Tax Reform Act of 1986: How the Measure Came Together; A Tax Bill for the Textbooks," *New York Times*, October 23, 1986, sec. D; David E. Rosenbaum, "Sweeping Tax Bill Approved in House by 292–136 Margin," *New York Times*, September 26, 1986, sec. A.
4. David Stephenson, "Fortune Is Strong with Alec's Estate," *Daily Express*, May 17, 2009; "Alec Guinness—1977 First Star Wars Interview—Michael Par-

kinson BBC TV," interview with Michael Parkinson, video, 6:36, posted by UKToyCollector1977 September 6, 2013, https://www.youtube.com/watch?time_continue=120&v=gyhO2uRA4FM.

5. Max H. Bazerman and Margaret A. Neale, "Heuristics in Negotiation: Limitations to Effective Dispute Resolution," in *Negotiating in Organizations*, ed. M. H. Bazerman and R. J. Lewicki (Beverly Hills, CA: Sage, 1983), 62–63; Max H. Bazerman and Margaret A. Neale, *Negotiating Rationally* (New York: Free Press, 1992), 16–22.
6. Leigh Thompson and Dennis Hrebec, "Lose-Lose Agreements in Interdependent Decision Making," *Psychological Bulletin* 120, no. 3 (1996): 396–409.

26. Solving the "Lemons" Problem

1. George A. Akerlof, "'The Market for Lemons': Quality Uncertainty and the Market Mechanism," *Quarterly Journal of Economics* 84, no. 3 (1970): 490.
2. George A. Akerlof, "Writing the 'The Market for Lemons': A Personal and Interpretive Essay," NobelPrize.org, accessed April 3, 2020.
3. 26 U.S. Code § 5000A (2010).
4. *Nat'l Fed'n of Indep. Bus. v. Sebelius*, 567 U.S. 519, 132 S. Ct. 2566 (2012).

27. Discouraging Shirking

1. Mnookin, Peppet, and Tulumello, *Beyond Winning*, 141.
2. Christopher S. Harrison, *Make the Deal: Negotiating Mergers and Acquisitions* (New York: John Wiley and Sons, 2016), 59.
3. Subramanian, *Negotiauctions*, 22–24.

28. Hard Bargaining at the Olympics

1. Dan Milmo, "Bus Strike over Olympic Pay Disrupts London Services," *The Guardian*, June 22, 2012.
2. Emma Clark, "Bus Drivers Bring London to a Halt as They Strike over Demands for £500 Olympics Bonus," *Daily Mail*, June 22, 2012.
3. "London Bus Workers Accept Olympic Bonus Offer," *The Guardian*, July 18, 2012.
4. Walter Isaacson, *Steve Jobs* (New York: Simon and Schuster, 2011), 284–92.
5. See, e.g., Vandra L. Huber and Margaret A. Neale, "Effects of Self- and Competitor Goals on Performance in an Interdependent Bargaining Task," *Journal of Applied Psychology* 72, no. 2 (1987): 197–203 (finding subjects assigned higher "requirements" for agreeing to a deal achieved better results); Margaret A. Neale and Max H. Bazerman, "The Effect of Externally Set Goals on Reaching Integrative Agreements in Competitive Markets," *Journal of Occupational Behavior* 6, no. 1 (1985): 19–32 (subjects told it was "against company policy" to accept a deal that would provide less than specified levels of profit in multi-issue negotiation earned more profit but took longer to reach agreements when given a high profit requirement than when

given a low profit requirement or no requirement). See also Gregory B. Northcraft et al., "Joint Effects of Assigned Goals and Training on Negotiator Performance," *Human Performance* 7, no. 4 (1994): 257–72.

29. A Beautiful Mind

1. In addition to capturing the Best Picture Oscar, the movie also won awards for Best Director, Best Adapted Screenplay, and Best Supporting Actress.
2. Nash's seminal article, published in 1950, describes a mathematically rational outcome of two parties who must agree to divide a particular item without making any assumptions about the bargaining process that they will employ. John F. Nash Jr., "The Bargaining Problem," *Econometrica* 18, no. 2 (1950): 155–62. In a subsequent article, Nash reaches a similar conclusion when assuming that two negotiators simultaneously make proposals to divide the cooperative surplus in a particular way, with the understanding that if the demands of both parties cannot be accommodated—that is, if the two parties' demands sum to more than the amount of cooperative surplus available—there will be no agreement and each negotiator will pursue his plan B. John Nash, "Two-Person Cooperative Games," *Econometrica* 21, no. 1 (1953): 128–40.

30. Bluffing

1. See Lawrence Bacow and Michael Wheeler, "Joint Problem Solving," in *Environmental Dispute Resolution* (New York: Springer Publishing, 1984), 73–74. The story is told slightly differently in different sources.
2. For Khrushchev's ultimatum, see U.S. State Department, "The Berlin Crisis, 1958–1961," January 10, 2017, https://history.state.gov/milestones/1953-1960/berlin-crises.
3. Don Oberdorfer, "Leaders Come to Grips with Post–Cold War Era," *Washington Post*, November 30, 1989.
4. Oberdorfer, "Leaders Come to Grips."

31. Playing "Chicken"

1. *Rebel without a Cause*, directed by Nicholas Ray (1955; Warner Bros.), motion picture.
2. Thomas Schelling, *The Strategy of Conflict* (Cambridge, MA: Harvard University Press, 1960).
3. Ian Ayres, "Founders," stickK.com, January 7, 2017, https://www.stickk.com/founders.
4. stickK.com, "What's an Anti-Charity?," accessed April 3, 2020, https://stickk.zendesk.com/hc/en-us/articles/206833337-What-s-an-Anti-Charity-.

32. Reputation and Rationality on the High Seas

1. Ishaan Tharoor, "How Somalia's Fishermen Became Pirates," *Time*, April 18, 2009.
2. *Captain Phillips*, directed by Paul Greengrass (2013; Columbia Pictures), motion picture; Richard Phillips and Stephan Talty, *A Captain's Duty* (New York: Hyperion Books, 2010).
3. Currun Singh and Arjun Singh Bedi, "War on Piracy: The Conflation of Somali Piracy with Terrorism in Discourse, Tactic, and Law," *Security Dialogue* 47, no. 5 (2016): 441.
4. Ingrid Melander and Lefteris Papadimas, "Somali Pirates Free Irene SL Tanker: Greek Coast Guard," Reuters, April 8, 2011.
5. Jay Bahadur, *The Pirates of Somalia: Inside Their Hidden World* (New York: Pantheon Books, 2011), 177–203.
6. Schelling, *The Strategy of Conflict*, 22.

33. Warm Lemonade and the Power of Patience

1. Ariel Rubinstein, "Perfect Equilibrium in a Bargaining Model," *Econometrica* 97, no. 1 (1982): 98–99; H. Peyton Young, "Negotiation Analysis," in *Negotiation Analysis* (Ann Arbor: University of Michigan Press, 1991), 6–7.
2. *Ozark*, "Kevin Cronin Was Here" episode, directed by Cherien Dabis, written by Ning Zhou and Paul Kolsby, aired March 27, 2020, on Netflix.
3. Bahadur, *The Pirates of Somalia*, 287–89.

34. Ultimatums and Dictators

1. Werner Güth, Rolf Schmittberger, and Bernd Schwarze, "An Experimental Analysis of Ultimatum Bargaining," *Journal of Economic Behavior and Organization* 3, no. 4 (1982): 367–88.
2. For a history, see Werner Güth and Martin G. Kocher, "More Than Thirty Years of Ultimatum Bargaining Experiments: Motives, Variations, and a Survey of the Recent Literature," *Journal of Economic Behavior and Organization* 108 (2014): 396–409.
3. See Güth and Kocher, "More Than Thirty Years of Ultimatum Bargaining Experiments."
4. Joseph Henrich et al., "In Search of Homo Economicus: Behavioral Experiments in 15 Small-Scale Societies," *American Economic Review* 91, no. 2 (2001): 73–78.
5. In *Getting to Yes*, Roger Fisher and William Ury advise negotiators to make a conscious tactic out of what seems to be a biologically ingrained attitude, telling negotiators who face threats to yield only if the other negotiator can provide an objective principle to justify his agreement proposal. Fisher, Ury, and Patton, *Getting to Yes*, 81–96.
6. Milmo, "Bus Strike over Olympic Pay"; Clark, "Bus Drivers Bring London to a Halt."
7. Milmo, "Bus Strike over Olympic Pay"; Clark, "Bus Drivers Bring London to a Halt."

8. An alternative conceptual approach is to understand Fairness Norms as directly affecting the negotiator's reservation point, because perceptions of whether or not an agreement is fair affect the utility generated by the agreement. For example, if Tube employees earn £27 per hour and the bus drivers believe that working for less than that would be deeply unfair, we could say that their reservation price is £27 because the *material utility* they would derive from a wage of £20–£26, minus the negative *transactional utility* they would suffer if they were to accept any wage of less than £27, would be less than the expected utility of striking. For the distinction between material and transactional utility, see Richard Thaler, "Mental Accounting and Consumer Choice," *Marketing Science* 4, no. 3 (1985): 199–214; Richard Thaler, "Transactional Utility Theory," in *Advances in Consumer Research*, ed. Richard P. Bagozzi and Alice M. Tybout (Ann Arbor, MI: Association for Consumer Research, 1983), 229–32.
9. A meta-analysis studying 129 dictator game papers finds these overall results. Christophe Engle, "Dictator Games: A Meta Study," *Experimental Economics* 14, no. 4 (2011): 583–610.

35. Distributive Justice

1. Economic Growth and Tax Relief Reconciliation Act of 2001, Pub. L. No. 107-16 (2001); Jobs and Growth Tax Relief Reconciliation Act of 2003, Pub. L. No. 108-27 (2003).
2. Tax Relief, Unemployment Insurance Reauthorization, and Job Creation Act of 2010, Pub. L. No. 111-312 (2010).
3. E. Klein, "Wonkbook: The Fiscal Cliff Is Finished," *Washington Post*, January 2, 2013. 89% of Senate Republicans voted yes, while only 36% of House Republicans voted yes. House vote Yes: 85 R, 172 D; House vote No: 151 R, 16 D; Senate vote Yes: 40 R, 49 D; Senate vote No: 5 R, 3 D.
4. Tax Cuts and Jobs Act of 2017, Pub. L. No. 115-97 (2017); The Joint Committee on Taxation, *Distributional Effects of the Conference Agreement for H.R.1, the "Tax Cuts and Jobs Act"* (Washington, DC: United States Congress, 2017); William G. Gale et al., "Effects of the Tax Cuts and Jobs Act, a Preliminary Analysis" (Washington, DC: Urban Institute and Brookings Institution, 2018), 33–36.
5. House vote Yes: 227 R, 0 D; House vote No: 13 R, 192 D; Senate vote Yes: 51 R, 0 D; Senate vote No: 1 R, 46 D, 2 I.
6. For a classic description of the principles of distributive justice, see Morton Deutsch, "Equity, Equality, and Need: What Determines Which Value Will Be Used as the Basis of Distributive Justice?," *Journal of Social Issues* 31, no. 3 (1975): 137–49.
7. See J. Stacy Adams, "Toward an Understanding of Inequity," *Journal of Abnormal and Social Psychology* 67, no. 5 (1963): 422–36.
8. Elizabeth A. Mannix et al., "Equity, Equality, or Need? The Effects of Organizational Culture on the Allocation of Benefits and Burdens," *Organizational Behavior and Human Decision Processes* 63, no. 3 (1995): 276–86.
9. Henrich et al., "In Search of Homo Economicus," 73–78.
10. Werner Güth and Reinhard Tietz, "Ultimatum Bargaining Behavior: A Survey

and Comparison of Experimental Results," *Journal of Economic Psychology* 11, no. 3 (1990): 417–49.

11. Elizabeth Hoffman et al., "Preferences, Property Rights, and Anonymity in Bargaining Games," *Games and Economic Behavior* 7, no. 3 (1994): 346–80.
12. Harris Sondak, Margaret A. Neale, and Robin L. Pinkley, "Relationship, Contribution, and Resource Constraints: Determinants of Distributive Justice in Individual Preferences and Negotiated Agreements," *Group Decision and Negotiation* 8, no. 6 (1999): 489–510.
13. Eugene Kiely, "'You Didn't Build That,' Uncut and Unedited," FactCheck.org, July 23, 2012; Juli Weiner, "The Rise of Romney's 'You Didn't Build That' Meme," *Vanity Fair*, July 18, 2012.

36. Convention

1. Robert C. Ellickson, *Order without Law* (Cambridge, MA: Harvard University Press, 1994).
2. Iris Bohnet and Richard Zeckhauser, "Social Comparisons in Ultimatum Bargaining," *Scandinavian Journal of Economics* 106, no. 3 (2004): 495–510.
3. Sarah F. Brosnan and Frans B. M. de Waal, "Monkeys Reject Unequal Pay," *Nature*, September 18, 2003, 297–99.

37. The Role of Market Price

1. Steven Lubet, "Notes on the Bedouin Horse Trade or 'Why Won't the Market Clear, Daddy?,'" *Texas Law Review* 74, no. 5 (1996): 1039–57.

38. Points of Comparison

1. Emily Yoffe, "A Wee Problem," Slate.com, August 12, 2014.
2. Bill Carter, "'Friends' Deal Will Pay Each of Its 6 Stars $22 Million," *New York Times*, February 12, 2002.
3. Bill Carter, "Saved by Timely Hit, NBC Is Ready for an Ad Kickoff," *New York Times*, May 17, 2004.
4. Brooks Barnes, "Reality Checks: Unscripted Shows Become a Money Pit," *Wall Street Journal*, July 27, 2004.
5. Scott Collins, "Trump Demonstrates How to Get Rich—Quick—He Wangles a Big Pay Bump for His Hit NBC Show, 'The Apprentice,'" *Los Angeles Times*, April 12, 2004.

39. Dancing through the Bazaar

1. *Monty Python's Life of Brian*, directed by Terry Jones, written by Graham Chapman et al. (1979; HandMade Films, 1999), DVD.
2. Raiffa, *The Art and Science of Negotiation*, 47.
3. Pink, *To Sell Is Human*, 11–12.
4. Samuel Bowles and Herbert Gintis, "Origins of Human Cooperation," in *Genetic and Cultural Evolution of Cooperation*, ed. Peter Hammerstein (Cambridge, MA: MIT Press, 2003), 429–42.
5. Jake Rossen, *Superman vs. Hollywood: How Fiendish Producers, Devious Directors, and Warring Writers Grounded an American Icon* (Chicago: Chicago Review Press, 2008), 71.
6. Dennis T. Regan, "Effects of a Favor and Liking on Compliance," *Journal of Experimental Social Psychology* 7, no. 6 (1971): 627–39.
7. Jerry M. Burger et al., "The Norm of Reciprocity as an Internalized Social Norm: Returning Favors Even When No One Finds Out," *Social Influence* 4, no. 1 (2009): 11–17.
8. Daniel Klerman and Lisa Klerman, "Inside the Caucus: An Empirical Analysis of Mediation from Within," *Journal of Empirical Legal Studies* 12, no. 4 (2015): 686–715.
9. Herbert R. Northrup, "The Case for Boulwarism," *Harvard Business Review* 41 (1963): 86–97.

40. Where You Stand Depends (Sometimes) on Where You Sit

1. Paloma Ubeda, "The Consistency of Fairness Rules: An Experimental Study," *Journal of Economic Psychology* 41 (2014): 88–100. See David M. Messick and Keith P. Sentis, "Fairness and Preference," *Journal of Experimental Social Psychology* 14, no. 4 (1979): 418; George Loewenstein et al., "Self-Serving Assessments of Fairness and Pretrial Bargaining," *Journal of Legal Studies* 22, no. 1 (1993): 135.
2. William Austin, "Friendship and Fairness: Effects of Type of Relationship and Task Performance on Choice of Distribution," *Personal and Social Psychology Bulletin* 6, no. 3 (1980).
3. Rufus E. Miles, "The Origin and Meaning of Miles' Law," *Public Administration Review* 38, no. 5 (1978): 399–403.

44. Negotiation as a Prisoner's Dilemma

1. The structure of the dilemma was first devised by Merrill Flood and Melvin Dresher at the RAND Corporation think tank in 1950. Mathematician Albert Tucker gave it its name.
2. The prisoner's dilemma story is told in many different ways. What is important is the structure of the payoffs that each "prisoner" receives based on the combination of his decision and the other prisoner's decision.

3. David Sally, "Conversation and Cooperation in Social Dilemmas: A Meta-analysis of Experiments from 1958–1992," *Rationality and Society* 7 (1995): 60.
4. Lax and Sebenius, *The Manager as Negotiator*, 29.
5. Stephen M. R. Covey, *The Speed of Trust: The One Thing That Changes Everything* (New York: Free Press, 2006), 15.
6. Joyce Berg, John Dickhaut, and Kevin McCabe, "Trust, Reciprocity, and Social History," *Games and Economic Behavior* 10 (1995): 122–42.

45. Who and When to Trust

1. Paul J. Zak and Stephen Knack, "Trust and Growth," *Economic Journal* 111 (April 2001): 316–18; David Dollar and Aart Kraay, "Institutions, Trade, and Growth," *Journal of Monetary Economics* 50, no. 1 (2003).
2. The results are described in Robert Axelrod, *The Evolution of Cooperation* (Cambridge, MA: Basic Books, 1984). In the tournaments run by Axelrod, the most successful strategy, which he called "Tit-for-Tat," involved cooperating in the first round of the game and then in each subsequent round mimicking the strategy of the other player in the previous round.
3. Dora L. Costa and Matthew E. Kahn, *Heroes and Cowards: The Social Face of War* (Princeton, NJ: Princeton University Press, 2008), 18–20, 120–31.
4. Costa and Kahn, *Heroes and Cowards*, 143–55.
5. Yuval Noah Harari, *Sapiens: A Brief History of Humankind* (New York: HarperCollins, 2015), 101–3.
6. Donald E. Brown, *Human Universals* (New York: McGraw Hill, 1991), 130–41.
7. Varda Liberman, Steven M. Samuels, and Lee Ross, "The Name of the Game: Predictive Power of Reputations versus Situational Labels in Determining Prisoner's Dilemma Game Moves," *Personality and Social Psychology Bulletin* 30 (September 2004): 1175–85.
8. Terence Burnham, Kevin McCabe, and Vernon L. Smith, "Friend-or-Foe Intentionality Priming in an Extensive Form Trust Game," *Journal of Economic Behavior and Organization* 43, no. 1 (2000): 57–73.
9. Lynn Stout, *Cultivating Conscience: How Good Laws Make Good People* (Princeton, NJ: Princeton University Press, 2011), 106–8.
10. Klerman and Klerman, "Inside the Caucus."
11. Maurice E. Schweitzer and Rachel Croson, "Curtailing Deception: The Impact of Direct Questions on Lies and Omissions," *International Journal of Conflict Management* 10, no. 3 (1999): 225–48.
12. See Gary Charness and Martin Dufwenberg, "Promises and Partnership," *Econometrica* 74, no. 6 (2006): 1579.
13. Ross and Ward, "Psychological Barriers to Dispute Resolution," 255.
14. Ernst Fehr and Herbert Gintis, "Human Motivation and Social Cooperation: Experimental and Analytical Foundations," *Annual Review of Sociology* 33 (2007).
15. Stout, *Cultivating Conscience*, 189–90, n. 23.

46. Trust-Building Strategies

1. Costa and Kahn, *Heroes and Cowards.*
2. Nancy Buchan and Rachel Croson, "The Boundaries of Trust: Own and Others' Actions in the U.S. and China," *Journal of Economic Behavior and Organization* 55, no. 4 (2004): 485.
3. Stout, *Cultivating Conscience*, 146–47.
4. Sally, "Conversation and Cooperation in Social Dilemmas," 78–83.
5. Paul J. Zak, *The Moral Molecule: How Trust Works* (New York: Dutton, 2012), 22–27.
6. Zak, *The Moral Molecule*, 44.
7. Amiee L. Drolet and Michael W. Morris, "Rapport in Conflict Resolution: Accounting for How Face-to-Face Contact Fosters Mutual Cooperation in Mixed-Motive Conflicts," *Journal of Experimental Social Psychology* 36, no. 1 (2000): 26, 42.
8. April H. Crusco and Christopher G. Wetzel, "The Midas Touch: Effects of Interpersonal Touch on Restaurant Tipping," *Personal and Social Psychology Bulletin* 10, no. 4 (1984): 512–17; Frank N. Willis and Helen K. Hamm, "The Use of Interpersonal Touch in Securing Compliance," *Journal of Nonverbal Behavior* 5, no. 1 (1980): 49–55; Damien Erceau and Nicolas Gueguen, "Tactile Contact and Evaluation of the Toucher," *Journal of Social Psychology* 147, no. 4 (2007): 441–44.
9. Don A. Moore et al., "Long and Short Routes to Success in Electronically Mediated Negotiations: Group Affiliation and Good Vibrations," *Organizational Behavior and Human Decision Processes* 77, no. 1 (1999): 22; Janice Nadler and Donna Shestowsky, "Negotiation, Information Technology, and the Problem of the Faceless Other," in *Negotiation Theory and Research*, ed. Leigh L. Thompson (New York: Psychology Press, 2006), 145, 162.
10. Zak, *The Moral Molecule*, 174–75.
11. Chris Voss and Tahl Raz, *Never Split the Difference: Negotiating as if Your Life Depended on It* (New York: HarperCollins, 2016), 15–16, 66–105.
12. Voss and Raz, *Never Split the Difference*, 35–36.
13. William W. Maddux, Elizabeth Mullen, and Adam D. Galinsky, "Chameleons Bake Bigger Pies and Take Bigger Pieces: Strategic Behavioral Mimicry Facilitates Negotiation Outcomes," *Journal of Experimental Social Psychology* 44, no. 2 (2008): 461–68.
14. Roderick I. Swaab, William W. Maddux, and Marwan Sinaceur, "Early Words That Work: When and How Virtual Linguistic Mimicry Facilitates Negotiation Outcomes," *Journal of Experimental Social Psychology* 47, no. 3 (2011): 616–21.
15. Meg Whitman and Joan O'C. Hamilton, *The Power of Many: Values for Success in Business and in Life* (New York: Three Rivers Press, 2010), 1–3.
16. Covey, *The Speed of Trust*, 155.
17. Johannes Abeler et al., "The Power of Apology," *Economics Letters* 107, no. 2 (2010): 233–35.
18. Florence R. LeCraw et al., "Changes in Liability Claims, Costs, and Resolution Times Following the Introduction of a Communication-and-Resolution Program in Tennessee," *Journal of Patient Safety and Risk Management* 23, no. 1 (2018): 13–18; Benjamin Ho and Elaine Liu, "What's an Apology Worth? Decomposing the Effect of Apologies on Medical Malpractice Payments Using State Apology Laws," *Journal of Empirical Studies* 8, no. S1 (2011): 179–99.

19. Zak, *The Moral Molecule*, 1–27.
20. Zak, *The Moral Molecule*, 84.

47. The Importance of the Stakes

1. Sally, "Conversation and Cooperation in Social Dilemmas."
2. *Golden Balls*, season 2, episode 4, aired March 14, 2008, on ITV.
3. Maxwell N. Burton-Chellew and Stuart A. West, "Correlates of Cooperation in a One-Shot High-Stakes Televised Prisoners' Dilemma," *PLoS ONE* 7, no. 4 (2012): e33344.
4. Neetzan Zimmerman, "Must Watch: Golden Balls Contestant Wins with Most Ballsy Move Ever," Gawker, April 20, 2012.

48. How to Continually Improve Your Skills

1. Jason Glatzer, "WSOP Stats: The Biggest Winners, the Best Country, the Most WSOP Bracelets," Pokernews, April 22, 2019; Seth Palansky, "Poker Hall of Fame Announces Class of 2019," WSOP, July 15, 2019.
2. Annie Duke, *Thinking in Bets: Making Smarter Decisions When You Don't Have All the Facts* (New York: Penguin Random House, 2018), 106.
3. George A. Miller, "The Magical Number Seven, Plus or Minus Two: Some Limits on Our Capacity for Processing Information," *Psychological Review* 63, no. 2 (1956): 81–97.

INDEX

Page numbers in *italics* refer to illustrations. The letter *n* after a page number refers to a footnote.